Endial

MODELS FOR WRITERS
SHORT ESSAYS FOR COMPOSITION

Second Edition

MODELS FOR WRITERS

SHORT ESSAYS FOR COMPOSITION
Second Edition

Editors

Alfred Rosa
Paul Eschholz
University of Vermont

ST. MARTIN'S PRESS   NEW YORK

Library of Congress Catalog Number: 85-61290
Copyright © 1986 by St. Martin's Press, Inc.
All rights reserved.
Manufactured in the United States of America.
09876
fedcba
For information, write St. Martin's Press, Inc.,
175 Fifth Avenue, New York, NY 10010

cover design: Darby Downey
cover art: "Western Flight," a woven hanging by
Dominie Nash

ISBN: 0-312-53592-9

Acknowledgments
Acknowledgments and copyrights continue at the back of the book on pages
388–391, which constitute an extension of the copyright page.

I. The Elements of an Essay
1. Thesis
"I'd Rather Be Black Than Female" by Shirley Chisholm and reprinted with
her permission. Originally appeared in *McCall's* August 1970.
"The Trouble With Television" by Robert MacNeil. © 1984 by Robert MacNeil.
From a speech delivered November 13, 1984 at the President's Leadership
Forum, State University of New York at Purchase. Reprinted in a condensed
version in *Reader's Digest*, March 1985.

2. Unity
"Intelligence" by Isaac Asimov (original title "What Is Intelligence, Anyway?").
Reprinted courtesy of Isaac Asimov.
"Don't Let Stereotypes Warp Your Judgments" by Robert Heilbroner and re-
printed with his permission.
"What Makes a Leader?" by Michael Korda. Copyright 1981, by Newsweek,
Inc. All Rights Reserved. Reprinted by Permission.

3. Organization
"Bugs Bunny Says They're Yummy" by Dawn Ann Kurth. Copyright © 1972 by
The New York Times Company. Reprinted by permission.
"Checks and Balances at the Sign of the Dove" by Jessica Mitford. Copyright ©
1977 by Jessica Mitford. Reprinted from *Poison Penmanship: The Gentle Art
of Muckraking*, by Jessica Mitford, by permission of Alfred A. Knopf, Inc.
"The Suicide-Pill Option" by Jason Salzman. Copyright 1985, by Newsweek,
Inc. All Rights Reserved.

4. Beginnings and Endings
"What Does a Woman Want?" by Susan Jacoby. Reprinted by permission of
Farrar, Straus and Giroux, Inc. "What Does a Woman Want?" from *The Pos-
sible She* by Susan Jacoby. Copyright © 1977, 1978, 1979 by Susan Jacoby.

Preface

Models for Writers offers sixty-five short, lively essays that represent particularly appropriate models for use by begining college writers. Most of our selections are comparable in length to the essays students will write themselves, and each clearly illustrates a basic rhetorical element, principle, or pattern. Just as important, the essays deal with subjects that we know from our own classroom experience will spark the interest of most college students. In making our selections, we have sought a level of readability that is neither so easy as to be condescending nor so difficult as to distract the reader's attention from the rhetorical issue under study. And, although we have included a few older classics, most of the essays have been written in the last ten years. Drawn from a wide range of sources, they represent a variety of contemporary prose styles.

This second edition of *Models for Writers* has been revised based on our own experiences as well as on the many suggestions made by instructors who adopted and liked the first edition. To begin, we have added an introduction that explains the purpose of the text and shows students how it can be used to help improve their writing. At the end of this new introduction is the final draft of an essay written by a student who used *Models for Writers* in one of our writing classes; marginal annotations show how various rhetorical techniques and patterns covered in the text can be put effectively to work and demonstrate for students some of the benefits of studying writing models. We have also added a section on beginnings and endings that addresses the problems students so often encounter in opening and closing their essays and in recognizing what characterizes an effective introduction or conclusion. In addition, we have significantly increased the number of suggested writing topics throughout the text, and, wherever called for by past users and reviewers, we have replaced selections with ones we feel will prove more workable, being careful in every case that the new essays meet the essential qualifications of brevity, clarity, and suitability for student writers.

As in the first edition, the essays in *Models for Writers*, Second Edition, are grouped into eighteen chapters, each devoted to a particular element or pattern. Chapters 1–7 focus on the concepts of thesis, unity, organization, beginnings and endings, paragraphs, transitions, and effective sentences. Next, Chapters 8 and 9 illustrate some aspects of language: the effects of diction and tone and the uses of figurative language. Finally, Chapters 10–18 explore the various types of writing most often required of college students: illustration, narration, description, process analysis, definition, division and classification, comparison and contrast, cause and effect, and argument. The arrangement of the chapters suggests a logical teaching sequence, moving from the elements of the essay to its language to the different types of essays. An alternative teaching strategy might be to structure the course around chapters 10–18, bringing in earlier chapters as necessary to illustrate various individual elements. Each chapter is self-contained, so that instructors may easily devise their own sequences, omitting or emphasizing certain chapters according to the needs of a particular group of students. Whatever sequence is followed, thematic comparisons among the selections will be facilitated by the alternate *Thematic Table of Contents* at the beginning of the book.

The chapters all follow a similar pattern. Each opens with an explanation of the element or principle to be considered, many including paragraph–length examples. We then present three or four essays, each of which has its own brief introduction providing information about the author and directing the student's attention to specific rhetorical features. Every essay is followed by study materials in three parts: *Questions for Study and Discussion*, *Vocabulary*, and *Suggested Writing Assignments*.

The *Questions for Study and Discussion* focus on the content, the author's purpose, and the rhetorical strategy used to achieve that purpose. Some questions allow brief answers, but most are designed to stimulate more searching analysis and to promote lively classroom discussion. In order to reinforce the lessons of other chapters and remind students that good writing is never one-dimensional, at least one question at the end of each series focuses on a writing concern other than the one highlighted in the chapter at hand. Whenever it seemed helpful, we have referred students to the *Glossary of Useful Terms*, which provides concise definitions of rhetorical and other terms. The *Vocabulary* exercise draws from each reading several words that students will find worth adding to their vocabularies. The exercise asks them to define each word as it is used in the context of the selection and then to use the word in a new sentence of their own.

The *Suggested Writing Assignments* provide two writing assignments for each essay. The first calls for an essay closely related to the content and style of the essay it follows, in effect encouraging the use of the reading selection as a direct model. The second writing assignment, while ranging a little further afield in subject, gives the student yet another opportunity to practice the particular rhetorical element or principle being illustrated.

We are indebted to many people for their criticism and advice as we prepared this second edition of *Models for Writers*. We are especially grateful to:

Mary F. Aldrich, Seattle Central Community College; Joy Barnes, University of Richmond; Paula Berggren, Baruch College—CUNY; Don Boes, Indiana University; Michelle Dolphin Bowan, Front Range Community College; Sally Broadbent, St. John Fisher College; Thomas J. Buchholz, University of Wisconsin at Stevens Point; Boyd Collins, Los Angeles City College; Marie K. Connelly, Case Western Reserve University; Walter Connolly, Central Connecticut State University; Linda Seidel Costic, University of Wisconsin at Whitewater; J.R. Crandall, West Valley College; Ian Cruickshank, St. Louis Community College at Florissant Valley; Ann Deprey, University of Wisconsin at Green Bay; Jim Dyer, Mohawk Valley Community College; Martha Edmonds, University of Richmond; Suzanne Eovaldi, Prairie State College; Karen Everett, Eastern Montana College; Carol Fitzpatrick, University of Maryland; Elaine Fitzpatrick, Massasoit Community College; Sandra M. Fluck, Franklin and Marshall College; Jo Ford, Mission College; Millicent Garcia, Creighton University; James Garmhauser, College of San Mateo; Vicente Gotera, Indiana University; Dorothy Greene, Community College of Rhode Island; Judith Hall, Monroe Community College; Mark Halperin, Central Washington University; Everett Hoagland, Southeastern Massachusetts University; Thomas Holbrook, University of Maryland; Brian Kent, University of Vermont; John P. Kent, West Chester University; Joyce Kesser, Villa Maria College; Linda Kitz, Cabrillo College; Ellen Kuiper, Rochester Institute of Technology; Bennie Lauve, Indiana University; Charles Lefcourt, SUNY College at Buffalo; Marcia Lipson, Hunter College—CUNY; Denise Lynch, Central Connecticut State University; Patricia J. McFarlane, Franklin and Marshall College; O. Victor Miller, Albany Junior College; Levonne Nelson, El Camino College; Kathryn O'Hare, Community College of Rhode Island; Jeanne Orentlicher, Queensborough Community College—CUNY; Janet K. Patlow, Rochester Institute of Technology; Fred F. Paulenich, Youngstown State University; Vincent F. Petronella, University of Massachusetts at Boston; Mary Anne Phillips, San Diego State University; Robert L. Piper, Southeastern Massachusetts University; John E. Reedy, SUNY College at Buffalo; Larry Robinson, California Polytechnic University at Pomona; Lorie Roth, Armstrong State College; H.M. Rubinstein, Hudson County Community College; E.A. Sachs, Western Connecticut State University; Brent Sargent, Community College of Vermont; Karen Schaafsma, University of California at Davis; Wayne Scheer, Atlanta Junior College; Robin Schore, Mercer County Community College; JoAnna Shayne, California State University at Los Angeles; Debra Sikes, Grayson County Junior College; M. Slavenes, SUNY College at Buffalo; Bruce Spiegelberg, Franklin B. Marshall College; Ellen Sternberg, St. John Fisher College; Edward Sundberg, Cabrillo College; Shirley Sykes, San Diego Mesa College; Robert Thacker, St. Lawrence University; Stanley Tick, San Francisco State University; Leon Ward, Grayson County Junior College; and James E. White, Rhode Island College.

It was once again our good fortune to have the editorial guidance of Nancy Perry and Mark Gallaher, both of St. Martin's Press, as we worked on this new edition. Our greatest debt, as always, is to our students, for all that they have taught us.

Alfred Rosa
Paul Eschholz

Table of Contents

Thematic Table of Contents

MODELS FOR WRITERS
SHORT ESSAYS FOR COMPOSITION
Second Edition

INTRODUCTION

Models for Writers is designed to help you learn to write by providing you with a collection of model essays, essays that are examples of good writing. We know that one of the best ways to learn to write and to improve our writing is to read. By reading we can begin to see how other writers have communicated their experiences, ideas, thoughts, and feelings. We can study how they have used the various elements of the essay—words, sentences, paragraphs, organizational patterns, transitions, examples, evidence, and so forth—and thus learn how we might effectively do the same. When we see, for example, how a writer like Shirley Chisholm develops an essay from a strong thesis statement, we can better appreciate the importance of having a clear thesis statement in our writing. When we see the way Russell Baker uses transitions to link key phrases and important ideas in order to make the parts of his essay work together in a pleasing and unified whole, we have a better idea of how to achieve unity in our writing.

But we do not learn only by observing, by reading. We also learn by doing, by writing, and in the best of all situations we engage in these two activities in conjunction with one another. *Models for Writers* encourages you, therefore, to write your essays, to practice what you are learning, as you are actually reading and analyzing the model essays in the text.

The kind of composition that you will be asked to write for your college writing instructor is most often referred to as an essay—a relatively short piece of nonfiction in which a writer attempts to develop one or more closely related points or ideas. An effective essay has a clear purpose, often provides useful information, has an effect on the reader's thoughts and feelings, and is usually a pleasure to read.

All well-written essays also share a number of structural and stylistic features that are illustrated by the various essays in

1

Models for Writers. One good way to learn what these features are and how you can involve them in your own writing is to look at each of them in isolation. For this reason we have divided *Models for Writers* first into three major sections and, within these sections, into eighteen chapters, each with its own particular focus and emphasis.

"The Elements of an Essay," the first section, includes chapters on the following subjects: thesis, unity, organization, beginnings and endings, paragraphs, transitions, and effective sentences. All these elements are essential to a well-written essay, but the concepts of thesis, unity, and organization underlie all the others and so come first in our sequence.

Briefly, "Thesis" shows how authors put forth or state the main ideas of their essays and how they use such statements to develop and control content; "Unity," how authors achieve a sense of wholeness in their essays; and "Organization," some important patterns that authors use to organize their thinking and writing. "Beginnings and Endings" offers advice and models of ways to begin and conclude essays, while "Paragraphs" concentrates on the importance of well-developed paragraphs and what is necessary to achieve them. "Transitions" concerns the various devices that writers use to move from one idea or section of an essay to the next. Finally, "Effective Sentences" focuses on techniques to make sentences more powerful and create stylistic variety.

"The Language of the Essay," the second major section of the text, includes a chapter on diction and tone and one on figurative language. "Diction and Tone" shows how carefully writers choose words either to convey exact meanings or to be purposefully suggestive. In addition, this chapter shows how the words a writer uses can create a particular tone or relationship between the writer and the reader, one of irony, for example, or humor or great seriousness. "Figurative Language" concentrates on the usefulness of the special devices of language, such as simile and metaphor, that add richness and depth to one's writing.

The final section of *Models for Writers*, "Types of Essays," includes chapters on the various types of writing most often required of college writing students: "Illustration" (how to use examples to illustrate a point or idea); "Narration" (how to tell a story or give an account of an event); "Description" (how to present a verbal picture); "Process Analysis" (how to explain how something is done or happens); "Definition" (how to explain what something is); "Division and Classification" (how to divide a subject into its parts and place items into appropriate categories); "Comparison and Contrast" (how to demonstrate likenesses and differences); "Cause and Effect" (how to explain the causes of an event or the effects of an action); and, finally, "Argument" (how to use reason and logic to persuade someone to your way of thinking).

All of the chapters follow a similar pattern. Each opens with an explanation of the element or principle under consideration. These introductions are intended to be brief, clear, and memorable. Here you will also usually find one or more short examples of the feature or principle being studied. Following the introduction, we present three or four model essays, each with a brief introduction of its own providing information about the author and directing your attention to the highlighted rhetorical features. Every essay is followed by study materials in three parts: *Questions for Study and Discussion, Vocabulary,* and *Suggested Writing Assignments.*

Models for Writers, then, provides information, instruction, and practice in writing essays. By reading carefully and intelligently and by applying what you learn, you can begin to have more and more control over your own writing.

Andy Pellett, one of our own writing students at the University of Vermont, found this to be true, and his work is a good example of what can be achieved from studying models. Andy was assigned to write a number of essays for class, one of them being an argument. He knew from his past experiences that in order to write a good essay he would have to write on a topic he cared about. He also knew that he should allow himself a reasonable amount of time to find such a topic and to gather his ideas. An avid sports fan, Andy immediately decided to write about some aspect of sports. After considering and rejecting several possible topics within that subject area—including professional salaries, Olympic basketball teams, and sports heros in advertisements—he decided that his strong feelings concerning artificial playing surfaces provided a good basis for an argumentative essay. Because of what he had read in the popular press and what he himself had seen, Andy had developed a longstanding dislike of artificial playing surfaces, and he determined that his major argument, the thesis of his essay, would be that such surfaces were bad for athletes and for sports.

Andy began by brainstorming about the topic. He made lists of all the ideas, facts, issues, arguments, and counterarguments that came to mind and that he thought he might want to include in his essay. Once he was confident that he had amassed enough information to begin writing, he made a rough outline of an organizational pattern that he felt would work well for him: first point out the weakness of the arguments put forth in favor of artificial turf, then conclude with his own strong arguments against. Keeping that organizational pattern in mind, Andy next wrote a first draft of his essay and proceeded to examine it carefully, assessing what still needed to be done to improve it.

Andy was writing this particular essay in the second half of the semester, after he read a good number of essays and had learned the importance of such matters as good paragraphing, unity, and transitions. In rereading his first draft, he discovered that there were several things he could still do to improve his essay. First he had failed to mention an important objection to artificial turf when he was writing the first draft (the high cost of installation and replacement), so he now included it. He also found places where phrases and even sentences could be added to make his meaning clearer. He changed the order of the sentences in his sixth paragraph, and he even improved his original organizational pattern by deciding to wait until just before his conclusion to bring up his argument about injuries. In addition, he inserted transitions (for example, in paragraph five) and changed a number of words, as in paragraph eight, to create a more forceful effect.

The final draft of Andy's paper illustrates how well he has learned how the parts of a well-written essay fit together, and how to make revisions based on what his reading and study of model essays has taught him. The following is the final draft of Andy's essay.

The Perils of AstroTurf

Andy Pellett

As a purist sports fan, I am suspicious of changes that occur in my favorite pastimes, namely baseball and football. In the past two decades, there have been many new developments--some good and some bad. But the most disturbing change has been the introduction of artificial turf as a playing surface.

This fake grass first appeared on the sporting scene in 1966. The grass in the Houston Astrodome was dying, so in a desperation move, it was replaced by artificial turf. This new surface, manufactured by the Monsanto Company, was appropriately called AstroTurf.

Since then, the living grass in stadiums and playing fields everywhere has been replaced with one form of artificial turf or another, usually made up of green nylon fibers stitched over a cushioned polyester mat. AstroTurf is still the most common.

What's so great about artificial turf? If real grass was good enough for the sports heroes of yesteryear, why shouldn't it be good enough for those of today? The proponents of artificial turf have at least two basic arguments.

The first argument uses a familiar line of reasoning: Artificial turf saves money. The field needs less maintenance, and rain

BEGINNING: establishes author's viewpoint and purpose

THESIS

DICTION: "artificial turf" vs. "fake grass"

PARAGRAPH UNITY: chronology/ repeated words (grass, turf, etc.)

RHETORICAL QUESTIONS

ORGANIZATION: proponents' first argument

water drains easily through small holes in the mat. Also, the field can be used for more than one sport. A football game won't tear up the turf, thereby making it possible to play a baseball game on the same field a day later.

This argument, however, overlooks several important problems. The cost of laying down a new synthetic field is very high--close to a million dollars. In addition, artificial turf deteriorates in appearance and condition. Tobacco juice spit onto the ground will soak in; on AstroTurf it makes an ugly stain that gives grounds-keeepers fits. In 1971, the artificial turf in Miami's Orange Bowl was decoratively painted for the Super Bowl. After the game, the paint couldn't be removed and remained on the field for months. For these and other reasons, older fields may have to be resurfaced. Such resurfacing increases, not decreases, the cost of field maintenance.

The second argument proponents of AstroTurf make is that traction is increased by artificial turf, thereby making it easier to play in inclement weather. But why should we make it easier to play in bad weather? A game like football is a tough sport, and playing in horrible conditions personifies that toughness. Most fans enjoy watching two football teams battle it out, with mud covering every part of their uniforms. Baseball, like football, was meant to be played outside on grass, and, if we take the natural element out of sport, we lose a sense of drama.

Transition: "however" sets up refutation

Illustration: examples used as evidence

Organization: proponents' second argument

It is evident that arguments in favor of artificial turf tend to ignore some important facts. Furthermore, these arguments appear even weaker when compared to the arguments put forth by the detractors of AstroTurf. Opponents of artificial turf make essentially two arguments: artificial turf causes the ball to hop unnaturally, which affects team statistics and strategy, and artificial turf causes more injuries to players.

TRANSITIONAL PARAGRAPH: introduces opposing arguments

In the major leagues the baseball diamond has been turned into a basketball court by the hard surface. The ball rockets off the turf as if being fired from a cannon. It rolls faster and further than on natural grass, thus allowing for more extra-base hits.

ORGANIZATION: first opposing argument

FIGURATIVE LANGUAGE

"Great," some fans will say; "we like to see more offense." But a baseball player's performance is measured by statistics. So it really isn't fair for a weak hitter to acquire more extra-base hits just because he plays on artificial turf.

Strategy is also affected. An outfielder must play back to prevent the ball from caroming over his head. This allows cheap bloop singles that ordinarily would be caught. And what about when the batter grounds the ball into the turf in front of home plate? Normally this should be an out; but by the time the ball comes down, the batter is standing on first base with a "Monsanto single."

DEFINITION: "Monsanto single"

EFFECTIVE SENTENCE

The other topic of debate has been injuries. Athletes have complained that

ORGANIZATION: second opposing argument

artificial turf is responsible for everything from friction burns to broken bones. Because of the hard surface, athletes must make adaptations in their running style, which can often result in painful foot ailments. Also, the greatly improved traction of AstroTurf means that, when a player plants his foot, it won't slide at all. Therefore, if a player is in an awkward position with his feet planted, and he gets hit, serious knee injuries can result. Earlier this year, Billy Sims of the Detroit Lions blamed his season-ending knee injury on the artificial turf. Years ago, Gale Sayers blamed artificial turf for delaying his comeback from knee surgery.

CAUSE AND EFFECT

EVIDENCE OF AUTHORITIES

My fervent, yet probably unrealistic, hope is that artificial turf be banned. There was never any controversy when real grass was the only surface on which outdoor games were played. If we stick with natural substances, we can't go wrong. Trying to improve on nature only causes trouble. Richie Allen, former baseball player, probably said it best: "If my horse can't eat it, I don't want to play on it."

ENDING: argument enforced by appropriate quotation

I

THE ELEMENTS OF AN ESSAY

1

THESIS

The thesis of an essay is its main idea, the point it is trying to make. The thesis is often expressed in a one- or two-sentence statement, although sometimes it is implied or suggested rather than stated directly. The thesis statement controls and directs the content of the essay: everything that the writer says must be logically related to the thesis statement.

Usually the thesis is presented early in an essay, sometimes in the first sentence. Here are some thesis statements that begin essays:

> New York is a city of things unnoticed.
>
> Gay Talese

> Most Americans are in terrible shape.
>
> James F. Fixx

> One of the most potent elements in body language is eye behavior.
>
> Flora Davis

Each of these sentences does what a good thesis statement should do—it identifies the topic and makes an assertion about it.

Often writers prepare readers for a thesis statement with one or several sentences that establish a context. Notice, in the following example, how the author eases the reader into his thesis about television instead of presenting it abruptly in the first sentence:

> With the advent of television, for the first time in history, all aspects of animal and human life and death, of societal and individual behavior have been condensed on the average to a 19 inch diagonal screen and a 30 minute time slot. Television, a unique medium, claiming to be neither a reality nor art, has become reality for many of us, particularly for our children who are growing up in front of it.
>
> Jerzy Kosinski

11

On occasion a writer may even purposefully delay the presentation of a thesis until the middle or end of an essay. If the thesis is controversial or needs extended discussion and illustration, the writer might present it later to make it easier for the reader to understand and accept it. Appearing near or at the end of an essay, a thesis also gains prominence.

Some kinds of writing do not need thesis statements. These include descriptions, narratives, and personal writing such as letters and diaries. But any essay that seeks to explain or prove a point has a thesis that is usually set forth in a thesis statement.

THE MOST IMPORTANT DAY

Helen Keller

Helen Keller (1880–1968) was afflicted by a disease that left her blind and deaf at the age of eighteen months. With the aid of her teacher, Anne Sullivan, she was able to overcome her severe handicaps, to graduate from Radcliffe College, and to lead a productive and challenging adult life. In the following selection from her autobiography, The Story of My Life *(1902), Keller tells of the day she first met Anne Sullivan, a day she regarded as the most important in her life. Notice that Keller states her thesis in the first paragraph and that it serves to direct and unify the remaining paragraphs.*

The most important day I remember in all my life is the one on which my teacher, Anne Mansfield Sullivan, came to me. I am filled with wonder when I consider the immeasurable contrast between the two lives which it connects. It was the third of March, 1887, three months before I was seven years old.

On the afternoon of that eventful day, I stood on the porch, dumb, expectant. I guessed vaguely from my mother's signs and from the hurrying to and fro in the house that something unusual was about to happen, so I went to the door and waited on the steps. The afternoon sun penetrated the mass of honeysuckle that covered the porch and fell on my upturned face. My fingers lingered almost unconsciously on the familiar leaves and blossoms which had just come forth to greet the sweet southern spring. I did not know what the future held of marvel or surprise for me. Anger and bitterness had preyed upon me continually for weeks and a deep languor had succeeded this passionate struggle.

Have you ever been at sea in a dense fog, when it seemed as if   3
a tangible white darkness shut you in, and the great ship, tense
and anxious, groped her way toward the shore with plummet
and sounding-line, and you waited with beating heart for something to happen? I was like that ship before my education began, only I was without compass or sounding-line, and had no
way of knowing how near the harbor was. "Light! give me
light!" was the wordless cry of my soul, and the light of love
shone on me in that very hour.

I felt approaching footsteps. I stretched out my hand as I sup-   4
posed to my mother. Someone took it, and I was caught up and
held close in the arms of her who had come to reveal all things
to me, and, more than all things else, to love me.

The morning after my teacher came she led me into her room   5
and gave me a doll. The little blind children at the Perkins Institution had sent it and Laura Bridgman had dressed it; but I did
not know this until afterward. When I had played with it a little
while, Miss Sullivan slowly spelled into my hand the word
"d-o-l-l." I was at once interested in this finger play and tried to
imitate it. When I finally succeeded in making the letters cor-
rectly I was flushed with childish pleasure and pride. Running
downstairs to my mother I held up my hand and made the letters for doll. I did not know that I was spelling a word or even
that words existed; I was simply making my fingers go in
monkeylike imitation. In the days that followed I learned to
spell in this uncomprehending way a great many words, among
them *pin, hat, cup* and a few verbs like *sit, stand* and *walk*. But
my teacher had been with me several weeks before I understood that everything has a name.

One day, while I was playing with my new doll, Miss Sullivan   6
put my big rag doll into my lap also, spelled "d-o-l-l" and tried
to make me understand that "d-o-l-l" applied to both. Earlier
in the day we had had a tussle over the words "m-u-g" and
"w-a-t-e-r." Miss Sullivan had tried to impress it upon me that
"m-u-g" is *mug* and that "w-a-t-e-r" is *water*, but I persisted in
confounding the two. In despair she had dropped the subject
for the time, only to renew it at the first opportunity. I became
impatient at her repeated attempts and, seizing the new doll, I
dashed it upon the floor. I was keenly delighted when I felt the

fragments of the broken doll at my feet. Neither sorrow nor regret followed my passionate outburst. I had not loved the doll. In the still, dark world in which I lived there was no strong sentiment or tenderness. I felt my teacher sweep the fragments to one side of the hearth, and I had a sense of satisfaction that the cause of my discomfort was removed. She brought me my hat, and I knew I was going out into the warm sunshine. This thought, if a wordless sensation may be called a thought, made me hop and skip with pleasure.

We walked down the path to the well-house, attracted by the fragrance of the honeysuckle with which it was covered. Some one was drawing water and my teacher placed my hand under the spout. As the cool stream gushed over one hand she spelled into the other the word *water*, first slowly, then rapidly. I stood still, my whole attention fixed upon the motions of her fingers. Suddenly I felt a misty consciousness as of something forgotten—a thrill of returning thought; and somehow the mystery of language was revealed to me. I knew then that "w-a-t-e-r" meant the wonderful cool something that was flowing over my hand. The living word awakened my soul, gave it light, hope, joy, set it free! There were barriers still, it is true, but barriers that could in time be swept away. 7

I left the well-house eager to learn. Everything had a name, and each name gave birth to a new thought. As we returned to the house every object which I touched seemed to quiver with life. That was because I saw everything with the strange, new sight that had come to me. On entering the door I remembered the doll I had broken. I felt my way to the hearth and picked up the pieces. I tried vainly to put them together. Then my eyes filled with tears; for I realized what I had done, and for the first time I felt repentance and sorrow. 8

I learned a great many new words that day. I do not remember what they all were; but I do know that *mother, father, sister, teacher* were among them—words that were to make the world blossom for me, "like Aaron's rod, with flowers." It would have been difficult to find a happier child than I was as I lay in my crib at the close of that eventful day and lived over the joys it had brought me, and for the first time longed for a new day to come. 9

Questions for Study and Discussion

1. What is Helen Keller's thesis in this essay?
2. What is Helen Keller's purpose in this essay? (Glossary: *Purpose*)
3. Helen Keller narrates the events of the day Anne Sullivan arrived (2–4), the morning after she arrived (5), and one day several weeks after her arrival (6–9). Describe what happens on each day, and explain how these separate incidents support her thesis.
4. Identify the figure of speech that Helen Keller uses in paragraph 3. Why is it effective? (Glossary: *Figures of Speech*)

Vocabulary

Refer to your dictionary to define the following words as they are used in this selection. Then use each word in a sentence of your own.

dumb (2)	plummet (3)
preyed (2)	tussle (6)
languor (2)	vainly (8)
passionate (2)	

Suggested Writing Assignments

1. Think about an important day in your own life. Using the thesis statement "The most important day of my life was _____," write an essay in which you show the significance of that day by recounting and explaining the events that took place.
2. For many people around the world, the life of Helen Keller stands as the symbol of what can be achieved by an individual despite seemingly insurmountable handicaps. Her achievements have also had a tremendous impact upon those who are not afflicted with handicaps, leading them to believe that they can accomplish more than they ever thought possible. Consider the role of handicapped people in our society, develop an appropriate thesis, and write an essay on the topic.

I'D RATHER BE BLACK
THAN FEMALE

Shirley Chisholm

Shirley Chisholm, a former member of the United States House of Representatives from Brooklyn, New York, is an outspoken advocate of the rights of all minorities, an authority on child welfare, and an educational consultant. Her books Unbought and Unbossed *(1970) and* The Good Fight *(1973) are records of her experiences as a black female politician. In the following essay, first published in the August 1970* McCall's, *it is Chisholm's thesis that in America today it is less of a disadvantage to be black than to be female.*

Being the first black woman elected to Congress has made me some kind of phenomenon. There are nine other blacks in Congress; there are ten other women. I was the first to overcome both handicaps at once. Of the two handicaps, being black is much less of a drawback than being female.

If I said that being black is a greater handicap than being a woman, probably no one would question me. Why? Because "we all know" there is prejudice against black people in America. That there is prejudice against women is an idea that still strikes nearly all men—and, I am afraid, most women—as bizarre.

Prejudice against blacks was invisible to most white Americans for many years. When blacks finally started to "mention" it, with sit-ins, boycotts, and freedom rides, Americans were incredulous. "Who, us?" they asked in injured tones. *"We're* prejudiced?" It was the start of a long, painful reeducation for white America. It will take years for whites—including those who think of themselves as liberals—to discover and eliminate the racist attitudes they all actually have.

How much harder will it be to eliminate the prejudice against women? I am sure it will be a longer struggle. Part of the problem is that women in America are much more brainwashed and content with their roles as second-class citizens than blacks ever were. 4

Let me explain. I have been active in politics for more than twenty years. For all but the last six, I have done the work—all the tedious details that make the difference between victory and defeat on election day—while men reaped the rewards, which is almost invariably the lot of women in politics. 5

It is still women—about three million volunteers—who do most of this work in the American political world. The best any of them can hope for is the honor of being district or county vice-chairman, a kind of separate-but-equal position with which a woman is rewarded for years of faithful envelope stuffing and card-party organizing. In such a job, she gets a number of free trips to state and sometimes national meetings and conventions, where her role is supposed to be to vote the way her male chairman votes. 6

When I tried to break out of that role in 1963 and run for the New York State Assembly seat from Brooklyn's Bedford-Stuyvesant, the resistance was bitter. From the start of that campaign, I faced undisguised hostility because of my sex. 7

But it was four years later, when I ran for Congress, that the question of my sex became a major issue. Among members of my own party, closed meetings were held to discuss ways of stopping me. 8

My opponent, the famous civil rights leader James Farmer, tried to project a black, masculine image; he toured the neighborhood with sound trucks filled with young men wearing Afro haircuts, dashikis, and beards. While the television crews ignored me, they were not aware of a very important statistic, which both I and my campaign manager, Wesley MacD. Holder, knew. In my district there are 2.5 women for every man registered to vote. And those women are organized—in PTAs, church societies, card clubs, and other social and service groups. I went to them and asked their help. Mr. Farmer still doesn't quite know what hit him. 9

When a bright young woman graduate starts looking for a 10

job, why is the first question always: "Can you type?" A history
of prejudice lies behind that question. Why are women thought
of as secretaries, not administrators? Librarians and teachers,
but not doctors and lawyers? Because they are thought of as
different and inferior. The happy homemaker and the con-
tented darky are both stereotypes produced by prejudice.

Women have not even reached the level of tokenism that   11
blacks are reaching. No women sit on the Supreme Court. Only
two have held Cabinet rank, and none do at present. Only two
women hold ambassadorial rank. But women predominate in
the lower-paying, menial, unrewarding, dead-end jobs, and
when they do reach better positions, they are invariably paid
less than a man gets for the same job.

If that is not prejudice, what would you call it?   12

A few years ago, I was talking with a political leader about a   13
promising young woman as a candidate. "Why invest time and
effort to build the girl up?" he asked me. "You know she'll only
drop out of the game to have a couple of kids just about the
time we're ready to run her for mayor."

Plenty of people have said similar things about me. Plenty of   14
others have advised me, every time I tried to take another upward step, that I should go back to teaching, a woman's voca-
tion, and leave politics to the men. I love teaching, and I am
ready to go back to it as soon as I am convinced that this country no longer needs a woman's contribution.

When there are no children going to bed hungry in this rich   15
nation, I may be ready to go back to teaching. When there is a
good school for every child, I may be ready. When we do not
spend our wealth on hardware to murder people, when we no
longer tolerate prejudice against minorities, and when the laws
against unfair housing and unfair employment practices are
enforced instead of evaded, then there may be nothing more for
me to do in politics.

But until that happens—and we all know it will not be this   16
year or next—what we need is more women in politics, because
we have a very special contribution to make. I hope that the example of my success will convince other women to get into
politics—and not just to stuff envelopes, but to run for office.

It is women who can bring empathy, tolerance, insight, pa-   17 tience, and persistence to government—the qualities we naturally have or have had to develop because of our suppression by men. The women of a nation mold its morals, its religion, and its politics by the lives they live. At present, our country needs women's idealism and determination, perhaps more in politics than anywhere else.

Questions for Study and Discussion

1. Where does Chisholm state her thesis?
2. Chisholm's purpose is to convince the reader that there is more prejudice against women than against blacks. How successful is she in convincing you?
3. Discuss Chisholm's use of comparison and contrast in this essay. (Glossary: *Comparison and Contrast*)
4. A *rhetorical question* is a question that requires no answer; it is often used for emphasis. In the context of the essay, what is the function of paragraph 12?

Vocabulary

Refer to your dictionary to define the following words as they are used in this selection. Then use each word in a sentence of your own.

bizarre (2)	menial (11)
incredulous (3)	vocation (14)
tedious (5)	empathy (17)
tokenism (11)	persistence (17)

Suggested Writing Assignments

1. Write an essay in which you use as your thesis the formula "I'd rather be _____ than _____." You may use one of the following topics or create one of your own:

   I'd rather be honest than successful.

   I'd rather be a spectator than an athlete.

I'd rather be a worker than a supervisor.
I'd rather take chances than lead a boring life.

2. Shirley Chisholm's essay first appeared in 1970. In your opinion have opportunities for women improved, stayed the same, or worsened since that time? Using your own experiences, your reading, and your own observations as a starting point, construct a thesis statement and write an essay which supports your thesis concerning opportunities for women to become leaders in important segments of our society.

THE TROUBLE WITH TELEVISION

Robert MacNeil

Robert MacNeil is best known today as the co-anchor of the Public Broadcasting Service's "MacNeil/Lehrer NewsHour," a news analysis program. Born in Montreal, Canada, he is the author of two books. In his first book, The People Machine: The Influence of Television on American Politics *(1968), MacNeil launches a criticism of the broadcast industry's emphasis on the entertainment value of news. In his second book,* The Right Place at the Right Time *(1982), he recounts his experiences as a journalist. In the following selection, MacNeil warns of TV's adverse effect on both our culture and our values.*

It is difficult to escape the influence of television. If you fit the statistical averages, by the age of 20 you will have been exposed to at least 20,000 hours of television. You can add 10,000 hours for each decade you have lived after the age of 20. The only things Americans do more than watch television are work and sleep.

Calculate for a moment what could be done with even a part of those hours. Five thousand hours, I am told, are what a typical college undergraduate spends working on a bachelor's degree. In 10,000 hours you could have learned enough to become an astronomer or engineer. You could have learned several languages fluently. If it appealed to you, you could be reading Homer in the original Greek or Dostoyevsky in Russian. If it didn't, you could have walked around the world and written a book about it.

The trouble with television is that it discourages concentration. Almost anything interesting and rewarding in life requires some constructive, consistently applied effort. The dullest, the least gifted of us can achieve things that seem miraculous to those who never concentrate on anything. But television encourages us to apply no effort. It sells us instant gratification. It diverts us only to divert, to make the time pass without pain.

This Television's variety becomes a narcotic, not a stimulus. Its 4 serial, kaleidoscopic exposures force us to follow its lead. The viewer is on a perpetual guided tour: 30 minutes at the museum, 30 at the cathedral, 30 for a drink, then back on the bus to the next attraction—except on television, typically, the spans allotted are on the order of minutes or seconds, and the chosen delights are more often car crashes and people killing one another. In short, a lot of television usurps one of the most precious of all human gifts, the ability to focus your attention yourself, rather than just passively surrender it.

Capturing your attention—and holding it—is the prime mo- 5 tive of most television programming and enhances its role as a profitable advertising vehicle. Programmers live in constant fear of losing anyone's attention—anyone's. The surest way to avoid doing so is to keep everything brief, not to strain the attention of anyone but instead to provide constant stimulation through variety, novelty, action and movement. Quite simply, television operates on the appeal to the short attention span.

It is simply the easiest way out. But it has come to be re- 6 garded as a given, as inherent in the medium itself; as an imperative, as though General Sarnoff, or one of the other august pioneers of video, had bequeathed to us tablets of stone commanding that nothing in television shall ever require more than a few moments' concentration.

In its place that is fine. Who can quarrel with a medium that 7 so brilliantly packages escapist entertainment as a mass-marketing tool? But I see its values now pervading this nation and its life. It has become fashionable to think that, like fast food, fast ideas are the way to get to a fast-moving, impatient public.

In the case of news, this practice, in my view, results in ineffi- 8 cient communication. I question how much of television's nightly news effort is really absorbable and understandable. Much of it is what has been aptly described as "machine-gunning with scraps." I think the technique fights coherence. I think it tends to make things ultimately boring and dismissable (unless they are accompanied by horrifying pictures) because almost anything is boring and dismissable if you know almost nothing about it.

I believe that TV's appeal to the short attention span is not only inefficient communication but decivilizing as well. Consider the casual assumptions that television tends to cultivate: that complexity must be avoided, that visual stimulation is a substitute for thought, that verbal precision is an anachronism. It may be old-fashioned, but I was taught that thought is words, arranged in grammatically precise ways. 9

There is a crisis of literacy in this country. One study estimates that some 30 million adult Americans are "functionally illiterate" and cannot read or write well enough to answer a want ad or understand the instructions on a medicine bottle. 10

Literacy may not be an inalienable human right, but it is one that the highly literate Founding Fathers might not have found unreasonable or even unattainable. We are not only not attaining it as a nation, statistically speaking, but we are falling further and further short of attaining it. And, while I would not be so simplistic as to suggest that television is the cause, I believe it contributes and is an influence. 11

Everything about this nation—the structure of the society, its forms of family organization, its economy, its place in the world—has become more complex, not less. Yet its dominating communications instrument, its principal form of national linkage, is one that sells neat resolutions to human problems that usually have no neat resolutions. It is all symbolized in my mind by the hugely successful art form that television has made central to the culture, the 30-second commercial: the tiny drama of the earnest housewife who finds happiness in choosing the right toothpaste. 12

*When before in human history has so much humanity collectively surrendered so much of its leisure to one toy, one mass diversion? When before has virtually an entire nation surrendered itself wholesale to a medium for selling? 13

Some years ago Yale University law professor Charles L. Black, Jr., wrote: ". . . forced feeding on trivial fare is not itself a trivial matter." I think this society is being force-fed with trivial fare, and I fear that the effects on our habits of mind, our language, our tolerance for effort, and our appetite for complexity are only dimly perceived. If I am wrong, we will 14 have done no harm to look at the issue skeptically and critically, to consider how we should be resisting it. I hope you will join with me in doing so.

Questions for Study and Discussion

1. What is MacNeil's thesis in this essay?
2. What specific criticisms does he make regarding the way television presents the news?
3. What do television commercials symbolize for MacNeil? (Glossary: *Symbol*)
4. How would you describe MacNeil's conclusion? What do you think he hopes to accomplish in his conclusion? (Glossary: *Beginnings/Endings*)

Vocabulary

Refer to your dictionary to define the following words as they are used in this selection. Then use each work in a sentence of your own.

dullest (3)	medium (6)
serial (4)	august (6)
kaleidoscopic (4)	anachronism (9)
usurps (4)	skeptically (14)

Suggested Writing Assignments

1. MacNeil's essay is almost totally negative about television's effects on its viewers. Write an essay in which you take the opposing view. Develop a thesis presenting the beneficial effects of television.
2. Write an essay in which you use the following sentence as a thesis statement:

   The best single source for daily news is the (television, radio, newspaper).

2

UNITY

A well-written essay should be unified; that is, everything in it should be related to its thesis, or main idea. The first requirement for unity is that the thesis itself be clear, either through a direct statement, called the thesis statement, or by implication. The second requirement is that there be no digressions, no discussion or information that is not shown to be logically related to the thesis. A unified essay stays within the limits of its thesis.

Here, for example, is a short essay called "Over-Generalizing" about the dangers of making generalizations. As you read, notice how carefully author Stuart Chase sticks to his point.

1
One swallow does not make a summer, nor can two or three cases often support a dependable generalization. Yet all of us, including the most polished eggheads, are constantly falling into this mental mantrap. It is the commonest, probably the most seductive, and potentially the most dangerous, of all the fallacies.

2
You drive through a town and see a drunken man on the sidewalk. A few blocks further on you see another. You turn to your companion: "Nothing but drunks in this town!" Soon you are out in the country, bowling along at fifty. A car passes you as if you were parked. On a curve a second whizzes by. Your companion turns to you: "All the drivers in this state are crazy!" Two thumping generalizations, each built on two cases. If we stop to think, we usually recognize the exaggeration and the unfairness of such generalizations. Trouble comes when we do not stop to think—or when we build them on a prejudice.

3
This kind of reasoning has been around for a long time. Aristotle was aware of its dangers and called it "reasoning by example," meaning too few examples. What it boils down to is failing to count your swallows before announcing that summer is here. Driving from my home to New Haven the other day, a distance of about forty miles, I caught

26

myself saying: "Every time I look around I see a new ranch-type house going up." So on the return trip I counted them; there were exactly five under construction. And how many times had I "looked around"? I suppose I had glanced to right and left—as one must at side roads and so forth in driving—several hundred times.

In this fallacy we do not make the error of neglecting   4 facts altogether and rushing immediately to the level of opinion. We start at the fact level properly enough, but *we do not stay there.* A case of two and up we go to a rousing over-simplification about drunks, speeders, ranch-style houses—or, more seriously, about foreigners, Negroes, labor leaders, teen-agers.

Why do we over-generalize so often and sometimes so di-   5 sastrously? One reason is that the human mind is a generalizing machine. We would not be men without this power. The old academic crack: "All generalizations are false, including this one," is only a play on words. We *must* generalize to communicate and to live. But we should beware of beating the gun; of not waiting until enough facts are in to say something useful. Meanwhile it is a plain waste of time to listen to arguments based on a few hand-picked examples.

Everything in the essay relates to Chase's thesis statement, which is included in the essay's first sentence: ". . . nor can two or three cases often support a dependable generalization." Paragraphs 2 and 3 document the thesis with examples; paragraph 4 explains how over-generalizing occurs; paragraph 5 analyzes why people over-generalize; and, for a conclusion, Chase restates his thesis in different words. An essay may be longer, more complex, and more wide-ranging than this one, but to be effective it must also avoid digressions and remain close to the author's main idea.

INTELLIGENCE

Isaac Asimov

Isaac Asimov was born in the Soviet Union in 1920 and came to the United States in 1923. Author of more than 300 books, he is internationally recognized as a great popularizer of science. In addition to his writings on science, he has written much science fiction as well as books on history, Shakespeare, and the Bible. Whatever kind of writing Asimov undertakes, he is both entertaining and lucid, as can be seen in the following selection. As you read the essay, notice how every paragraph is related to Asimov's thesis that intelligence is a relative matter.

What is intelligence, anyway? When I was in the army I   1
received a kind of aptitude test that all soldiers took and, against a normal of 100, scored 160. No one at the base had ever seen a figure like that, and for two hours they made a big fuss over me. (It didn't mean anything. The next day I was still a buck private with KP as my highest duty.)

All my life I've been registering scores like that, so that I have   2
the complacent feeling that I'm highly intelligent, and I expect other people to think so, too. Actually, though, don't such scores simply mean that I am very good at answering the type of academic questions that are considered worthy of answers by the people who make up the intelligence tests—people with intellectual bents similar to mine?

For instance, I had an auto-repair man once, who, on these in-   3
telligence tests, could not possibly have scored more than 80, by my estimate. I always took it for granted that I was far more intelligent than he was. Yet, when anything went wrong with my car I hastened to him with it, watched him anxiously as he explored its vitals, and listened to his pronouncements as though they were divine oracles—and he always fixed my car.

Well, then, suppose my auto-repair man devised questions   4
for an intelligence test. Or suppose a carpenter did, or a

farmer, or, indeed, almost anyone but an academician. By every one of those tests, I'd prove myself a moron. And I'd *be* a moron, too. In a world where I could not use my academic training and my verbal talents but had to do something intricate or hard, working with my hands, I would do poorly. My intelligence, then, is not absolute but is a function of the society I live in and of the fact that a small subsection of that society has managed to foist itself on the rest as an arbiter of such matters.

Consider my auto-repair man, again. He had a habit of telling   5
me jokes whenever he saw me. One time he raised his head from under the automobile hood to say: "Doc, a deaf-and-dumb guy went into a hardware store to ask for some nails. He put two fingers together on the counter and made hammering motions with the other hand. The clerk brought him a hammer. He shook his head and pointed to the two fingers he was hammering. The clerk brought him nails. He picked out the sizes he wanted, and left. Well, doc, the next guy who came in was a blind man. He wanted scissors. How do you suppose he asked for them?"

Indulgently, I lifted my right hand and made scissoring mo-   6
tions with my first two fingers. Whereupon my auto-repair man laughed raucously and said, "Why, you dumb jerk, he used his *voice* and asked for them." Then he said, smugly, "I've been trying that on all my customers today." "Did you catch many?" I asked. "Quite a few," he said, "but I knew for sure I'd catch *you.*" "Why is that?" I asked. "Because you're so goddamned educated, doc, I *knew* you couldn't be very smart."

And I have an uneasy feeling he had something there.   7

Questions for Study and Discussion

1. The main point of this essay is that intelligence is a relative matter. How is each paragraph in the essay related to this thesis?
2. Discuss how Asimov achieves coherence in this essay by using transitions to link paragraphs. (Glossary: *Transitions*)
3. What is the author's purpose in telling the auto-repair man's joke? What distinction does the auto-repair man make between "educated" and "smart"?

4. Why, in your opinion, does Asimov make the final sentence a separate paragraph instead of including it in the preceding one?

Vocabulary

Refer to your dictionary to define the following words as they are used in this selection. Then use each word in a sentence of your own.

aptitude (1)   foist (4)
complacent (2)   indulgently (6)
oracles (3)   raucously (6)

Suggested Writing Assignments

1. Write an essay in which you attempt to come to an understanding of intelligence or of another elusive abstract term—creativity, charm, courage, or professionalism, for example. Make sure that your essay, like Asimov's, is unified; that is, your examples and discussions must relate to your thesis.

2. Make a generalization about a topic of your choice and write an essay in which you use multiple examples to support it. Make sure that your essay is unified; choose your examples carefully and relate them to your thesis.

DON'T LET STEREOTYPES
WARP YOUR JUDGMENTS

Robert L. Heilbroner

The economist Robert L. Heilbroner was educated at Harvard and at the New School for Social Research, where he has been the Norman Thomas Professor of Economics since 1972. He has written The Future as History *(1960),* A Primer of Government Spending: Between Capitalism and Socialism *(1970), and* An Inquiry into the Human Prospect *(1974). "Don't Let Stereotypes Warp Your Judgments" first appeared in* Reader's Digest. *As you read this essay, pay particular attention to its unity—the relationships of the paragraphs to the thesis.*

Is a girl called Gloria apt to be better-looking than one called   1
Bertha? Are criminals more likely to be dark than blond?
Can you tell a good deal about someone's personality from
hearing his voice briefly over the phone? Can a person's nation-
ality be pretty accurately guessed from his photograph? Does
the fact that someone wears glasses imply that he is intelligent?

The answer to all these questions is obviously, "No."   2

Yet, from all the evidence at hand, most of us believe these   3
things. Ask any college boy if he'd rather take his chances with
a Gloria or a Bertha, or ask a college girl if she'd rather blind-
date a Richard or a Cuthbert. In fact, you don't have to ask:
college students in questionnaires have revealed that names
conjure up the same images in their minds as they do in
yours—and for as little reason.

Look into the favorite suspects of persons who report "suspi-   4
cious characters" and you will find a large percentage of them
to be "swarthy" or "dark and foreign-looking"—despite the tes-
timony of criminologists that criminals do *not* tend to be dark,
foreign or "wild-eyed." Delve into the main asset of a telephone

stock swindler and you will find it to be a marvelously confidence-inspiring telephone "personality." And whereas we all think we know what an Italian or a Swede looks like, it is the sad fact that when a group of Nebraska students sought to match faces and nationalities of 15 European countries, they were scored wrong in 93 percent of their identifications. Finally, for all the fact that horn-rimmed glasses have now become the standard television sign of an "intellectual," optometrists know that the main thing that distinguishes people with glasses is just bad eyes.

Stereotypes are a kind of gossip about the world, a gossip   5
that makes us prejudge people before we ever lay eyes on them. Hence it is not surprising that stereotypes have something to do with the dark world of prejudice. Explore most prejudices (note that the word means prejudgment) and you will find a cruel stereotype at the core of each one.

For it is the extraordinary fact that once we have typecast the   6
world, we tend to see people in terms of our standardized pictures. In another demonstration of the power of stereotypes to affect our vision, a number of Columbia and Barnard students were shown 30 photographs of pretty but unidentified girls, and asked to rate each in terms of "general liking," "intelligence," "beauty" and so on. Two months later, the same group were shown the same photographs, this time with fictitious Irish, Italian, Jewish and "American" names attached to the pictures. Right away the ratings changed. Faces which were now seen as representing a national group went down in looks and still farther down in likability, while the "American" girls suddenly looked decidedly prettier and nicer.

Why is it that we stereotype the world in such irrational and   7
harmful fashion? In part, we begin to type-cast people in our childhood years. Early in life, as every parent whose child has watched a TV Western knows, we learn to spot the Good Guys from the Bad Guys. Some years ago, a social psychologist showed very clearly how powerful these stereotypes of childhood vision are. He secretly asked the most popular youngsters in an elementary school to make errors in their morning gym exercises. Afterwards, he asked the class if anyone had noticed any mistakes during gym period. Oh, yes, said the children. But

it was the *unpopular* members of the class—the "bad guys"—they remembered as being out of step.

We not only grow up with standardized pictures forming in-   8
side of us, but as grown-ups we are constantly having them thrust upon us. Some of them, like the half-joking, half-serious stereotypes of mothers-in-law, or country yokels, or psychiatrists, are dinned into us by the stock jokes we hear and repeat. In fact, without such stereotypes, there would be a lot fewer jokes. Still other stereotypes are perpetuated by the advertisements we read, the movies we see, the books we read.

And finally, we tend to stereotype because it helps us make   9
sense out of a highly confusing world, a world which William James once described as "one great, blooming, buzzing confusion." It is a curious fact that if we don't *know* what we're looking at, we are often quite literally unable to *see* what we're looking at. People who recover their sight after a lifetime of blindness actually cannot at first tell a triangle from a square. A visitor to a factory sees only noisy chaos where the superintendent sees a perfectly synchronized flow of work. As Walter Lippmann has said, "For the most part we do not first see, and then define; we define first, and then we see."

Stereotypes are one way in which we "define" the world in   10
order to see it. They classify the infinite variety of human beings into a convenient handful of "types" towards whom we learn to act in stereotyped fashion. Life would be a wearing process if we had to start from scratch with each and every human contact. Stereotypes economize on our mental effort by covering up the blooming, buzzing confusion with big recognizable cut-outs. They save us the "trouble" of finding out what the world is like—they give it its accustomed look.

Thus the trouble is that stereotypes make us mentally lazy.   11
As S. I. Hayakawa, the authority on semantics, has written: "The danger of stereotypes lies not in their existence, but in the fact that they become for all people some of the time, and for some people all the time, *substitutes for observation*." Worse yet, stereotypes get in the way of our judgment, even when we do observe the world. Someone who has formed rigid preconceptions of all Latins as "excitable," or all teenagers as "wild," doesn't alter his point of view when he meets a calm and delib-

erate Genoese, or a serious-minded high school student. He brushes them aside as "exceptions that prove the rule." And, of course, if he meets someone true to type, he stands triumphantly vindicated. "They're all like that," he proclaims, having encountered an excited Latin, an ill-behaved adolescent.

Hence, quite aside from the injustice which stereotypes do to others, they impoverish ourselves. A person who lumps the world into simple categories, who type-casts all labor leaders as "racketeers," all businessmen as "reactionaries," all Harvard men as "snobs," and all Frenchmen as "sexy," is in danger of becoming a stereotype himself. He loses his capacity to be himself—which is to say, to see the world in his own absolutely unique, inimitable and independent fashion. 12

Instead, he votes for the man who fits his standardized picture of what a candidate "should" look like or sound like, buys the goods that someone in his "situation" in life "should" own, lives the life that others define for him. The mark of the stereotype person is that he never surprises us, that we do indeed have him "typed." And no one fits this strait-jacket so perfectly as someone whose opinions about *other people* are fixed and inflexible. 13

Impoverishing as they are, stereotypes are not easy to get rid of. The world we type-cast may be no better than a Grade B movie, but at least we know what to expect of our stock characters. When we let them act for themselves in the strangely unpredictable way that people do act, who knows but that many of our fondest convictions will be proved wrong? 14

Nor do we suddenly drop our standardized pictures for a blinding vision of the Truth. Sharp swings of ideas about people often just substitute one stereotype for another. The true process of change is a slow one that adds bits and pieces of reality to the pictures in our heads, until gradually they take on some of the blurriness of life itself. Little by little, we learn not that Jews and Negroes and Catholics and Puerto Ricans are "just like everybody else"—for that, too, is a stereotype—but that each and every one of them is unique, special, different and individual. Often we do not even know that we have let a stereotype lapse until we hear someone saying, "all so-and-so's are like such-and-such," and we hear ourselves saying, "Well—maybe." 15

Can we speed the process along? Of course we can.   16

First, we can become *aware* of the standardized pictures in   17
our heads, in other peoples' heads, in the world around us.

Second, we can become suspicious of all judgments that we   18
allow exceptions to "prove." There is* no more chastening
thought than that in the vast intellectual adventure of science,
it takes but one tiny exception to topple a whole edifice of
ideas.

Third, we can learn to be chary of generalizations about peo-   19
ple. As F. Scott Fitzgerald once wrote: "Begin with an individual, and before you know it you have created a type; begin with
a type, and you find you have created—nothing."

Most of the time, when we type-cast the world, we are not in   20
fact generalizing about people at all. We are only revealing the
embarrassing facts about the pictures that hang in the gallery
of stereotypes in our own heads.

Questions for Study and Discussion

1. What is Heilbroner's main point, or thesis, in this essay?
   (Glossary: *Thesis*)
2. Study paragraphs 6, 8, and 15. Each paragraph illustrates
   Heilbroner's thesis. How? What does each paragraph contribute to support the thesis?
3. Transitional devices indicate relationships between paragraphs and thus help to unify the essay. Identify three transitions in this essay. Explain how they help to unify the essay. (Glossary: *Transitions*)
4. Heilbroner uses the word *picture* in his discussion of stereotypes. Why is this an appropriate word in this discussion?
   (Glossary: *Diction*)

Vocabulary

Refer to your dictionary to define the following words as they
are used in this selection. Then use each word in a sentence of
your own.

irrational (7)   impoverish (12)
perpetuated (8)   chastening (18)
infinite (10)   edifice (18)
preconceptions (11)   chary (19)
vindicated (11)

Suggested Writing Assignments

1. Write an essay in which you attempt to convince your readers that it is not in their best interests to perform a particular act—for example, smoke, take stimulants to stay awake, go on a crash diet, make snap judgments. In writing your essay, follow Heilbroner's lead: First identify the issue; then explain why it is a problem; and, finally, offer a solution or some advice. Remember to unify the various parts of your essay.

2. Have you ever been considered as a stereotype—a student, a member of a particular sex, class, ethnic, national, or racial group? Write a unified essay that examines how stereotyping has affected you, how it has perhaps changed you, and how you regard the process.

WHAT MAKES A LEADER?

Michael Korda

Michael Korda is the author of such bestsellers as Male Chauvinism *(1979),* Power *(1975),* Charmed Lives *(1979), and* Queenie *(1985). In this essay, which first appeared in* Newsweek, *Korda discusses the qualities that all good leaders have in common. Notice how Korda uses the topic sentence in each paragraph to focus our attention on these qualities and how these topic sentences contribute to an overall sense of unity.*

Not every President is a leader, but every time we elect a President we hope for one, especially in times of doubt and crisis. In easy times we are ambivalent—the leader, after all, makes demands, challenges the status quo, shakes things up.

Leadership is as much a question of timing as anything else. The leader must appear on the scene at a moment when people are looking for leadership, as Churchill did in 1940, as Roosevelt did in 1933, as Lenin did in 1917. And when he comes, he must offer a simple, eloquent message.

Great leaders are almost always great simplifiers, who cut through argument, debate and doubt to offer a solution everybody can understand and remember. Churchill warned the British to expect "blood, toil, tears and sweat"; FDR told Americans that "the only thing we have to fear is fear itself"; Lenin promised the war-weary Russians peace, land and bread. Straightforward but potent messages.

We have an image of what a leader ought to be. We even recognize the physical signs: leaders may not necessarily be tall, but they must have bigger-than-life, commanding features— LBJ's nose and ear lobes, Ike's broad grin. A trademark also comes in handy: Lincoln's stovepipe hat, JFK's rocker. We expect our leaders to stand out a little, not to be like ordinary men. Half of President Ford's trouble lay in the fact that, if you closed your eyes for a moment, you couldn't remember his face, figure or clothes. A leader should have an unforgettable identity, instantly and permanently fixed in people's minds.

It also helps for a leader to be able to do something most of us can't: FDR overcame polio; Mao swam the Yangtze River at the age of 72. We don't want our leaders to be "just like us." We want them to be like us but better, special, more so. Yet if they are *too* different, we reject them. Adlai Stevenson was too cerebral. Nelson Rockefeller, too rich.

Even television, which comes in for a lot of knocks as an image-builder that magnifies form over substance, doesn't altogether obscure the qualities of leadership we recognize, or their absence. Television exposed Nixon's insecurity, Humphrey's fatal infatuation with his own voice.

A leader must know how to use power (that's what leadership is about), but he also has to have a way of showing that he does. He has to be able to project firmness—no physical clumsiness (like Ford), no rapid eye movements (like Carter).

A Chinese philosopher once remarked that a leader must have the grace of a good dancer, and there is a great deal of wisdom to this. A leader should know how to appear relaxed and confident. His walk should be firm and purposeful. He should be able, like Lincoln, FDR, Truman, Ike and JFK, to give a good, hearty, belly laugh, instead of the sickly grin that passes for good humor in Nixon or Carter. Ronald Reagan's training as an actor showed to good effect in the debate with Carter, when by his easy manner and apparent affability, he managed to convey the impression that in fact he was the President and Carter the challenger.

If we know what we're looking for, why is it so difficult to find? The answer lies in a very simple truth about leadership. *People can only be led where they want to go.* The leader follows, though a step ahead. Americans *wanted* to climb out of the Depression and needed someone to tell them they could do it, and FDR did. The British believed that they could still win the war after the defeats of 1940, and Churchill told them they were right.

A leader rides the waves, moves with the tides, understands the deepest yearnings of his people. He cannot make a nation that wants peace at any price go to war, or stop a nation determined to fight from doing so. His purpose must match the national mood. His task is to focus the people's energies and desires, to define them in simple terms, to inspire, to make what people already want seem attainable, important, within their grasp.

Above all, he must dignify our desires, convince us that we 11 are taking part in the making of great history, give us a sense of glory about ourselves. Winston Churchill managed, by sheer rhetoric, to turn the British defeat and the evacuation of Dunkirk in 1940 into a major victory. FDR's words turned the sinking of the American fleet at Pearl Harbor into a national rallying cry instead of a humiliating national scandal. A leader must stir our blood, not appeal to our reason. . . .

A great leader must have a certain irrational quality, a stub- 12 born refusal to face facts, infectious optimism, the ability to convince us that all is not lost even when we're afraid it is. Confucius suggested that, while the advisers of a great leader should be as cold as ice, the leader himself should have fire, a spark of divine madness.

He won't come until we're ready for him, for the leader is 13 like a mirror, reflecting back to us our own sense of purpose, putting into words our own dreams and hopes, transforming our needs and fears into coherent policies and programs.

Our strength makes him strong; our determination makes 14 him determined; our courage makes him a hero; he is, in the final analysis, the symbol of the best in us, shaped by our own spirit and will. And when these qualities are lacking in us, we can't produce him; and even with all our skill at image-building, we can't fake him. He is, after all, merely the sum of us.

Questions for Study and Discussion

1. What is Korda's thesis in this essay and where is it stated? Why do you suppose he states his thesis where he does instead of elsewhere in the essay? (Glossary: *Thesis*)

2. Explain how Korda uses parallelism to achieve unity in this essay. (Glossary: *Parallelism*)

3. Identify the topic sentence in paragraph 4. What would be gained or lost if the topic sentence were placed elsewhere in the paragraph?

4. Korda's knowledge of history and great leaders is reflected in the examples he uses to support his topic sentences. Using paragraphs 2, 4, 8, and 11 explain how Korda's examples develop his topic sentences. (Glossary: *Example*)

5. What would be gained or lost if paragraphs 13 and 14 were combined?

6. At the beginning of paragraph 9 Korda asks a rhetorical question, one that requires no answer and that is often used for emphasis. What is the purpose of this question in the context of his essay?

Vocabulary

Refer to your dictionary to define the following words as they are used in this selection. Then use each word in a sentence of your own.

ambivalent (1)   cerebral (5)
status quo (1)   affability (8)
eloquent (2)   infectious (12)

Suggested Writing Assignments

1. In his essay, Michael Korda presents his views on what makes a great leader. Most people would agree, however, that for a leader to lead there must be those who are willing to be led, to be good team players. Write an essay in which you explain what it takes to be a willing and productive participant in a group effort, whether the group be as small as a class or a basketball team or as large as a major corporation. While writing be especially conscious of achieving unity in your work.

2. Select one of the following topics for a short essay:

    What makes a good teacher?
    What makes a good student?
    What makes a good team captain?
    What makes a good parent?

  Make sure that your essay is unified.

3

ORGANIZATION

In an essay, ideas and information cannot be presented all at once; they have to be arranged in some order. That order is the essay's organization.

The pattern of organization in an essay should be suited to the writer's subject and purpose. For example, if you are writing about your experience working in a fast-food restaurant, and your purpose is to tell about the activities of a typical day, you might present those activities in chronological order. If, on the other hand, you wish to argue that working in a bank is an ideal summer job, you might proceed from the least rewarding to the most rewarding aspect of this job; this is called "climactic" order.

Some often-used patterns of organization are time order, space order, and logical order. Time order, or chronological order, is used to present events as they occurred. A personal narrative, a report of a campus incident, or an account of a historical event can be most naturally and easily related in chronological order. The description of a process, such as the refinishing of a table, the building of a stone wall, or the way to serve a tennis ball, almost always calls for a chronological organization. Of course, the order of events can sometimes be rearranged for special effect. For example, an account of an auto accident may begin with the collision itself and then go back in time to tell about the events leading up to it. Essays that are models of chronological order include Dick Gregory's "Shame" and Bernard Gladstone's "How to Build a Fire in a Fireplace."

Space order is used when describing a person, place, or thing. This organizational pattern begins at a particular point and moves in some direction, such as left to right, top to bottom, east to west, outside to inside, front to back, near to far, around, or over. In describing a house, for example, a writer could move from top to bottom, from outside to inside, or in a circle around the outside. Gilbert Highet's "Subway Station"

(p. 231) is an essay in which space is used as the organizing principle.

Logical order can take many forms depending on the writer's purpose. These include: general to specific, most familiar to least familiar, and smallest to biggest. Perhaps the most common type of logical order is order of importance. Notice how the writer uses this order in the following paragraph:

> The Egyptians have taught us many things. They were excellent farmers. They knew all about irrigation. They built temples which were afterwards copied by the Greeks and which served as the earliest models for the churches in which we worship nowadays. They invented a calendar which proved such a useful instrument for the purpose of measuring time that it has survived with a few changes until today. But most important of all, the Egyptians learned how to preserve speech for the benefit of future generations. They invented the art of writing.

By organizing the material according to the order of increasing importance, the writer places special emphasis on the final sentence. In writing a descriptive essay you can move from the least striking to the most striking detail, so as to keep your reader interested and involved in the description. In an explanatory essay you can start with the point that readers will find least difficult to understand, and move on to the most difficult; that's how teachers organize many courses. Or, in writing an argumentative essay, you can move from your least controversial point to the most controversial, preparing your reader gradually to accept your argument.

BUGS BUNNY SAYS THEY'RE YUMMY

Dawn Ann Kurth

In 1972 eleven-year-old Dawn Ann Kurth was a surprise witness at a Senate subcommittee hearing on television advertising. She believes that television commercials, especially those shown on Saturday-morning television, take unfair advantage of children. The following is a transcript of her statement to the committee. As you read it, pay particular attention to the way her examples of television advertising are arranged.

Mr. Chairman: [1]
My name is Dawn Ann Kurth. I am 11 years old and in the fifth grade at Meadowlane Elementary School in Melbourne, Florida. This year I was one of the 36 students chosen by the teachers out of 20,000 5th-through-8th graders to do a project in the Talented Student Program in Brevard County. We were allowed to choose a project in any field we wanted. It was difficult to decide. There seem to be so many problems in the world today. What could I do?

A small family crisis solved my problem. My sister Martha, [2] who is 7, had asked my mother to buy a box of Post Raisin Bran so that she could get the free record that was on the back of the box. It had been advertised several times on Saturday morning cartoon shows. My mother bought the cereal, and we all (there are four children in our family) helped Martha to eat it so she could get the record. It was after the cereal was eaten and she had the record that the crisis occurred. There was no way the record would work.

Martha was very upset and began crying and I was angry too. [3] It just didn't seem right to me that something could be shown on TV that worked fine and people were listening and dancing to the record and when you bought the cereal, instead of laughing and dancing, we were crying and angry. Then I realized that perhaps here was a problem I could do something about or, if I

44

couldn't change things, at least I could make others aware of deceptive advertising practices to children.

To begin my project I decided to keep a record of the number of commercials shown on typical Saturday morning TV shows. There were 25 commercial messages during one hour, from 8 to 9 A.M., not counting ads for shows coming up or public service ads. I found there were only 10 to 12 commercials during shows my parents like to watch. For the first time, I really began to think about what the commercials were saying. I had always listened before and many times asked my mother to buy certain products I had seen advertised, but now I was listening and really thinking about what was being said. Millions of kids are being told:

"Make friends with Kool-Aid. Kool-Aid makes good friends."

"People who love kids have to buy Fritos."

"Hershey chocolate makes milk taste like a chocolate bar." Why should milk taste like a chocolate bar anyway?

"Cheerios make you feel groovy all day long." I eat them sometimes and I don't feel any different.

"Libby frozen dinners have fun in them." Nothing is said about the food in them.

"Cocoa Krispies taste like a chocolate milk shake only they are crunchy."

"Lucky Charms are magically delicious with sweet surprises inside." Those sweet surprises are marshmallow candy.

I think the commercials I just mentioned are examples of deceptive advertising practices.

Another type of commercial advertises a free bonus gift if you buy a certain product. The whole commercial tells about the bonus gift and says nothing about the product they want you to buy. Many times, as in the case of the record, the bonus gift appears to be worthless junk or isn't in the package. I wrote to the TV networks and found it costs about $4,000 for a 30-second commercial. Many of those ads appeared four times in each hour. I wonder why any company would spend $15,000 or $20,000 an hour to advertise worthless junk.

The ads that I have mentioned I consider deceptive. However, I've found others I feel are dangerous.

Bugs Bunny vitamin ads say their vitamins "taste yummy" and taste good.

Chocolate Zestabs say their product is "delicious" and compare taking it with eating a chocolate cookie. 16

If my mother were to buy those vitamins, and my little sister 17
got to the bottles, I'm sure she would eat them just as if they were candy.

I do not know a lot about nutrition, but I do know that my 18
mother tries to keep our family from eating so many sweets. She says they are bad for our teeth. Our dentist says so too. If they are bad, why are companies allowed to make children want them by advertising on TV? Almost all of the ads I have seen during children's programs are for candy, or sugar-coated cereal, or even sugar-coated cereal with candy in it.

I know people who make these commercials are not bad. I 19
know the commercials pay for TV shows and I like to watch TV. I just think that it would be as easy to produce a good commercial as a bad one. If there is nothing good that can be said about a product that is the truth, perhaps the product should not be sold to kids on TV in the first place.

I do not know all the ways to write a good commercial, but I 20
think commercials would be good if they taught kids something that was true. They could teach about good health, and also about where food is grown. If my 3-year-old sister can learn to sing, "It takes two hands to handle a whopper 'cause the burgers are better at Burger King," from a commercial, couldn't a commercial also teach her to recognize the letters of the alphabet, numbers, and colors? I am sure that people who write commercials are much smarter than I and they should be able to think of many ways to write a commercial that tells the truth about a product without telling kids they should eat it because it is sweeter or "shaped like fun" (what shape *is* fun, anyway?) or because Tony Tiger says so.

I also think kids should not be bribed to buy a product by 21
commercials telling of the wonderful free bonus gift inside.

I think kids should not be told to eat a certain product be- 22
cause a well-known hero does. If this is a reason to eat something, then, when a well-known person uses drugs, should kids try drugs for the same reason?

Last of all, I think vitamin companies should never, never be 23
allowed to advertise their product as being delicious, yummy, or in any way make children think they are candy. Perhaps

these commercials could teach children the dangers of taking drugs or teach children that, if they do find a bottle of pills, or if the medicine closet is open, they should run and tell a grown-up, and never, never eat the medicine.

I want to thank the Committee for letting me appear. When I leave Washington, the thing that I will remember for the rest of my life is that some people *do* care what kids think. I know I could have led a protest about commercials through our shopping center and people would have laughed at me or thought I needed a good spanking or wondered what kind of parents I had that would let me run around in the streets protesting. I decided to gather my information and write letters to anyone I thought would listen. Many of them didn't listen, but some did. That is why I am here today. Because some people cared about what I thought. I hope now that I can tell every kid in America that when they see a wrong, they shouldn't just try to forget about it and hope it will go away. They should begin to do what they can to change it.   24

People will listen. I know, because you're listening to me.   25

Questions for Study and Discussion

1. What disturbs Kurth about advertisements directed at children?
2. Why does the writer include the incident about her sister and the Post Raisin Bran record?
3. Which of the three patterns of organization does she use in presenting her examples of TV advertising? Support your answers with examples.
4. Where is the writer's argument summarized?

Vocabulary

Refer to your dictionary to define the following words as they are used in this selection. Then use each word in a sentence of your own.

deceptive (3)   nutrition (18)
bonus (13)   bribed (21)

Suggested Writing Assignments

1. No one who watches television can remain unaware of television advertising. Write an essay in which you discuss your attitude toward television commercials. Do you find them entertaining, annoying, mildly amusing, representative of our society, indicative of what's right or wrong with America, offensive? Cite examples of television commercials in your essay, being sure to organize them in such a way as to serve your thesis and overall purpose.

2. Think of a commonplace subject that people might take for granted, but that you find interesting. Write an essay on that subject, using one of the following types of logical order:

   least important to most important
   most familiar to least familiar
   smallest to biggest
   oldest to newest
   easiest to understand to most difficult to understand
   good news to bad news
   general to specific

CHECKS AND BALANCES
AT THE SIGN OF THE DOVE

Jessica Mitford

*Jessica Mitford was born in 1917 in Batsford,
Gloucestershire, England. A* Time *reviewer
called her the "Queen of the Muckrakers" for
her cleverness and tenacity in writing exposes of
society's less-than-honest people and businesses.
In* The American Way of Death *Mitford examines the American funeral industry and exposes
the technical and business practices used by un-
dertakers to take advantage of unsuspecting consumers. Mitford is respected as a tireless researcher and a simple but inventive writer. In
the following selection from* New York *magazine, Mitford recounts what happened when she
and a friend decided to have dinner at a posh
New York restaurant. As you read, notice the
way Mitford has organized her experiences into
the form of a mini-play.*

This is a cautionary tale in five acts for out-of-towners, as   1
New Yorkers call provincials, like me, who venture into
Manhattan only once in a great while. (I should hasten to hedge:
some of my happiest moments have been spent in New York
restaurants, from plain to fancy.)

Act I. I invite a friend who works in the fashion industry to   2
have dinner with me. As she is (I presume) a sophisticate who
knows the city, I ask her to choose the restaurant. "Let's go
somewhere *really* nice," I say expansively. She proposes the
Sign of the Dove, once recommended to her by somebody; so
thither we repair at 8 p.m.

Act II. We are seated in an absurdly done-up place, its décor   3
like a pink wedding scene, but, determined to enjoy ourselves,
we remark how very elegant it is. Menus arrive; rather to my
sorrow, I note the entrées are in the range of $16 to $18.50. We
order frugally: one drink each; my friend gets the $18.50 lamb

chops, I get the plat du jour (not on the menu), which is shad
roe; half a bottle of Chablis to share; no starters or desserts.
She has two small coffees, I none. The shad roe is overcooked,
with a charred piece of bacon on top; my friend's potatoes are
cold. We ask for some proper bacon and some string beans to
replace the cold potatoes. After a longish interval, these are
brought. The restaurant, fairly empty when we first arrived, is
filling up rapidly with persons of the gold-brocade-pantsuit
type and their male counterparts, who blend nicely with the
décor.

Act III. The bill comes; it is for $76.10. I am inwardly fuming, 4
especially since the two entrées are lumped as $50, with no fur-
ther explanation. (Was the unlisted shad roe $31.50? Had the
restaurant charged extra for the new piece of bacon? For the
string beans in lieu of the unacceptable potatoes?) The two
drinks are $5.50; the half-bottle of Chablis, $10.50; my friend's
coffee, $3.50. Cover charge and sales tax account for the bal-
ance. Not wishing to embarrass my friend—TSOTD having
been her suggestion—I choke down my fury, say nothing, and
write a check (with a measly $9 tip) for $85. My only desire now
is to get out of this beastly place and write the whole thing off
as one of life's more dismal experiences.

Act IV. Waiter says he cannot accept a personal check. I 5
counter crossly that I haven't got that much cash. Manager
looms; have I no credit card? No, but I have tons of identifica-
tion. He says *on no account* will he take personal checks—a
check is just a piece of paper. So is a dollar bill, I point out. He
beckons us into the lobby, where we are surrounded by menacing waiters, acting with the precision of trained guards. The
manager, directing this B-movie scene, says he is going to call
the police. I furiously demand that he should do so immediately; we'll wait until they come and *then* he'll find out what
trouble is. He changes his mind about the police but swoops up
our coat checks and says we won't get our coats until we pay
cash. I snatch back my $85 check, which he is holding, and we
storm out, coatless, into the cold night.

Act V. Back at the apartment, we start telephoning, first to a 6
lawyer renowned for his consistent, militant defense of the un-
derdog, then to a famous food columnist. The lawyer grumpily
says I should have realized there's no law requiring a business-
man to accept a personal check, and there's nothing he can do.

The food columnist says I should have known better than to go there, that the place is notorious for its absurd prices and awful food. I am beginning to feel like the rape victim who is told she asked for it.

Epilogue. My friend, who went back the next day bearing cash to ransom our coats, demanded an itemized breakdown of the $76.10 bill. After a long, whispered huddle between manager and waiters, this was produced. Except for its total, it bore no relation to our original bill. The "two entrées, $50" had disappeared, replaced by chops and roe at $18.50 apiece. Coffee, previously charged at $3.50, was now $4.50, and two desserts had been added for $10. My persevering friend managed to make them knock off the unordered, unserved desserts plus a dollar for the coffee. The new total, including tax and cover charge, was $63.72, already a saving of $12.38 over the original bill. But this time my friend proffered not even the mingiest tip; thus, if one deducts $63.72 from the $85 I tried to pay, I saved a grand total of $21.28—thanks entirely to the inhospitable behavior of the management. What a windfall! Nevertheless, I think I shall not soon return to the Sign of the Dove.

Questions for Study and Discussion

1. What is Mitford's primary purpose in this essay? (Glossary: *Purpose*) Why does she call it a "cautionary tale"?

2. Which of the three types of organizational patterns (time order, space order, and logical order) has Mitford used in her essay? Do you think that Mitford's decision to tell her story in five acts and an Epilogue was a good idea? Why, or why not?

3. In a published commentary Mitford wrote that the five act, Epilogue format of her essay was a strategy she devised to keep the article within the space limitations given by *New York* magazine. How precisely did her division of the essay into acts help her save words? Give examples to support your points.

4. What is the purpose of paragraph 1? Why do you think Mitford put her second sentence in parentheses?

5. What is the significance of Mitford's title? (Glossary: *Title*)

What is ironic about the name of the restaurant? (Glossary: *Irony*)

Vocabulary

Refer to your dictionary to define the following words as they are used in this selection. Then use each word in a sentence of your own.

provincials (1)   beckons (5)
hedge (1)   militant (6)
sophisticate (2)   notorious (6)
expansively (2)   epilogue (7)
thither (2)   proffered (7)
brocade (3)   inhospitable (7)

Suggested Writing Assignments

1. Using the organization of Mitford's essay as a model, write an account of an event that you yourself have experienced that begins quietly enough, but soon builds in tension until it reaches a climax, and then ends. Depending on the story you tell, you may or may not see the need for an epilogue.
2. Write an essay on one of the following topics:

    local restaurants
    reading materials
    television shows
    ways of financing a college education
    types of summer jobs

    Be sure to use an organizational pattern that is well thought out and suited to both your material and your purpose.

THE SUICIDE-PILL OPTION

Jason Salzman

When he wrote the following essay, published as a "My Turn" column in Newsweek on Campus, Jason Salzman was a junior at Brown University. He is the founder of Students for Suicide Tablets, and in the fall of 1984 he headed an anti-nuclear suicide-pill campaign at Brown. In his essay Salzman explains why he thinks his campaign was worthwhile, using the types of reactions he has received to his proposal as his basis of organization. Note how this organizational pattern allows him to present his reasons in order of importance.

B rown University students overwhelmingly passed a refer- 1
endum on our student-council election ballot last fall asking our infirmary "to stockpile suicide pills for optional use by
students only after a nuclear war." I call on college students
across the country to put the same measure up for a vote at
their schools.

Although Brown officials refused to stockpile the suicide 2
pills, the referendum was in no way a failure. Most students
voted for it as a symbol anyway. Although the original intent of
the organizers was literal, the referendum does not have to be
viewed that way. And the absurdity of requesting suicide pills
fades away when one thinks about the consequences of a nuclear war and the way we deal with the thought of nuclear war
in general.

I get four types of reactions when I propose that students 3
adopt a suicide-pill referendum: (1) It's nothing but a crazy
joke. (2) It's an offensive idea that does more harm than good.
(3) It's worth supporting. (4) What it says is irrelevant; it's not
worth the time to listen to the idea.

Students who think that the suicide-pill proposal is a joke are 4
easily dealt with. They discover that I'm serious and ask some-

53

thing about the logistics of the program, such as where the pills would be guarded or distributed. For people who have not thought about it, just verbalizing the idea of suicide after a nuclear war is important. The prospect makes them understand a little bit more about what nuclear war means. This educational value alone makes the suicide-pill proposal worthwhile.

Another group of students either find the plan personally offensive or a poor way to show concern. First, they argue that it is defeatist; it encourages people to accept nuclear war as suicide so that they will do nothing to prevent it. But I think that the first step in preventing nuclear war is to make people realize, as much as is humanly possible, what it means. 5

Some students also say that suicide is too serious a subject to use in this way. I argue that this belief shows how good the approach is. People should be just as upset by the prospect of nuclear war as by the prospect of suicide. How better to show the degree of destruction that a nuclear war would inflict than to point out how it would affect our most sacred value, our value of life itself? Suicide, like life, would take on a whole new meaning. Our "never give up, never cop out" ethic would be meaningless after a nuclear war. If a nuclear war occurs, we will be robbed of our humanity. All this is hard to imagine because the destructive power of nuclear war is unimaginable. But we must try to face it. 6

Some students also ask what would happen if there were a limited nuclear war. Although I believe limited nuclear war is like limited pregnancy or limited death, I respond that the suicide pills would be optional and that a student could make up his or her mind when the time comes. 7

Students needn't agree with all the possible justifications to accept the suicide-pill option. Most people don't. 8

Some people support it for the same reasons that they support the freeze—as an important symbol. It shows their concern about the problems of nuclear war and disarmament. It shows that we are scared. 9

The suicide option emphasizes people's belief that surviving nuclear war is a dangerous illusion. If it is believed that a nuclear war will be won by the side with the most survivors or by the side which can rebuild the fastest, then waging a nuclear war becomes a realistic, not theoretical, idea. Opting for suicide pills would debunk the "nuclear winners" hypothesis. 10

Similarly, nuclear war is often associated with words such as 11
"victory," "survival," and "recovery." The suicide-pill program
links more appropriate words to nuclear war such as "death"
and "suicide."

On an even more theoretical level, the suicide-pill program is 12
a logical way to stabilize the arms race. It would demonstrate
to the Soviet Union that people in the United States are absolutely serious about preventing nuclear war. By denying the in-
stinctive desire for life after nuclear war, we would be making
the strongest possible statement for peace and disarmament.

Perhaps one of the best reasons is also the most simple: life 13
after nuclear war, if possible, would be undesirable. As the
phrase goes, "the living will envy the dead."

Students also support the suicide-pill option because it is a 14
good response to the government's civil-defense programs. The
emergency-evacuation plan, a scheme designed to move people
from the cities to the farms before the bombs start falling (in
other words, "back to the garden"), and the "in-place option,"
hiding from nuclear war in the basements of buildings around
campus, are both absurd projects that our government expends
too much energy on. The number and destructive power of Soviet nuclear missiles make any shelter plan useless. Civil defense is a prenuclear-age concept that cannot be transplanted
into the nuclear age.

Now, about those students who will not even listen to the 15
idea. Sometimes I try to catch their attention by asking them,
"Do you think you can survive a nuclear war?" Students have
replied with something like this, "If I can make it through college I can survive anything." Although clearly spoken in jest,
this response illustrates an unspoken mind-set. Asked about
survival, the first thing these students think about is college. In
many ways this is understandable. It is hard to realize that political problems, including the threat of nuclear weapons, can
be almost as immediate as what's right in front of us. It is easy
to forget that the bombs could start falling from the sky before
your next exam starts.

Because of the suicide-pill referendum, Brown students have 16
engaged in intense debate about the complex moral, political
and philosophical questions that are bound up with the arms
race. By sponsoring a similar referendum at your college, you
can ignite important discussion in this terribly apathetic age.

Questions for Study and Discussion

1. What is Salzman asking for in this essay?
2. How does he organize his essay? It may help to answer this question if you outline the essay. On which type of reaction does Salzman spend the most time? Why?
3. How might Salzman have organized his essay differently? What could be gained or lost with the new organization?

Vocabulary

Refer to your dictionary to define the following words as they are used in this selection. Then use each word in a sentence of your own.

referendum (1)   debunk (10)
logistics (4)   jest (15)
defeatist (5)   apathetic (16)
ethic (6)

Suggested Writing Assignments

1. Write an essay explaining why you would or would not vote for the Suicide-Pill Option if a referendum were held on your campus. Pay particular attention to the way in which you organize your thoughts and information.
2. Like Martin Gansberg's "38 Who Saw Murder Didn't Call Police," Salzman's essay addresses the problem of public apathy. Write an essay in which you analyze the problem of public apathy concerning important social and humanitarian issues and suggest what can be done to encourage thought and action. Again, give special consideration to the various possibilities for organizing your essay.

4

BEGINNINGS AND ENDINGS

"Begin at the beginning and go on till you come to the end: then stop," advised the King of Hearts in *Alice in Wonderland*. "Good advice, but more easily said than done," you might be tempted to reply. Certainly, no part of writing essays can be more daunting than coming up with effective beginnings and endings. In fact, many writers feel these are the most important parts of any piece of writing regardless of its length. Even before coming to your introduction proper, your readers will usually know something about your intentions from your title. Titles like "The Case Against Euthanasia," "How to Buy a Used Car," or "What Is a Migraine Headache?" indicate both your subject and approach and prepare your readers for what is to follow.

But what makes for an effective beginning? Not unlike a personal greeting, a good beginning should catch a reader's interest and then hold it. The experienced writer realizes that most readers would rather do almost anything than make a commitment to read, so the opening or "lead," as journalists refer to it, requires a lot of thought and much revising to make it right and to keep the reader's attention from straying. The inexperienced writer knows that the beginning is important but tries to write it first and to perfect it before moving on to the rest of the essay. Although there are no "rules" for writing introductions, we can offer one bit of general advice: wait until the writing process is well underway or almost completed before focusing on your lead. Following this advice will keep you from spending too much time on an introduction that you will probably revise. More importantly, once you actually see how your essay develops, you will know better how to introduce it to your reader.

In addition to capturing your reader's attention, a good beginning frequently introduces your thesis and either suggests or actually reveals the structure of the composition. Keep in mind that the best beginning is not necessarily the most catchy or the most shocking but the one most appropriate for the job you are trying to do.

Beginnings

The following examples from published essays show you some effective beginnings:

Short Generalization

It is a miracle that New York works at all.

E. B. White

Startling Claim

It is possible to stop most drug addiction in the United States within a very short time.

Gore Vidal

Questions

Just how interconnected *is* the animal world? Is it true that if we change any part of that world we risk unduly damaging life in other, larger parts of it?

Matthew Douglas

Humor/Apt Quotation

The right to pursue happiness is issued to Americans with their birth certificates, but no one seems quite sure which way it ran. It may be we are issued a hunting license but offered no game. Jonathan Swift seemed to think so when he attacked the idea of happiness as "the possession of being well-deceived," the felicity of being "a fool among knaves." For Swift saw society as Vanity Fair, the land of false goals.

John Ciardi

Startling Fact

Charles Darwin and Abraham Lincoln were born on the same day—February 12, 1809. They are also linked in another curious way—for both must simultaneously play, and for similar reasons, the role of man and legend.

Stephen Jay Gould

Dialogue

"This would be excellent, to go in the ocean with this thing," says Dave Gembutis, fifteen.

He is looking at a $170 Sea Cruiser raft.

"Great," says his companion, Dan Holmes, also fifteen.

This is at Herman's World of Sporting Goods, in the middle of the Woodfield Mall in Schaumburg, Illinois.

Bob Greene

Statistics/Question

In the 40 years from 1939 to 1979 white women who work full time have with monotonous regularity made slightly less than 60 percent as much as white men. Why?

Lester C. Thurow

Irony

In Moulmein, in lower Burma, I was hated by large numbers of people—the only time in my life that I have been important enough for this to happen to me.

George Orwell

There are many more excellent ways to begin an essay, but there are also some ways of beginning that should be avoided. Some of these follow:

Apology

I am a college student and do not consider myself an expert on the computer industry, but I think that many computer companies make false claims about just how easy it is to learn to use a computer.

Complaint

I'd rather write about a topic of my own choice than the one that is assigned, but here goes.

Webster's Dictionary

Webster's New Collegiate Dictionary defines the verb *to snore* as follows: "to breathe during sleep with a rough hoarse noise due to vibration of the soft palate."

Platitude

America is the land of opportunity and no one knows it better than Lee Iacocca.

Reference to Title

As you can see from my title, this essay is about why we should continue to experiment with human heart transplants.

Endings

An effective ending does more than simply indicate where the writer stopped writing. A conclusion may summarize; may inspire the reader to further thought or even action; may return to the beginning by repeating key words, phrases, or ideas; or may surprise the reader by providing a particularly convincing example to support a thesis. Indeed, there are, as with beginnings, many ways to write a conclusion, but the effectiveness of any choice really must be measured by how appropriately it fits what has gone before it. In the following conclusion to a long chapter on weasel words, a form of deceptive advertising language, writer Paul Stevens summarizes the points that he has made:

A weasel word is a word that's used to imply a meaning that cannot be truthfully stated. Some weasels imply meanings that are not the same as their actual definition, such as "help," "like," or "fortified." They can act as qualifiers and/or comparatives. Other weasels, such as "taste" and "flavor," have no definite meanings, and are simply subjective opinions offered by the manufacturer. A weasel of omission is one that implies a claim so strongly that it forces you to supply the bogus fact. Adjectives are weasels used to convey feelings and emotions to a greater extent than the product itself can.

In dealing with weasels, you must strip away the innuendos and try to ascertain the facts, if any. To do this, you need to ask questions such as: How? Why? How many? How much? Stick to basic definitions of words. Look them up if you have to. Then, apply the strict definition to the text of the advertisement or commercial. "Like" means similar to, but not the same as. "Virtually" means the same in essence, but not in fact.

Above all, never underestimate the devious qualities of a weasel. Weasels twist and turn and hide in dark shadows. You must come to grips with them, or advertising will rule you forever.

My advice to you is: Beware of weasels. They are nasty and untrainable, and they attack pocketbooks.

If you are having trouble with your conclusion—and this is not an uncommon problem—it may be because of problems with your essay itself. Frequently, writers do not know when to end because they are not sure about their overall purpose in the first place. For example, if you are taking a trip and your purpose is to go to Chicago, you'll know when you get there and will stop. But if you don't really know where you are going, it's very difficult to know when to stop.

It's usually a good idea in your conclusion to avoid such over-worked expressions as "In conclusion," "In summary," "I hope I have shown," or "Finally." Your conclusion should also do more than simply repeat what you've said in your opening paragraph. The most satisfying essays are those in which the conclusion provides an interesting way of wrapping up ideas introduced in the beginning and developed throughout.

WHAT DOES A WOMAN WANT?

Susan Jacoby

*When Susan Jacoby became a newspaper re-
porter in 1963 at the age of seventeen, she had no
intention of writing about "women's subjects."
"To write about women was to write about triv-
ia: charity balls, cake sales, and the like," she
recalls. "I would have laughed at anyone who
tried to tell me that one day I would believe the
members of my own sex were important enough
to write about." But times have changed. And Jacoby has, in fact, written extensively about wom-
en's subjects, often in* The New York Times *and*
McCall's. *Many of these pieces have been collected in her book,* The Possible She *(1979). Pay
particular attention to the way Jacoby sets up
her opening and then cleverly returns to it in her
conclusion.*

"Candy and flowers, dear," Ellen had said time and 1
again, "and perhaps a book of poetry or an album or a
small bottle of Florida water are the only things a lady may accept from a gentleman. Never, never any expensive gift, even
from your fiancé. And never any gifts of jewelry or wearing ap-
parel, not even gloves or handkerchiefs. Should you accept
such gifts, men would know you were no lady and would try to
take liberties."

"Oh, dear," thought Scarlett, looking first at herself in the 2
mirror and then at Rhett's unreadable face. "I simply can't tell
him I won't accept it. It's too darling. I'd—I'd almost rather he
took a liberty, if it was a very small one."

Such was Scarlett O'Hara's moral dilemma when Rhett But- 3
ler presented her with a green silk bonnet. I should be so lucky.
The last gift I received from a man was not a silk frippery or a
bottle of Florida water, whatever that is, but an eminently
practical electronic calculator.

The calculator was certainly presented with the best of intentions. I had been complaining for weeks about what a drag it was to add up my business expenses and do my bank statements. I don't know what Scarlett's mother would have said about calculators, but I do know how I felt: I wanted to clobber the man who brought me the infernal machine. 4

Even now, the calculator blinks at me reproachfully, reminding me of its indispensability by its very proximity to my typewriter. Why do I resent this handy gadget? Because, every time I look at it, I wonder what it means when a man gives a woman a calculator instead of a fragile gold necklace or a dozen roses. Because there is no romance in its electronic innards. Because I can't stroke it or sniff it or wear it to bed. Because, damn, damn, damn, it's just not the sort of thing you expect a man to give a sex object. Poor calculator, symbol of the confusion that arises from a woman's dual desire to be admired for her gender-free mind and to be lusted after (and not only in the heart) for her female body. 5

It is impossible to overestimate the symbolic importance of gifts. When my mother sends me a beach dress marked "Large"—ignoring the fact that I've only worn "Smalls" since I shed my teen-age fat—I assume there's a message buried in the tissue paper. When I send her a pallid blue blouse with a bow at the neck—in a fussy style she has not worn since the early 1950's—I assume she finds a message too. 6

The tiffs inspired by gifts from members of the same sex are insignificant in comparison to the emotional storms triggered by gifts from members of the opposite sex. Men who are wondering what to give their sweethearts on Valentine's Day would do well to ponder the symbolic message of their gifts on this hokey romantic occasion. My father once made a terrible mistake by presenting my mother with a new stainless-steel frying pan. The fight that ensued remains a famous one, even in a family much given to shouting and breaking crockery in the heat of domestic battle. In all fairness, I must admit that my mother's complaints about her old frying pans were as loud as my recent complaints about having to do my own arithmetic. Nevertheless, I don't see how my father could have thought Mother's complaints meant she really wanted pots and pans for her birthday or wedding anniversary or Valentine's Day. 7

Men who want to arouse tender emotions rather than the ire   8
of the women in their lives might begin with Jacoby's Law: The
more intelligent and competent a woman is in her adult life, the
less likely she is to have received an adequate amount of romantic attention in adolescence. If a girl was smart, and if she
attended an American high school between 1930 and 1965,
chances are that no one paid attention to anything but her
brains unless she took the utmost care to conceal them.

Until I was fourteen, I attended parochial schools in which   9
the nuns made a great effort to shield their charges from the
brutal world of adolescent courtship. When we exchanged gifts
at our eighth-grade Christmas party, Sister Cyril Therese made
sure the unpopular kids would not be forgotten. Instead of giving presents to the people we liked best, everyone drew a name
out of a hat. I was thrilled when the card on my package
showed that it came from Bob Wheeler, who was generally
thought to have the most sex appeal of any boy in the class. Bob
didn't know I was alive; he was interested in the girls who knew
how to tighten the belts of their green serge uniforms in a way
that showed off their budding figures without attracting the
wrath of the nuns.

It seemed to me that the happy accident of Bob's drawing my   10
name for the Christmas party might form the basis for a whole
new relationship. When I opened the box (carefully wrapped by
his mother), I almost wept when I saw a sturdy pen-and-pencil
set. Girls around me were opening little bottles of perfume and
chains with artificial pearl drops. So much for the efforts of the
nuns to shield us from the mysteries of sexual attraction.

Things didn't change in high school. When I was a junior, the   11
movie *Breakfast at Tiffany's* was released; we all sighed when
Audrey Hepburn's romantic fate was sealed with a ring from a
Cracker Jack box. My best friend Wendy had an enterprising
boyfriend who sent her flimsy ring off to Tiffany's with the request that it be polished and engraved. How we envied her
when that ring came back in a velvet box. (Years later, a salesman at Tiffany's told me thousands of people had the same idea
after the movie was released. The store decided it would be
good public relations to polish all the rings at no charge. I can
well believe that thousands of diamond rings were ultimately
purchased at Tiffany's by the former Cracker Jack set.)

The year Wendy got her ring from Tiffany's, I did get a strange present I thought was intended as a romantic gesture. It was an eyelash curler. As it turned out, the boy who gave me the curler was picked up on charges of shoplifting at the local drugstore. Eyelash curlers, hanging loose on the Maybelline racks with eyebrow pencils and mascara, were irresistible bait for a kleptomaniac. 12

Which brings us to Valentine's Day. If a man is interested in a woman who was a cheerleader and was always invited to high school proms, he probably doesn't need to worry about the romantic portion of her ego. He can give her a tool kit or a calculator or a jack for tire changing and she will no doubt be thrilled that he appreciates her for something other than her looks. But if a woman was once sneered at for being a "brain," she would probably prefer the adult equivalent of a Cracker Jack ring. In return for such a gift, she might even allow a man a liberty—if it were a very small one. 13

Questions for Study and Discussion

1. Study the beginning of Jacoby's essay. Why do you suppose that she begins with an excerpt from *Gone with the Wind*?
2. What is Jacoby's thesis in this essay? (Glossary: *Thesis*)
3. What is Jacoby's Law? (8) Do you think that it is a realistic law? Why or why not?
4. Jacoby narrates an incident that occurred at a Christmas party she attended in eighth grade. What does the story show? (Glossary: *Narration*)
5. Consider Jacoby's conclusion. Do you think it is fitting for her essay? Why or why not?

Vocabulary

Refer to your dictionary to define the following words as they are used in this selection. Then use each word in a sentence of your own.

eminently (3)   tiffs (7)
reproachfully (5)   hokey (7)
proximity (5)   kleptomaniac (12)
innards (5)

Suggested Writing Assignments

1. Jacoby writes, "It is impossible to overestimate the . . . importance of gifts." If you agree, use Jacoby's statement as your thesis and write an essay supporting the thesis with your experiences in both giving and receiving gifts. Pay particular attention to the beginning and ending of your essay, perhaps even using suggestions for each given in the introduction of this chapter.

2. How we say "Hello" and "Goodbye" can be extremely important in interpersonal relationships. Write an essay using your own experiences to examine the importance of various kinds of greetings and farewells. Your essay should have an effective lead and a fitting conclusion.

HOW TO TAKE A JOB INTERVIEW

Kirby W. Stanat

*A former personnel recruiter and placement offi-
cer at the University of Wisconsin-Milwaukee,
Kirby W. Stanat has helped thousands of people
get jobs.* His book Job Hunting Secrets and Tac-
tics *(1977) tells readers what they need to know
in order to get the jobs they want. In this selection Stanat analyzes the campus interview, a
process that hundreds of thousands of college
students undergo each year as they seek to enter
the job market. Notice how Stanat begins and
how the "snap" of his ending echoes back
through his essay.*

To succeed in campus job interviews, you have to know   1
where that recruiter is coming from. The simple answer is
that he is coming from corporate headquarters.

That may sound obvious, but it is a significant point that too   2
many students do not consider. The recruiter is not a free spirit
as he flies from Berkeley to New Haven, from Chapel Hill to
Boulder. He's on an invisible leash to the office, and if he is
worth his salary, he is mentally in corporate headquarters all
the time he's on the road.

If you can fix that in your mind—that when you walk into   3
that bare-walled cubicle in the placement center you are walking into a branch office of Sears, Bendix or General Motors—
you can avoid a lot of little mistakes and maybe some big ones.

If, for example, you assume that because the interview is on   4
campus the recruiter expects you to look and act like a student,
you're in for a shock. A student is somebody who drinks beer,
wears blue jeans and throws a Frisbee. No recruiter has jobs
for student Frisbee whizzes.

A cool spring day in late March, Sam Davis, a good recruiter   5
who has been on the college circuit for years, is on my campus
talking to candidates. He comes out to the waiting area to meet

the student who signed up for an 11 o'clock interview. I'm standing in the doorway of my office taking in the scene.

Sam calls the candidate: "Sidney Student." There sits Sidney. He's at a 45 degree angle, his feet are in the aisle, and he's almost lying down. He's wearing well-polished brown shoes, a tasteful pair of brown pants, a light brown shirt, and a good looking tie. Unfortunately, he tops off this well-coordinated outfit with his Joe's Tavern Class A Softball Championship jacket, which has a big woven emblem over the heart.   6

If that isn't bad enough, in his left hand is a cigarette and in his right hand is a half-eaten apple.   7

When Sam calls his name, the kid is caught off guard. He ditches the cigarette in an ashtray, struggles to his feet, and transfers the apple from the right to the left hand. Apple juice is everywhere, so Sid wipes his hand on the seat of his pants and shakes hands with Sam.   8

Sam, who by now is close to having a stroke, gives me that what-do-I-have-here look and has the young man follow him into the interviewing room.   9

The situation deteriorates even further—into pure Laurel and Hardy. The kid is stuck with the half-eaten apple, doesn't know what to do with it, and obviously is suffering some discomfort. He carries the apple into the interviewing room with him and places it in the ashtray on the desk—right on top of Sam's freshly lit cigarette.   10

The interview lasts five minutes . . .   11

Let us move in for a closer look at how the campus recruiter operates.   12

Let's say you have a 10 o'clock appointment with the recruiter from the XYZ Corporation. The recruiter gets rid of the candidate in front of you at about 5 minutes to 10, jots down a few notes about what he is going to do with him or her, then picks up your résumé or data sheet (which you have submitted in advance) . . .   13

Although the recruiter is still in the interview room and you are still in the lobby, your interview is under way. You're on. The recruiter will look over your sheet pretty carefully before he goes out to call you. He develops a mental picture of you.   14

He thinks, "I'm going to enjoy talking with this kid," or "This one's going to be a turkey." The recruiter has already begun to make a screening decision about you.   15

His first impression of you, from reading the sheet, could come from your grade point. It could come from misspelled words. It could come from poor erasures or from the fact that necessary information is missing. By the time the recruiter has finished reading your sheet, you've already hit the plus or minus column. 16

Let's assume the recruiter got a fairly good impression from your sheet. 17

Now the recruiter goes out to the lobby to meet you. He almost shuffles along, and his mind is somewhere else. Then he calls your name, and at that instant he visibly clicks into gear. He just went to work. 18

As he calls your name he looks quickly around the room, waiting for somebody to move. If you are sitting on the middle of your back, with a book open and a cigarette going, and if you have to rebuild yourself to stand up, the interest will run right out of the recruiter's face. You, not the recruiter, made the appointment for 10 o'clock, and the recruiter expects to see a young professional come popping out of that chair like today is a good day and you're anxious to meet him. 19

At this point, the recruiter does something rude. He doesn't walk across the room to meet you halfway. He waits for you to come to him. Something very important is happening. He wants to see you move. He wants to get an impression about your posture, your stride, and your briskness. 20

If you slouch over him, sidewinderlike, he is not going to be impressed. He'll figure you would probably slouch your way through your workdays. He wants you to come at him with lots of good things going for you. If you watch the recruiter's eyes, you can see the inspection. He glances quickly at shoes, pants, coat, shirt; dress, blouse, hose—the whole works. 21

After introducing himself, the recruiter will probably say, "Okay, please follow me," and he'll lead you into his interviewing room. 22

When you get to the room, you may find that the recruiter will open the door and gesture you in—with him blocking part of the doorway. There's enough room for you to get past him, but it's a near thing. 23

As you scrape past, he gives you a closeup inspection. He looks at your hair; if it's greasy, that will bother him. He looks at your collar; if it's dirty, that will bother him. He looks at 24 your shoulders; if they're covered with dandruff, that will bother him. If you're a man, he looks at your chin. If you didn't get a close shave, that will irritate him. If you're a woman, he checks your makeup. If it's too heavy, he won't like it.

Then he smells you. An amazing number of people smell bad.   25 Occasionally a recruiter meets a student who smells like a canal horse. That student can expect an interview of about four or five minutes.

Next the recruiter inspects the back side of you. He checks   26 your hair (is it combed in front but not in back?), he checks your heels (are they run down?), your pants (are they baggy?), your slip (is it showing?), your stockings (do they have runs?).

Then he invites you to sit down.   27

At this point, I submit, the recruiter's decision on you is 75 to   28 80 percent made.

Think about it. The recruiter has read your résumé. He   29 knows who you are and where you are from. He knows your marital status, your major and your grade point. And he knows what you have done with your summers. He has inspected you, exchanged greetings with you and smelled you. There is very little additional hard information that he must gather on you. From now on it's mostly body chemistry.

Many recruiters have argued strenuously with me that they   30 don't make such hasty decisions. So I tried an experiment. I told several recruiters that I would hang around in the hall outside the interview room when they took candidates in.

I told them that as soon as they had definitely decided not to   31 recommend (to department managers in their companies) the candidate they were interviewing, they should snap their fingers loud enough for me to hear. It went like this.

First candidate: 38 seconds after the candidate sat down: 32 Snap!

Second candidate: 1 minute, 42 seconds: Snap!   33

Third candidate: 45 seconds: Snap!   34

One recruiter was particularly adamant, insisting that he   35 didn't rush to judgment on candidates. I asked him to participate in the snapping experiment. He went out in the lobby, picked up his first candidate of the day, and headed for an interview room.

As he passed me in the hall, he glared at me. And his fingers   36 went "Snap!"

Questions for Study and Discussion

1. Explain the appropriateness of the beginning and ending of Stanat's essay.
2. What are Stanat's purpose and thesis in telling the reader how the recruitment process works? (Glossary: *Purpose* and *Thesis*)
3. In paragraphs 12–29 Stanat explains how the campus recruiter works. Make a list of the steps in that process.
4. Identify the transitional devices that Stanat uses in paragraphs 12–29 to mark clearly the sequence of steps in the recruitment process. (Glossary: *Transitions*)
5. For what audience has Stanat written this essay? What in the essay leads you to this conclusion? (Glossary: *Audience*)
6. Stanat's tone—his attitude toward his subject and audience—in this essay is informal. What in his sentence structure and diction creates this informality? Cite examples. How might the tone be made more formal for a different audience?

Vocabulary

Refer to your dictionary to define the following words as they are used in this selection. Then use each word in a sentence of your own.

cubicle (3)   résumé (13)
deteriorates (10)   adamant (35)

Suggested Writing Assignments

1. Stanat's purpose is to offer practical advice to students interviewing for jobs. Determine a subject about which you could offer advice to a specific audience. Present your advice in the form of an essay, being careful to provide an attention-grabbing beginning and a convincing conclusion.
2. Stanat gives us an account of the interview process from the viewpoint of the interviewer. If you have ever been interviewed and remember the experience well, write an essay on your feelings and thoughts as the interview took

place. What were the circumstances of the interview? What questions were asked of you, how did you feel about them, and how comfortable was the process? How did the interview turn out? What precisely, if anything, did you learn from the experience? What advice would you give anyone about to be interviewed?

Rush Week

Bob Greene

Bob Greene was born in 1947 in Columbus, Ohio. He is a syndicated columnist for the Chicago Tribune, *and his column appears in over 150 newspapers throughout the United States. Greene has written seven books, the most recent being his best-selling chronicle of his daughter's first year of life,* Good Morning, Merry Sunshine *(1984). The following selection is taken from* American Beat *(1983), a collection of Greene's essays. Notice the way Greene sets up the story he tells in his opening paragraph and the sense of finality he achieves in his ending.*

This is a story that happened ten years ago. It bears retell- 1
ing today.

The story should be repeated because, all of a sudden, frater- 2
nities are very big on the college campuses once again. A movie
called *Animal House* has a lot to do with it. For a few years fraternities suffered a lull in popularity, but now they are back.
National magazines are devoting feature stories to fraternity
pranks, and television news shows are filming fraternity parties. The country is being told about the fun and craziness of
the college fraternity system.

But there is another side. As long as the fraternities exist, 3
there will be another side.

The boy's name was Jon. He was a bright kid. He came to 4
Northwestern in that autumn of 1968 for his freshman year,
and he signed up for fraternity rush.

He had something wrong with the way his body was formed. 5
It made him look unusual. Maybe he didn't know what lay in
store for him during rush week; maybe he did know, but had
determined that he would do his best anyway.

His best wasn't very good. At the first house where he 6
showed up for a rush date, one of the rush chairmen saw Jon

and grinned. Jon didn't look like all of the other freshmen who were going through rush, so he made an easy target.

He was placed in a corner, by himself, and he was allowed to sit there for two hours. No one greeted him, no one talked to him. When the others went downstairs to the dining room for their meal, Jon was left to stay by himself in the living room. 7

He waited the whole time, and when the meal was over and all of the other freshmen were leaving the house, Jon got up and walked out with the rest. He went on to the next house on his schedule, and again he was sized up at the door, and again he was shunted aside. 8

At some of the houses it was more subtle than at others. Some fraternities had entire rooms where young men like Jon were placed, so as not to disturb the other freshmen who were judged to be fraternity material. Not all of them had physical disabilities such as Jon's, of course; most were simply not handsome, or were awkward, or were dressed poorly. They were extraneous; they got in the way of rush week. 9

At one house, Jon was led out onto a fire escape and made to stand there for over an hour. It was an astonishing kind of cruelty; maybe things are different in fraternity rush now. Maybe things have changed. 10

And then, one night, two active members of one of the fraternities were assigned to make a rush call on a good prospect in a freshman dorm. The two were seniors; they were becoming disillusioned with the fraternity system, but they were going through with rush week this last time. They looked through the dorm for the boy they wanted, and somehow they went to the wrong room, and there was Jon, crying on his bed. 11

The two seniors could have turned and walked out, but for some reason they didn't. They sat down and they asked Jon what was wrong. He was reluctant to discuss it, but then he told them; told them what had happened to him during rush week, and how it was breaking his heart. 12

He told them about how he hadn't been given even a sliver of a chance, even by one house. He told them how desperately afraid he was of college. They listened to him and they understood that Jon's story was the story of so many boys who signed up for fraternity rush, and were then casually humili- 13 ated because, for various small reasons, they were not judged suitable. It was a hurt that would stay for years, and they knew it.

The two seniors listened, and they talked quietly to Jon, and   14
after they had left him in his dorm they knew they would have to do something about it. Jon was determined to continue with rush week, and they knew they could not let him go through it alone.

So they went to the central rush office, and they got a copy of   15
Jon's rush schedule for the rest of the week. And that night they started to visit the houses where Jon would be going in the days to come.

At every house, the two of them asked to talk to the fraternity   16
members. They explained what they had come for. They told the fraternity men about Jon, and the way he looked. And they said: We are not asking you to take him into your fraternity. We are just asking you not to hurt him anymore.

Surprisingly, the fraternity men listened. There were a few   17
snickers, but not many, and by the time the two of them were through they had talked to every house where Jon was scheduled to go. The two of them didn't talk much to each other about it; they didn't know exactly why they were doing this. But it was the first grown-up thing they had ever done, and it felt right.

Jon went through the rest of rush week. He was not asked to   18
join a house, but he was treated with decency. The fraternities he visited assigned members to talk to him, to eat with him, and to make him feel welcome. Perhaps the pain was lessened a little.

The two seniors ended up quitting their fraternity. Part of it   19
had to do with Jon, and part of it had to do with other aspects of the fraternity system. They just wanted no part of it anymore.

They lived in an apartment off campus. As far as they knew,   20
Jon didn't know about what they had done. They completed their senior year, and in the spring they prepared to graduate.

And then, one day, a congratulatory graduation card came   21
addressed to them in the mail. They opened it. It was from Jon.

"Thank you," it said. . . .   22

Questions for Study and Discussion

1. What is Greene's purpose in this essay? Why does he tell Jon's story? (Glossary: *Purpose*)
2. What is Greene's attitude toward the fraternity system on college campuses? What in particular in the essay reveals his attitude? (Glossary: *Attitude*)
3. How might Greene have begun his essay differently? What would be gained or lost with a different beginning?
4. How effective do you find the ending of Greene's essay? Were you surprised by the ending, disappointed by it? What would be gained or lost if the essay ended with paragraph 16? 17? 18?
5. How would you characterize Greene's sentences?

Vocabulary

Refer to your dictionary to define the following words as they are used in this selection. Then use each word in a sentence of your own.

shunted (8)   prospect (11)
extraneous (9)   disillusioned (11)

Suggested Writing Assignments

1. Attitudes toward fraternities and sororities vary widely among students. If you have fraternities and sororities on your college campus, write an essay examining the prevailing attitude toward them among the student body. Have attitudes changed recently? How so? Are there some pleasant surprises? Some unpleasant surprises? Pay particular attention to the way you begin and conclude your essay.
2. Bob Greene's "Rush Week" is an account that bears a strong relationship to the subjects of other essays in *Models for Writers*: Helen Keller's "The Most Important Day," Robert Heilbroner's "Don't Let Stereotypes Warp Your Judgments," Dick Gregory's "Shame," and Peter Farb's "Children's Insults," among others. The message in these essays

seems, in part, to be that we Americans need to improve our social consciousness regarding the handicapped and that the schools should help prevent stereotyping and social injustices. Write an essay in which you speculate why the handicapped are so frequently stereotyped and even victimized and suggest what our schools might do to help improve the situation. Be sure to consider the effectiveness of both the opening and concluding sections of your essay.

HUGH TROY: PRACTICAL JOKER

Alfred Rosa and Paul Eschholz

Alfred Rosa and Paul Eschholz are both professors of English at the University of Vermont, where they teach courses in composition, the English language, and American literature. In the following article, which first appeared in The People's Almanac #2 *in 1978, Rosa and Eschholz draw a portrait of a man who believed that in the hands of an expert a practical joke was more than just a good laugh. As you read, notice how the opening serves to build interest and how the conclusion works to reflect the point of the essay.*

Nothing seemed unusual. In fact, it was a rather common occurrence in New York City. Five men dressed in overalls roped off a section of busy Fifth Avenue in front of the old Rockefeller residence, hung out MEN WORKING signs, and began ripping up the pavement. By the time they stopped for lunch, they had dug quite a hole in the street. This crew was different, however, from all the others that had descended upon the streets of the city. It was led by Hugh Troy—the world's greatest practical joker.

For lunch, Troy led his tired and dirty crew into the dining room of a fashionable Fifth Avenue hotel that was nearby. When the headwaiter protested, Troy took him into his confidence. "It's a little gag the manager wants to put over," he told the waiter. The men ate heartily and seemed not to notice that indignant diners were leaving the premises. After lunch Troy and his men returned to their digging, and by late afternoon they had greatly enlarged the hole in the avenue. When quitting time arrived, they dutifully hung out their red lanterns, left the scene, and never returned. City officials discovered the hoax the next day, but they never learned who the pranksters were.

Hugh Troy was born in Ithaca, N.Y., where his father was a

professor at Cornell University. After graduating from Cornell, Troy left for New York City, where he became a successful illustrator of children's books. When W.W. II broke out, he went into the army and eventually became a captain in the 21st Bomber Command, 20th Air Force, under Gen. Curtis LeMay. After the war he made his home in Garrison, N.Y., for a short while before finally settling in Washington, D.C., where he lived until his death.

As a youngster Troy became a friend of the painter Louis   4
Agassiz Fuertes, who encouraged Troy to become an artist and may have encouraged the boy to become a practical joker as well. While Fuertes and Troy were out driving one day, Fuertes saw a JESUS SAVES sign and swiped it. Many a good laugh was had when several days later people saw the sign firmly planted in front of the Ithaca Savings Bank. The boy put up a few signs of his own. Fascinated by the word *pinking*, he posted a sign in front of his house: PINKING DONE. No one needed pinking done, but curiosity got the best of some, who stopped to ask what pinking was. "It's a trade secret," Troy quipped. The boy was also a member of a skating club, and when he needed some pocket money, he tacked an old cigar box near the entrance of the clubhouse, along with a PLEASE HELP sign. People naturally began dropping change into the box, change which Troy routinely pocketed.

The fun for Troy really began when he entered Cornell. Some   5
of his celebrated antics involved a phony plane crash, reports on the campus radio station of an enemy invasion, an apparent ceiling collapse, and a cherry tree which one year miraculously bore apples. Troy's most successful stunt at Cornell concerned a rhinoceros. Using a wastebasket made from the foot of a rhinoceros, which he borrowed from his friend Fuertes, Troy made tracks across the campus and onto the frozen reservoir, stopping at the brink of a large hole in the ice. Nobody knew what to make of the whole thing until campus zoologists confirmed the authenticity of the tracks. Townspeople then began to complain that their tap water tasted of rhinoceros. Not until the truth surfaced did the complaints subside.

Troy's antics did not stop when he graduated from Cornell.   6
Shortly after moving to New York, he purchased a park bench, an exact duplicate of those used by the city. With the help of a

friend, he hauled it into Central Park. As soon as Hugh and his cohort spied a policeman coming down the path, they picked up the bench and started off with it. In no time the mischievous pair were in the local hoosegow. At that point the clever Troy produced his bill of sale, forcing the embarrassed police to release him and his pal. The two men repeated the caper several times before the entire force finally caught on.

Often Troy's pranks were conceived on the spur of the moment. For example, on a whim Troy bought a dozen copies of the 1932 election-night extra announcing Roosevelt's victory. The papers remained in mothballs until New Year's Eve, 1935, when Hugh and a group of merrymakers rode the city's subways, each with a copy of the newspaper. Other passengers, most of whom were feeling no pain, did a double take at the bold headline: ROOSEVELT ELECTED.   7

When the Museum of Modern Art sponsored the first American showing of Van Gogh's work in 1935, Hugh was on the scene again. The exhibit attracted large crowds of people who Troy suspected were more interested in the sensational aspects of the artist's life than in his paintings. To test his theory, Troy fashioned a replica of an ear out of chipped beef and had it neatly mounted in a blue velvet display case. A small card telling the grisly story was attached: "This was the ear which Vincent Van Gogh cut off and sent to his mistress, a French prostitute, Dec. 24, 1888." The "chipped beef ear" was then placed on a table in the gallery where Van Gogh's paintings were displayed. Troy got immediate results. New York's "art lovers" flocked to the ear, which, as Troy suspected, was what they really wanted to see after all.   8

Hugh Troy's pranks were never vindictive, but once, when irked by the operator of a Greenwich Village movie theater, he got the last laugh. One evening he took a jar full of moths into the theater and released them during the show. The moths flew directly for the light from the projector and made it impossible for anyone to see the picture. While the manager tried to appease the angry moviegoers, Hugh looked on with satisfaction.   9

To protest the tremendous amount of paperwork in the army during W.W. II, Troy invented the special "flypaper report." Each day he sent this report to Washington to account for the number of flies trapped on the variously coded flypaper rib-   10 bons hanging in the company's mess hall. Soon the Pentagon, as might be expected, was asking other units for their flypaper reports. Troy was also responsible for "Operation Folklore." While stationed in the South Pacific, he and two other intelligence officers coached an island youngster in fantastic Troy-devised folktales, which the child then told to a gullible visiting anthropologist.

While some of his practical jokes were pure fun, many were designed to expose the smugness and gullibility of the American public. Annoyed by a recently announced course in ghostwriting at American University, Troy placed the following ad in the *Washington Post:* "Too Busy to Paint? Call on The Ghost Artists. We Paint It—You Sign It!! Why Not Give an Exhibition?" The response was more than he had bargained for. The hundreds of letters and phone calls only highlighted the fact that Americans' pretentiousness about art and their attempts to buy their way into "arty circles" had not waned since the Van Gogh escapade. 11

Whether questioning the values of American society or simply relieving the monotony of daily life, Hugh Troy always managed to put a little bit of himself into each of his stunts. One day he attached a plaster hand to his shirt sleeve and took a trip through the Holland Tunnel. As he approached the tollbooth, with his toll ticket between the fingers of the artificial hand, Troy left both ticket and hand in the grasp of the stunned tollbooth attendant and sped away. 12

Questions for Study and Discussion

1. Reread the first two paragraphs of this essay. Are they a fitting introduction to the essay? Why, or why not? What would be gained or lost if the essay began with paragraph 3?

2. Reread the last paragraph of the essay. Is this paragraph a fitting conclusion? Why, or why not?

3. What in particular made Hugh Troy the world's greatest practical joker: that is, what put him in a different league than the ordinary prankster?

4. Briefly describe the organization of Rosa and Eschholz's essay. Would the essay be as effective if the paragraphs were rearranged in a different order? Explain. (Glossary: *Organization*)

Vocabulary

Refer to your dictionary to define the following words as they are used in this selection. Then use each word in a sentence of your own.

hoax (2)	vindictive (9)
pinking (4)	irked (9)
hoosegow (6)	appease (9)
caper (6)	smugness (11)
whim (7)	waned (11)

Suggested Writing Assignments

1. If you yourself are a practical joker, or if you have ever known one, write an essay modeled after Rosa and Eschholz's "Hugh Troy." Try to recount in detail the pranks that have been carried out and, most importantly, try to assess their significance. Give extra time and attention to the opening and concluding portions of your essay, making sure they do their jobs well.

2. Write an essay in which you discuss the need for humor in our lives. Draw upon your experiences, as well as those of classmates, to recount humorous situations, events, and statements in order to analyze how they have served to ease tensions, tone down aggressive behavior, or lighten an otherwise dark moment. Be sure that the beginning of your essay grabs and holds the reader's attention and that the ending provides a conclusion rather than just a stopping point.

5

PARAGRAPHS

Within an essay, the paragraph is the most important unit of thought. Like the essay, it has its own main idea, often stated directly in a topic sentence. Like a good essay, a good paragraph is unified: It avoids digressions and develops its main idea. Paragraphs use many of the rhetorical techniques that essays use, techniques such as classification, comparison and contrast, and cause and effect. In fact, many writers find it helpful to think of the paragraph as a very small, compact essay.

Here is a paragraph from an essay on testing:

> Multiple-choice questions distort the purposes of education. Picking one answer among four is very different from thinking a question through to an answer of one's own, and far less useful in life. Recognition of vocabulary and isolated facts makes the best kind of multiple-choice questions, so these dominate the tests, rather than questions that test the use of knowledge. Because schools want their children to perform well, they are often tempted to teach the limited sorts of knowledge most useful on the tests.

This paragraph, like all well-written paragraphs, has several distinguishing characteristics: It is unified, coherent, and adequately developed. It is unified in that every sentence and every idea relate to the main idea, stated in the topic sentence, "Multiple-choice questions distort the purposes of education." It is coherent in that the sentences and ideas are arranged logically and the relationships among them are made clear by the use of effective transitions. Finally, the paragraph is adequately developed in that it presents a short but persuasive argument supporting its main idea.

How much development is "adequate" development? The answer depends on many things: how complicated or controversial the main idea is; what readers already know and believe; how much space the writer is permitted. Everyone, or nearly everyone, agrees that the earth circles around the sun; a single sentence would be enough to make that point. A writer trying to prove that the earth does *not* circle the sun, however, would need many sentences, indeed many paragraphs, to develop that idea convincingly.

Here is another model of an effective paragraph. As you read this paragraph about the resourcefulness of pigeons in evading attempts to control them, pay particular attention to its controlling idea, unity, development, and coherence.

> Pigeons [and their human friends] have proved remarkably resourceful in evading nearly all the controls, from birth-control pellets to carbide shells to pigeon apartment complexes, that pigeon-haters have devised. One of New York's leading museums once put large black rubber owls on its wide ledges to discourage the large number of pigeons that roosted there. Within the day the pigeons had gotten over their fear of owls and were back perched on the owls' heads. A few years ago San Francisco put a sticky coating on the ledges of some public buildings, but the pigeons got used to the goop and came back to roost. The city then tried trapping, using electric owls, and periodically exploding carbide shells outside a city building, hoping the noise would scare the pigeons away. It did, but not for long, and the program was abandoned. More frequent explosions probably would have distressed the humans in the area more than the birds. Philadelphia tried a feed that makes pigeons vomit, and then, they hoped, go away. A New York firm claimed it had a feed that made a pigeon's nervous system send "danger signals" to the other members of its flock.

The controlling idea is stated at the beginning in a topic sentence. Other sentences in the paragraph support the controlling idea with examples. Since all the separate examples illustrate how pigeons have evaded attempts to control them, the paragraph is unified. Since there are enough examples to convince the reader of the truth of the topic statement, the paragraph is adequately developed. Finally, the regular use of transitional words and phrases such as *once, within the day, a few years ago,* and *then,* lends the paragraph coherence.

How long should a paragraph be? In modern essays most paragraphs range from 50 to 250 words, but some run a full page or more and others may be only a few words long. The best answer is that a paragraph should be long enough to develop its main idea adequately. Some authors, when they find a paragraph running very long, may break it into two or more paragraphs so that readers can pause and catch their breath. Other writers forge ahead, relying on the unity and coherence of their paragraph to keep their readers from getting lost.

Articles and essays that appear in magazines and newspapers often have relatively short paragraphs, some of only one or two sentences. This is because they are printed in very narrow columns, which make paragraphs of average length appear very long. But often you will find that these journalistic "paragraphs" could be joined together into a few, longer, more normal paragraphs. Longer, more normal paragraphs are the kind you should use in all but journalistic writing.

CLAUDE FETRIDGE'S INFURIATING LAW

H. Allen Smith

H. Allen Smith (1907–1976) wrote many humorous books, among them Low Man on the Totem Pole *(1941),* Life in a Putty Knife Factory *(1943), and* Larks in the Popcorn *(1948). As can be seen in the following selection, Smith perceived the humor in everyday life and captured this humor in his writing. Notice the way in which Smith's topic sentences serve to control and focus the material in each of the essay's five paragraphs.*

Fetridge's Law, in simple language, states that important 1 things that are supposed to happen do not happen, especially when people are looking; or, conversely, things that are supposed not to happen do happen, especially when people are looking. Thus a dog that will jump through a hoop a thousand times a day for his owner will not jump through a hoop when a neighbor is called in to watch; and a baby that will say "Dada" in the presence of its proud parents will, when friends are summoned, either clam up or screech like a jaybird.

Fetridge's Law takes its name from a onetime radio engineer 2 named Claude Fetridge. Back in 1936, Mr. Fetridge though up the idea of broadcasting the flight of the famous swallows from San Juan de Capistrano mission in Southern California. As is well known, the swallows depart from the mission each year on St. John's Day, October 23, and return on March 19, St. Joseph's Day. Claude Fetridge conceived the idea of broadcasting the flutter of wings of the departing swallows on October 23. His company went to considerable expense to set up its equipment at the mission; then, with the whole nation waiting anxiously for the soul-stirring event, it was discovered that this year the swallows, out of sheer orneriness, had departed a day ahead of schedule. Thus did a flock of birds lend immortality to Claude Fetridge.

Television sets, of course, are often subject to the workings 3 of Fetridge's Law. If a friend tells me he is going to appear on a television show and asks me to watch it, I groan inwardly, knowing this is going to cost me money. The moment his show comes on the air, my screen will snow up or acquire the look of an old-school-tie pattern. I turn it off and call the repairman. He travels three miles to my house and turns the set on. The picture emerges bright and clear, the contrast exactly right, a better picture than I've ever had before. It's that way always and forever, days without end.

An attractive woman neighbor of mine drives her husband to   4 the railroad station every morning. On rare occasions she has been late getting her backfield in motion, and hasn't had time to get dressed. These times she has thrown a coat over her nightgown and, wearing bedroom slippers, headed for the depot. Fetridge's Law always seems to give her trouble. Once she clashed fenders with another car on the highway and had to go to the police station in her night shift. Twice she has had motor trouble in the depot plaza, requiring that she get out of her car in robe and slippers and pincurlers. The last I heard, she was considering sleeping in her street clothes.

Fetridge's Law operates fiercely in the realm of dentistry. In   5 my own case, I have often noted that whenever I develop a raging toothache it is a Sunday and the dentists are all on the golf course. Not long ago, my toothache hung on through the weekend, and Monday morning it was still throbbing and pulsating like a diesel locomotive, I called my dentist, proclaimed an emergency, and drove to his office. As I was going up the stairway, the ache suddenly vanished. By the time I got into his chair, I was confused and embarrassed and unable to tell him with certainty which tooth it was that had been killing me. The X ray showed no shady spots, though it would have several if he had pointed the thing at my brain. Claude Fetridge's law clearly has its good points; it can exasperate, but it can also cure toothaches.

Questions for Study and Discussion

1. How does Fetridge's Law work?
2. Identify the topic sentences in paragraphs 1, 3, and 5 of the essay. (Glossary: *Topic Sentence*)

3. How, specifically, do the other sentences in each paragraph support and/or develop the topic sentence?
4. Explain how Smith achieves coherence in paragraph 2. (Glossary: *Coherence*)
5. Briefly describe the organization of the essay. Would the essay be as effective if the paragraphs were arranged in a different order? Explain. (Glossary: *Organization*)
6. Do you think that the last sentence is an effective ending for the essay? Why, or why not? (Glossary: *Beginnings/Endings*)

Vocabulary

Refer to your dictionary to define the following words as they are used in this selection. Then use each word in a sentence of your own.

conversely (1)   pulsating (5)
orneriness (2)   exasperate (5)

Suggested Writing Assignments

1. Using several examples from your own experience, write a short essay illustrating the validity of Fetridge's Law. Make sure that each of your paragraphs has a clearly identifiable topic sentence.
2. Fetridge's Law grew out of Claude Fetridge's observations of events around him, events that showed remarkable consistency in the way they occurred or failed to occur. If you have observed similarly consistent patterns of behavior in the people around you or in the events of everyday life, formulate a law of your own. For example, do your favorite sports teams lose when you personally attend the games? Do your friends ask you to go out only on the nights when you have an important exam the next day? Do you always do well on exams when you wear your favorite old sweatshirt? Write an essay in which you give examples of how your law works. Be sure your paragraphs are well developed.

AMERICANS AND PHYSICAL FITNESS

James F. Fixx

James F. Fixx was one of the country's best-known authorities on running. The Complete Book of Running *(1977) has been an international bestseller and is in part responsible for popularizing running as a healthy everyday activity. In the following essay, taken from* The Complete Book of Running, *Fixx offers a series of well-developed paragraphs to support his thesis that "Most Americans are in terrible shape."*

Most Americans are in terrible shape. We smoke and drink too much, weigh too much, exercise too little and eat too many of the wrong things. A California pathologist, Thomas J. Bassler, says on the basis of autopsies he has performed that two out of every three deaths are premature; they are related to what he calls loafer's heart, smoker's lung and drinker's liver. Thomas K. Cureton, a professor at the University of Illinois Physical Fitness Laboratory, has said, "The average American young man has a middle-aged body. He can't run the length of a city block, he can't climb a flight of stairs without getting breathless. In his twenties, he has the capacity that a man is expected to have in his forties."

What about people who aren't so young? Cureton goes on: "The average middle-aged man in this country is close to death. He is only one emotional shock or one sudden exertion away from a serious heart attack." If that strikes you as overdramatic, for the next few days notice the ages in the obituary columns.

But isn't there a contradiction here? Participation in sports has been increasing since World War II: from 1946 to 1963 the numbers of participants doubled, and a glance at any tennis court or golf course is enough to suggest that the rate of growth since then has accelerated. Unfortunately, only a fraction of the population does most of the participating. The rest of us are spectators. Certainly more than half of all Americans do not exercise enough to do themselves any good, and fifty million adult Americans never exercise at all.

The experience of Neil Carver, a Philadelphia criminal lawyer, is typical. Carver is tall, rangy and sturdily built, but at thirty-three he was out of shape. "I was carrying my two kids upstairs one night to put them to bed," he told me. "I got so winded I could hardly breathe. I said to myself, I've got to do something about this." Carver started running. Today, seven or eight years later, he has not only competed in an eight-mile race but spends part of every summer climbing with his wife and children in New Hampshire's rugged Presidential Range. 4

Even American kids are out of shape. In one Massachusetts school only eight fifth-graders out of a class of fifty-two were fit enough to earn presidential physical fitness awards. In a class in Connecticut, only two students out of forty qualified. Not long ago a study at Massachusetts General Hospital showed that 15 percent of 1,900 seventh-graders had high cholesterol levels and 8 percent had high blood pressure. (Both conditions are associated with an increased likelihood of heart attacks and strokes.) Nor, despite our growing interest in sports, is our children's physical fitness getting any better. When 12,000,000 youngsters ten to seventeen years old were tested by the University of Michigan for the U.S. Office of Education, strength, agility and speed showed no improvement over a ten-year period. (The one exception: Girls had slightly more endurance.) 5

The very people we might reasonably look to for guidance—physicians—are in no better shape than the rest of us. In Southern California not long ago, fifty-eight doctors were given physical exams. Most were found to be in poor physical condition. One out of five smoked; two out of three were overweight; one in four had high blood pressure; one in five had an abnormal electrocardiogram while exercising; more than half had high serum lipid levels. Their condition may reflect the attitude of a young physician friend of mine who smokes heavily. "I don't worry about lung cancer," he told me. "By the time I get it they'll have a cure for it." 6

The fact that our doctors often don't offer the rest of us a very inspiring example may be because, as John F. Moe, a thoughtful Indianapolis physician, put it, "The problems of phy- 7 sician ignorance and physician apathy are closely tied together. To compound the situation, there has been a great lack of impetus from the medical schools. When I was in school ten years ago, very little (if any) time was devoted to the serious study of physical fitness in the sense that you and I know it. I strongly suspect that the situation has not changed much.

"The underexercised, coronary-prone physician sees himself   8
as the authority on health matters. He tends to reflect to others his own life style and thinks he is giving good, sound advice. Because he views himself as an authority figure, he finds it difficult to accept ideas foreign to his own concepts, especially when they differ radically from what he believes to be sound, conservative practice."

Can the federal government help make us fit? It's not likely,   9
despite the example of several European countries. Although the government undeniably takes an interest in our health—to the tune of about a billion and a quarter dollars a year—it doesn't in truth do much good. "Health problems today are an instructive paradigm of the limits of government . . . ," George F. Will wrote in *Newsweek*. "It is to be prayerfully hoped, but not reasonably expected, that some political leader will find the gumption to blurt out the melancholy truth: each additional dollar spent on medical care is producing a declining marginal benefit."

If neither our doctors nor the government can be expected to   10
bring us good health, to whom can we look? The answer is plain: to ourselves.

Questions for Study and Discussion

1. According to Fixx, in what ways are most Americans out of shape?
2. Identify the topic sentences in paragraphs 1, 5, and 6. (Glossary: *Topic Sentence*) How does Fixx develop these topic sentences?
3. How does Fixx achieve coherence in paragraph 6? (Glossary: *Coherence*)

4. Paragraphs 2, 3, 9, and 10 begin with rhetorical questions. How does Fixx use these questions to emphasize his points? (Glossary: *Coherence*)

5. In the context of the whole essay, what is the function of paragraph 4?

Vocabulary

Refer to your dictionary to define the following words as they are used in this selection. Then use each word in a sentence of your own.

obituary (2)	impetus (7)
agility (5)	paradigm (9)
apathy (7)	gumption (9)

Suggested Writing Assignments

1. Fixx argues in paragraph 9 that it is "not likely" that "the federal government (can) help make us fit." Write a short essay in which you disagree with Fixx and propose a plan whereby the federal government could encourage and/or give incentives to Americans who follow a regular routine of physical fitness. Make sure that each of your paragraphs is well developed and has a clearly identifiable topic sentence.

2. Select one of the following statements as the thesis for a short essay. Make sure that each paragraph of your essay is unified, coherent, and adequately developed.

   Car pooling is beneficial but makes demands of people.

   Social activities for freshmen are limited.

   A college is a community, just like a city or a town.

   College is expensive.

SIMPLICITY

William Zinsser

William Zinsser was born in New York City in 1922. After graduating from Princeton University, he worked for the New York Herald Tribune, *first as a feature writer and later as its drama editor and film critic. Currently the Executive Editor of the Book-of-the-Month Club, Zinsser has written a number of books including* The City Dwellers, Pop Goes America, The Lunacy Boom, *and* Writing with a Word Processor, *as well as other social and cultural commentaries. In this selection from his popular book* On Writing Well, *Zinsser, reminding us of Thoreau before him, exhorts the writer to "Simplify, simplify." Notice that Zinsser's paragraphs are unified and logically developed, and consequently work well together to support his thesis.*

Clutter is the disease of American writing. We are a society   1
strangling in unnecessary words, circular constructions,
pompous frills and meaningless jargon.

Who can understand the viscous language of everyday Amer-   2
ican commerce and enterprise: the business letter, the interoffice memo, the corporation report, the notice from the bank explaining its latest "simplified" statement? What member of an insurance or medical plan can decipher the brochure that tells him what his costs and benefits are? What father or mother can put together a child's toy—on Christmas Eve or any other eve—from the instructions on the box? Our national tendency is to inflate and thereby sound important. The airline pilot who announces that he is presently anticipating experiencing considerable precipitation wouldn't dream of saying that it may rain. The sentence is too simple—there must be something wrong with it.

But the secret of good writing is to strip every sentence to its 3
cleanest components. Every word that serves no function, every long word that could be a short word, every adverb that carries the same meaning that's already in the verb, every passive construction that leaves the reader unsure of who is doing what—these are the thousand and one adulterants that weaken the strength of a sentence. And they usually occur, ironically, in proportion to education and rank.

During the late 1960s, the president of a major university 4
wrote a letter to mollify the alumni after a spell of campus unrest. "You are probably aware," he began, "that we have been experiencing very considerable potentially explosive expressions of dissatisfaction on issues only partially related." He meant that the students had been hassling them about different things. I was far more upset by the president's English than by the students' potentially explosive expressions of dissatisfaction. I would have preferred the presidential approach taken by Franklin D. Roosevelt when he tried to convert into English his own government's memos, such as this blackout order of 1942:

> Such preparations shall be made as will completely obscure all Federal buildings and non-Federal buildings occupied by the Federal government during an air raid for any period of time from visibility by reason of internal or external illumination.

"Tell them," Roosevelt said, "that in buildings where they 5
have to keep the work going to put something across the windows."

Simplify, simplify. Thoreau said it, as we are so often re- 6
minded, and no American writer more consistently practiced what he preached. Open *Walden* to any page and you will find a man saying in a plain and orderly way what is on his mind:

> I love to be alone. I never found the companion that was so companionable as solitude. We are for the most part more lonely when we go abroad among men than when we stay in our chambers. A man thinking or working is always alone, let him be where he will. Solitude is not measured by the miles of space that intervene between a man and his fellows. The really diligent student in one of the crowded hives of Cambridge College is as solitary as a dervish in the desert.

How can the rest of us achieve such enviable freedom from clutter? The answer is to clear our heads of clutter. Clear thinking becomes clear writing: one can't exist without the other. It is impossible for a muddy thinker to write good English. He may get away with it for a paragraph or two, but soon the reader will be lost, and there is no sin so grave, for he will not easily be lured back.

Who is this elusive creature the reader? He is a person with an attention span of about twenty seconds. He is assailed on every side by forces competing for his time: by newspapers and magazines, by television and radio, by his stereo and videocassettes, by his wife and children and pets, by his house and his yard and all the gadgets that he has bought to keep them spruce, and by that most potent of competitors, sleep. The man snoozing in his chair with an unfinished magazine open on his lap is a man who was being given too much unnecessary trouble by the writer.

It won't do to say that the snoozing reader is too dumb or too lazy to keep pace with the train of thought. My sympathies are with him. If the reader is lost, it is generally because the writer has not been careful enough to keep him on the path.

This carelessness can take any number of forms. Perhaps a sentence is so excessively cluttered that the reader, hacking his way through the verbiage, simply doesn't know what it means. Perhaps a sentence has been so shoddily constructed that the reader could read it in any of several ways. Perhaps the writer has switched pronouns in mid-sentence, or has switched tenses, so the reader loses track of who is talking or when the action took place. Perhaps Sentence B is not a logical sequel to Sentence A—the writer, in whose head the connection is clear, has not bothered to provide the missing link. Perhaps the writer has used an important word incorrectly by not taking the trouble to look it up. He may think that "sanguine" and "sanguinary" mean the same thing, but the difference is a bloody big one. The reader can only infer (speaking of big differences) what the writer is trying to imply.

Faced with these obstacles, the reader is at first a remarkably tenacious bird. He blames himself—he obviously missed something, and he goes back over the mystifying sentence, or over the whole paragraph, piecing it out like an ancient rune, making guesses and moving on. But he won't do this for long.

The writer is making him work too hard, and the reader will look for one who is better at his craft.

The writer must therefore constantly ask himself: What am I trying to say? Surprisingly often, he doesn't know. Then he must look at what he has written and ask: Have I said it? Is it clear to someone encountering the subject for the first time? If it's not, it is because some fuzz has worked its way into the machinery. The clear writer is a person clear-headed enough to see this stuff for what it is: fuzz. 12

I don't mean that some people are born clear-headed and are therefore natural writers, whereas others are naturally fuzzy and will never write well. Thinking clearly is a conscious act that the writer must force upon himself, just as if he were embarking on any other project that requires logic: adding up a laundry list or doing an algebra problem. Good writing doesn't come naturally, though most people obviously think it does. The professional writer is forever being bearded by strangers who say that they'd like to "try a little writing sometime" when they retire from their real profession. Or they say, "I could write a book about that." I doubt it. 13

Writing is hard work. A clear sentence is no accident. Very few sentences come out right the first time, or even the third time. Remember this as a consolation in moments of despair. If you find that writing is hard, it's because it *is* hard. It's one of the hardest things that people do. 14

Questions for Study and Discussion

1. What exactly does Zinsser mean by clutter? How does Zinsser feel that we can free ourselves of clutter?
2. How do Zinsser's first and last paragraphs serve to introduce and conclude his essay? (Glossary: *Beginnings/ Endings*)
3. What is the function of paragraphs 4–6 in the context of the essay?
4. How do the questions in paragraph 2 further Zinsser's purpose? (Glossary: *Rhetorical Question*)

5. How would you characterize Zinsser's tone? Comment on the appropriateness of the tone for his subject and audience. (Glossary: *Tone*)

Vocabulary

Refer to your dictionary to define the following words as they are used in this selection. Then use each word in a sentence of your own.

pompous (1)   enviable (7)
decipher (2)   tenacious (11)
adulterants (3) bearded (13)
mollify (4)

Suggested Writing Assignments

1. The following pages show a passage from the final manuscript for Zinsser's essay. Carefully study the manuscript and Zinsser's changes, and then write several well-developed paragraphs analyzing the ways he has eliminated clutter.

is too dumb or too lazy to keep pace with the ~~writer's~~ train
of thought. My sympathics are ~~entirely~~ with him. ~~He's not
so dumb.~~ (If the reader is lost, it is generally because the
writer ~~of the article~~ has not been careful enough to keep
him on the ~~proper~~ path.

This carelessness can take any number of ~~different~~ forms.
Perhaps a sentence is so excessively ~~long and~~ cluttered that
the reader, hacking his way through ~~all~~ the verbiage, simply
doesn't know what it ~~the writer~~ means. Perhaps a sentence has
been so shoddily constructed that the reader could read it in
any of several ~~two or three different~~ ways. ~~He thinks he knows what
the writer is trying to say, but he's not sure.~~ Perhaps the
writer has switched pronouns in mid-sentence, or ~~perhaps he~~

has switched tenses, so the reader loses track of who is
talking ~~to whom~~ or ~~exactly~~ when the action took place. Perhaps Sentence B is not a logical sequel to Sentence A -- the
writer, in whose head the connection is ~~perfectly~~ clear, has
not bothered to provide ~~given enough thought to providing~~ the missing link. Perhaps the writer has used an important word incorrectly by not
taking the trouble to look it up ~~and make sure.~~ He may think
that "sanguine" and "sanguinary" mean the same thing, but)
~~I can assure you that~~ (the difference is a bloody big one ~~to the~~
~~reader.~~ The reader can only ~~try to~~ infer ~~what~~ (speaking of big differences) what the writer is trying to imply.

Faced with these ~~such a variety of~~ obstacles, the reader
is at first a remarkably tenacious bird. He ~~tends to~~ blames
himself. ~~He~~ obviously missed something, ~~he thinks,~~ and he goes
back over the mystifying sentence, or over the whole paragraph,
piecing it out like an ancient rune, making guesses and moving
on. But he won't do this for long. ~~He will soon run out of~~
~~patience.~~ (The writer is making him work too hard ~~-- harder~~
~~than he should have to work --~~ (and the reader will look for
one ~~a writer~~ who is better at his craft.

The writer must therefore constantly ask himself: What am
I trying to say? ~~in this sentence?~~ (Surprisingly often, he
doesn't know.) ~~And~~ Then he must look at what he has ~~just~~
written and ask: Have I said it? Is it clear to someone
encountering ~~who is coming upon~~ the subject for the first time? If it's
not, ~~clear,~~ it is because some fuzz has worked its way into the
machinery. The clear writer is a person ~~who is~~ clear-headed
enough to see this stuff for what it is: fuzz.

I don't mean ~~to suggest~~ that some people are born
clear-headed and are therefore natural writers, whereas
others ~~other people~~ are naturally fuzzy and will ~~therefore~~ never write

well. Thinking clearly is ~~an entirely~~ **force** conscious act that the
writer must ~~keep forcing~~ upon himself, just as if he were
embarking ~~starting out~~ on any other ~~kind of~~ project that ~~calls for~~ **requires** logic:
adding up a laundry list or doing an algebra problem ~~or playing chess.~~
Good writing doesn't ~~just~~ come naturally, though most
people obviously think ~~it's as easy as walking.~~ **it does.** The professional

2. If what Zinsser writes about clutter is an accurate assessment, we should easily find numerous examples of clutter all around us. During the next few days, make a point of looking for clutter in the written materials you come across. Choose one example that you find—an article, an essay, a form letter, or a chapter from a textbook, for example—and write an extended analysis explaining how it might have been written more simply. Develop your paragraphs well, make sure they are coherent, and try not to "clutter" your own writing.

6

TRANSITIONS

Transitions are words and phrases that are used to signal the relationships between ideas in an essay and to join the various parts of an essay together. Writers use transitions to relate ideas within sentences, between sentences, and between paragraphs. Perhaps the most common type of transition is the so-called transitional expression. Following is a list of transitional expressions categorized according to their functions.

ADDITION: and, again, too, also, in addition, further, furthermore, moreover, besides

CAUSE AND EFFECT: therefore, consequently, thus, accordingly, as a result, hence, then, so

COMPARISON: similarly, likewise, by comparison

CONCESSION: to be sure, granted, of course, it is true, to tell the truth, certainly, with the exception of, although this may be true, even though, naturally

CONTRAST: but, however, in contrast, on the contrary, on the other hand, yet, nevertheless, after all, in spite of

EXAMPLE: for example, for instance

PLACE: elsewhere, here, above, below, farther on, there, beyond, nearby, opposite to, around

RESTATEMENT: that is, as I have said, in other words, in simpler terms, to put it differently, simply stated

SEQUENCE: first, second, third, next, finally

SUMMARY: in conclusion, to conclude, to summarize, in brief, in short

TIME: afterward, later, earlier, subsequently, at the same time, simultaneously, immediately, this time, until now, before, meanwhile, shortly, soon, currently, when, lately, in the meantime, formerly

Besides transitional expressions, there are two other important ways to make transitions: by using pronoun reference, and by repeating key words and phrases. This paragraph begins with the phrase "Besides transitional expressions": the phrase contains the transitional word *besides* and also repeats an earlier idea. Thus the reader knows that this discussion is moving toward a new but related idea. Repetition can also give a word or idea emphasis: "Foreigners look to America as a land of freedom. Freedom, however, is not something all Americans enjoy."

Pronoun reference avoids monotonous repetition of nouns and phrases. Without pronouns, these two sentences are wordy and tiring to read: "Jim went to the concert, where he heard some of Beethoven's music. Afterwards, Jim bought a recording of some of Beethoven's music." A more graceful and readable passage results if two pronouns are substituted in the second sentence: "Afterwards, he bought a recording of it." The second version has another advantage in that it is now more tightly related to the first sentence. The transition between the two sentences is smoother.

In the following example, notice how Rachel Carson uses transitional expressions, repetition of words and ideas, and pronoun reference:

Under primitive agricultural conditions the farmer had few insect problems. *These* arose `pronoun reference` with the intensification of agriculture—the devotion of immense acreages to a single crop. `repeated key idea` *Such a system* set the stage for explosive increases in specific insect populations. Single-crop farming does not take advantage of the principles by which nature works; *it* is agriculture `pronoun reference` as an engineer might conceive it to be. Nature has introduced great variety into the landscape, but man has displayed a passion for

pronoun reference

repeated key word

repeated key idea

simplifying *it. Thus he* undoes the built-in checks and balances by which nature holds the species within bounds. One important natural *check* is a limit on the amount of suitable habitat for each species. *Obviously then,* an insect that lives on wheat can build up its population to much higher levels on a farm devoted to wheat than on one in which wheat is intermingled with other crops to which the insect is not adapted.

The same thing happens in other situations. A generation or more ago, the towns of large areas of the United States lined their streets with the noble elm tree. *Now* the beauty *they* hopefully created is threatened with complete destruction as disease sweeps through the elms, carried by a beetle that would have only limited chance to build up large populations and to spread from tree to tree if the elms were only occasional trees in a richly diversified planting.

transitional expression; pronoun reference

transitional expression

transitional expression; pronoun reference

Carson's transitions in this passage enhance its *coherence*—that quality of good writing that results when all sentences, paragraphs, and longer divisions of an essay are effectively and naturally connected.

FRESH START

Evelyn Herald

Evelyn Herald wrote the following essay for Nut-shell magazine, a publication written for college students and distributed free on college campuses. In the essay, Herald tells of her thoughts and feelings as she experiences her first few days of college life. As you read her account, notice how Herald makes effective use of transitions to link the parts of her essay.

I first began to wonder what I was doing on a college campus anyway when my parents drove off, leaving me standing piti-fully in a parking lot, wanting nothing more than to find my way safely to my dorm room. The fact was that no matter how mature I liked to consider myself, I was feeling just a bit first-gradish. Adding to my distress was the distinct impression that everyone on campus was watching me. My plan was to keep my ears open and my mouth shut and hope no one would notice I was a freshman.

With that thought in mind, I raised my head, squared my shoulders, and set off in the direction of my dorm, glancing twice (and then ever so discreetly) at the campus map clutched in my hand. It took everything I had not to stare when I caught my first glimpse of a real live college football player. What confidence, what reserve, what muscles! I only hoped his attention was drawn to my air of assurance rather than to my shaking knees. I spent the afternoon seeking out each of my classrooms so that I could make a perfectly timed entrance before each lecture without having to ask dumb questions about its where-abouts.

The next morning I found my first class and marched in. Once I was in the room, however, another problem awaited me. Where to sit? Freshman manuals advised sitting near the front, showing the professor an intelligent and energetic demeanor. After much deliberation I chose a seat in the first row and to the side. I was in the foreground (as advised), but out of the professor's direct line of vision.

I cracked my anthology of American literature and scribbled   4
the date at the top of a crisp ruled page. "Welcome to Biology
101," the professor began. A cold sweat broke out on the back
of my neck. I groped for my schedule and checked the room
number. I *was* in the right room. Just the wrong building.

So now what? Get up and leave in the middle of the lecture?   5
Wouldn't the professor be angry? I knew everyone would stare.
Forget it. I settled into my chair and tried to assume the scientific pose of a biology major, bending slightly forward, tensing
my arms in preparation for furious notetaking, and cursing under my breath. The bottled snakes along the wall should have
tipped me off.

After class I decided my stomach (as well as my ego) needed a   6
little nourishment, and I hurried to the cafeteria. I piled my
tray with sandwich goodies and was heading for the salad bar
when I accidentally stepped in a large puddle of ketchup. Keeping myself upright and getting out of the mess was not going to
be easy, and this flailing of feet was doing no good. Just as I decided to try another maneuver, my food tray tipped and I lost
my balance. As my rear end met the floor, I saw my entire life
pass before my eyes; it ended with my first day of college
classes.

In the seconds after my fall I thought how nice it would be if   7
no one had noticed. But as all the students in the cafeteria
came to their feet, table by table, cheering and clapping, I knew
they had not only noticed, they were determined that I would
never forget it. Slowly I kicked off my ketchup-soaked sandals
and jumped clear of the toppled tray and spilled food. A
cleanup brigade came charging out of the kitchen, mops in
hands. I sneaked out of the cafeteria as the cheers died down
behind me.

For three days I dined alone on nothing more than humilia-   8
tion, shame, and an assortment of junk food from a machine
strategically placed outside my room. On the fourth day I
couldn't take another crunchy-chewy-salty-sweet bite. I needed
some real food. Perhaps three days was long enough for the
campus population to have forgotten me. So off to the cafeteria
I went.

I made my way through the food line and tiptoed to a table, 9
where I collapsed in relief. Suddenly I heard a crash that
sounded vaguely familiar. I looked up to see that another poor
soul had met the fate I'd thought was reserved only for me. I
was even more surprised when I saw who the poor soul was:
the very composed, very upperclass football player I'd seen
just days before (though he didn't look quite so composed wearing spaghetti on the front of his shirt). My heart went out to
him as people began to cheer and clap as they had for me. He
got up, hands held high above his head in a victory clasp, grinning from ear to ear. I expected him to slink out of the cafeteria
as I had, but instead he turned around and began preparing another tray. And that's when I realized I had been taking myself
far too seriously.

What I had interpreted as a malicious attempt to embarrass 10
a naive freshman had been merely a moment of college fun.
Probably everyone in the cafeteria had done something equally
dumb when he or she was a freshman—and had lived to tell
about it.

Who cared whether I dropped a tray, where I sat in class, or 11
even whether I showed up in the wrong lecture? Nobody. This
wasn't like high school. Popularity was not so important; running with the crowd was no longer a law of survival. In college,
it didn't matter. This was my big chance to do my own thing, be
my own woman—if I could get past my preoccupation with doing everything perfectly.

Once I recognized that I had no one's expectations to live up 12
to but my own, I relaxed. The shackles of self-consciousness
fell away, and I began to view college as a wonderful experiment. I tried on new experiences like articles of clothing,
checking their fit and judging their worth. I broke a few rules
to test my conscience. I dressed a little differently until I found
the Real Me. I discovered a taste for jazz, and I decided I liked
going barefoot.

I gave up trying to act my way through college (this wasn't 13
drama school) and began not acting at all. College, I decided,
was probably the only time I would be completely forgiven for
massive mistakes (including stepping in puddles of ketchup
and dropping food trays). So I used the opportunity to make all
the ones I thought I'd ever make.

Three years after graduation, I'm still making mistakes. And   14
I'm even being forgiven for a few.

Questions for Study and Discussion

1. What is Herald's thesis in this essay? (Glossary: *Thesis*)
2. How are paragraphs 1 and 2 linked? How are paragraphs 6 and 7 linked? Identify the transitions Herald uses in paragraph 3.
3. What purpose is served by the questions that begin paragraph 5? (Glossary: *Rhetorical Question*)
4. How soon after the experiences she describes did Herald write this account? How do you know?

Vocabulary

Refer to your dictionary to define the following words as they are used in this selection. Then use each word in a sentence of your own.

demeanor (3)   malicious (10)
groped (4)   naive (10)
flailing (6)   shackles (12)
slink (9)

Suggested Writing Assignments

1. Write an essay explaining what your first few days in college were like. Did you feel self-conscious? Anxious? Self-assured? Give specific examples of events that occurred. Remember to use transitions to connect your ideas logically both within paragraphs and from one paragraph to another.
2. In *The New York Times Complete Manual of Home Repair*, Bernard Gladstone gives directions for applying blacktop sealer to a driveway. His directions appear below in scrambled order. First, carefully read all of Gladstone's sentences. Next, arrange the sentences in what seems to you

the correct sequence, paying attention to transitional devices. Be prepared to explain the reasons for your particular arrangement of the sentences.

1. A long-handled pushbroom or roofing brush is used to spread the coating evenly over the entire area.
2. Care should be taken to make certain the entire surface is uniformly wet, though puddles should be swept away if water collects in low spots.
3. Greasy areas and oil slicks should be scraped up, then scrubbed thoroughly with a detergent solution.
4. With most brands there are just three steps to follow.
5. In most cases one coat of sealer will be sufficient.
6. The application of blacktop sealer is best done on a day when the weather is dry and warm, preferably while the sun is shining on the surface.
7. This should not be applied until the first coat is completely dry.
8. First sweep the surface absolutely clean to remove all dust, dirt and foreign material.
9. To simplify spreading and to assure a good bond, the surface of the driveway should be wet down thoroughly by sprinkling with a hose.
10. However, for surfaces in poor condition a second coat may be required.
11. The blacktop sealer is next stirred thoroughly and poured on while the surface is still damp.
12. The sealer should be allowed to dry overnight (or longer if recommended by the manufacturer) before normal traffic is resumed.

BABY BIRDS

Gale Lawrence

*Gale Lawrence was born in Springfield, Ver-
mont. A free-lance writer, teacher, and naturalist, Lawrence writes a weekly column on nature
and has published* The Beginning Naturalist
(1979) and Field Guide to the Familiar *(1984). In
the following essay, Lawrence turns her attention to the "baby bird crisis" that occurs every
spring, and she offers sound advice for those
who don't know how to deal with a baby bird
that has fallen from its nest. As you read the essay, notice the way Lawrence uses transitional
words and expressions to tie her words and
thoughts together logically and to achieve coherence.*

Every spring the "baby bird crisis" occurs. By May many 1
birds have hatched their first broods and are feeding
them in the nest while they grow their feathers and learn to fly.
Baby birds have a way of tumbling out of their nests, and children have a way of finding them and bringing them home. What
should a family do if faced with this "crisis"?

First, take the baby bird back to the exact spot where it was 2
found. Look carefully for a nest nearby. If you find the nest and
it is accessible, put the bird gently back into the nest. Contrary
to popular belief, the mother bird will not reject a baby that
has been handled by human beings. A deer, which has a keen
sense of smell and fears the human scent, will reject a fawn
that has been handled, but birds are different. If you find the
nest and return the baby, you have done the best you can do.

As a next-best measure, tie a small box onto a branch of a tree 3
or shrub near where the bird was found, and put the baby bird
in the box. The bird will thus be off the ground and out of the
reach of neighborhood cats and dogs.

The third best thing you can do is simply to leave the bird in 4
the exact spot where it was found. Parent birds are accustomed
to having their young fall out of the nest, and they will feed
them on the ground. Of course, the baby bird is more vulnerable on the ground than it is in the nest or in a box, but it still
stands a better chance of surviving under its own parents' care
than under human care. If the baby bird is found near a house,
it is better to keep pet dogs and cats indoors than to bring the
baby bird indoors in an attempt to protect it.

If the baby is truly abandoned or orphaned—something you 5
can learn only by watching it from a distance for an hour or
more—you have a decision to make. You can leave it there to
die a natural death—which might in fact be the most humane
thing to do. Or you can take it indoors. If you decide to care for
it yourself, you are making a substantial commitment. And,
even if you live up to your commitment, there is no guarantee
that the bird will survive.

Two major problems are involved in trying to parent a baby 6
bird. One is feeding it, and the other is preparing it for life in
the wild. Parent birds do it all as a matter of course, but a human parent will have to drop other activities for a period of
weeks and perhaps install a screened porch or aviary to do the
job right.

Before you can even address yourself to the problem of feed- 7
ing, however, you have the more immediate problem of the
bird's shock and fright to contend with. Perhaps this is the time
to send one member of the family for a book on the care of wild
animal young, while another rigs up a heating pad or hot water
bottle to warm the baby bird. One good book is *Care of the Wild
Feathered and Furred: A Guide to Wildlife Handling and Care*
(Santa Cruz: Unity Press, 1973) by Mae Hickman and Maxine
Guy. Another is Ronald Rood's *The Care and Feeding of Wild
Pets* (New York: Pocket Books, 1976). A third book that is spe-
cifically about birds is *Bird Ambulance* (New York: Charles
Scribner's Sons, 1971) by Arline Thomas.

Now comes the problem of feeding. The warm milk in an eye 8
dropper that seems to be everyone's immediate impulse when
it comes to feeding animal young may be appropriate for baby
mammals, but it will come as a complete surprise to the baby

bird. Its parents were probably feeding it mashed worms, cat-
erpillars, insects, and other delicious odds and ends. Therefore, you'll need to do the same. At first you should supply the
baby bird with protein-rich foods. Eventually you're going to
have to identify the species and learn something about its food
habits in the wild if you want the bird to grow up properly.
Whether the bird is a seedeater, an insect eater, or a predator
will make a difference.

Parent birds feed their babies about every ten or fifteen min-   9
utes from sunrise to sunset. They also feed them exactly what
they need to keep their bowels regulated and their bodies growing properly. They also keep the nest clean by removing the babies' excrement, which usually appears shortly after each feeding. In brief, between finding and preparing appropriate food,
feeding, and cleaning up after meals you're not going to have
much time for anything else for a while if you decide to parent
a baby bird.

If you do manage to keep the young bird fed properly and   10
growing, your next problem is providing it with enough space
for it to practice flying. You cannot expect a bird to go from
your kitchen to the wild with one swoop of its wings. You will
need to continue feeding and protecting the bird while it is ad-
justing to the outdoors. If it had stayed with its parents, it
would have had adult birds to follow and imitate, but, with
nothing but human beings to encourage it, it will have to make
sense out of its environment alone. The young bird that has
been raised by humans is at a disadvantage when it comes to
competing for food and avoiding the attacks of predators. So
even if you do manage to raise a fledgling to adulthood, you
have not guaranteed its survival in the wild.

If you think I'm trying to sound discouraging, I am. The adop-   11
tion of a baby bird will probably result in failure. You might
even cause a death that would not have occurred had you left
the baby bird where it was. Your intentions might be good; the
ethical impulse that motivates your actions might be of the
best kind. But you should know that even experienced veteri-
narians have a low success rate in caring for wild animals.

Perhaps the most important thing a child or adult can learn   12
from an encounter with a baby bird is the difference between
wild animals and domestic pets. Whereas puppies and kittens

warm to human attention and become very much a part of the family, a wild bird never will. Attempting to make a pet out of a wild animal is a serious disservice to that animal—so serious, in fact, that there are laws against it. Life in the wild does not consist of friendly humans, readily available meals, and a protected environment. Wild animals must remain wild to survive.

Rather than adopt a baby bird, why not "adopt" a whole bird family—from a distance? Chances are there is a bird's nest somewhere near your home. Or you can build birdhouses to attract birds to your yard. Learn to watch the bird family from a distance. If human beings get too close, the parent birds won't come to the nest. So practice sitting quietly, perhaps with a pair of binoculars, far enough away from the nest that the adult birds won't feel threatened. 13

Watching birds in the wild is a much healthier and more realistic activity than fantasizing that a bird will become your special friend because you raised it. Unfortunately, movies, television, and children's books have created a "Bambi syndrome" in us. The young of most species are precious and adorable, but the desire to fondle and caress and make pets out of wildlings is dangerously romantic. It should not be encouraged. We'd be much wiser if we were content to be observers of wildlife. If we truly care about wild animals, we should be protectors of their wildness, which enables the best of them to survive. 14

Questions for Study and Discussion

1. In paragraphs 2–4 Lawrence offers advice on what a family should do if faced with an abandoned baby bird. Identify the transitions Lawrence uses to link these paragraphs.

2. How are paragraphs 5 and 6 linked together? What sentence in paragraph 5 serves as the transition into paragraph 6?

3. What is the "Bambi syndrome" mentioned in paragraph 14? On what false notions is it based?

4. What alternatives to caring for wild animals does Lawrence suggest to her readers?

Vocabulary

Refer to your dictionary to define the following words as they are used in this selection. Then use each word in a sentence of your own.

keen (2)   fledgling (10)
aviary (6)   romantic (14)
predator (8)

Suggested Writing Assignments

1. Write an essay in which you examine the differences between domestic and wild animals. How do they differ in their habitats, eating and reproductive patterns, and predatory instincts? How do we as humans regard each group? Be sure that you have linked the various elements of your essay by using transitional words and expressions.

2. Gale Lawrence's essay treats the problem of people who in meaning well may actually do things that are harmful. If you know of another situation in which this is true, write an essay using examples you have come across that illustrate this occurrence. Be sure that your transitions effectively and logically link your ideas.

AUTO SUGGESTION

Russell Baker

*After graduating from Johns Hopkins University
in 1947, Russell Baker joined the staff of the* Baltimore Sun *and later worked in the Washington
bureau of* The New York Times. *Since 1962 he
has written a syndicated column for the* Times
*for which he was awarded a Pulitzer Prize in
1979. "Auto Suggestion," first published in the*
Times *on April 1, 1979, presents Baker's techniques for not buying a car. As you read, notice
how the author's transitions give coherence to
the essay.*

Many persons have written asking the secret of my tech-   1
nique for not buying a new car. Aware that it could destroy the American economy and reduce the sheiks of OPEC to
prowling the streets with pleas for baksheesh, I divulge it here
with the greatest reluctance.

In extenuation, let me explain that my power to resist buying   2
a new car does not derive from a resentment of new cars. In
fact, I bought a new car 10 years ago and would buy another at
any moment if the right new car came along.

When seized by new-car passion, however, I do not deal with   3
it as most people do. To conquer the lust and escape without a
new car, you must have a program. The first step is to face the
philosophical question: Is a new car really going to give you
less trouble than your old car?

In most cases the notion that a new car will free its owner of   4
auto headache will not hold water. Common experience shows
that all cars, old or new, are trouble. The belief that a change of
vintage will relieve the headache is a mental exercise in willful
self-deception.

A new car simply presents a new set of troubles, which may   5
be more disturbing than the beloved, familiar old troubles the
old car presented. With your old car, strange troubles do not

113

take you by surprise, but a new car's troubles are invariably terrifying for being strange and unexpected.

Before entering the new-car bazaar, I always remind myself 6 that I am about to acquire an entirely new set of troubles and that it is going to take me months, maybe years, to learn to live happily with them.

Step Two is to place a sensible limit on the amount you will 7 pay for a new car. As a guide to value, I use the price my parents paid for the house in which I grew up. To own a car that costs more than a house is vulgar and reflects an alarming disproportion in one's sense of values. Wheels may be splendid but they should not be valued more highly than four bedrooms, dining room, bath and cellar.

The price of my parents' house, purchased in 1940, was 8 $5,900. This becomes my limit, effectively ruling out the kind of new car you have to drive to get to a business appointment in Los Angeles, as well as most other new cars on the market today.

After setting a price limit, the next step is to study the car's 9 capacity to perform its duties. For this purpose I always go to the car dealer's place with two large children, a wife, a grandmother, two cats, six suitcases, an ice chest and a large club suitable for subduing quarrelsome children on the turnpike.

Loading all the paraphernalia and people into the car under 10 study, I then ask myself whether I could drive 400 miles in this environment without suffering mental breakdown.

Since most cars within the $5,900 price limit nowadays are 11 scarcely commodious enough to transport two persons and a strand of spaghetti, I am now approaching very close to the goal I despise, which is to avoid buying a new car.

Suppose, however, that you pack everything inside—chil- 12 dren, wife, cats, club and grandmother—and it seems just barely possible that you might cover 400 miles despite the knees from the back seat grinding into your kidneys. Now is the time to take out your checkoff list.

Can you slide in behind the wheel without denting the skull 13 against the door frame? Will you be able to do it at night when you have had a drink and aren't thinking about it?

If the car passes this test, which is unlikely unless you're get- 14 ting an incredible deal on a pickup truck—and cats and grandmothers, remember, don't much like riding in the open beds of pickup trucks, especially when it rains—if the car passes this test, you must give it the cascading rainwater test.

For this purpose I take a garden hose to the car lot, spray the top of the car heavily and then, upon opening the door try to slide in without being drenched in a cascade of water pouring into the driver's seat. If the car soaks you with hose water, imagine what it will do with a heavy dose of rain. 15

If the car passes this examination, the final test is to slip a fingernail under the plastic sheathing on the dashboard and see if the entire piece peels away easily. If it does not, I buy the new car immediately. The last time I had to do so was in 1969. 16

Questions for Study and Discussion

1. What are the steps in Baker's program for not buying a car? Give examples of transitions he uses to move from one step to the next.

2. In explaining how not to buy a new car, Baker pokes fun at the economy and at the auto industry. What aspects of each does he criticize?

3. What transitional device does Baker use to link paragraphs 7, 8, and 9?

4. Baker's essay provides an interesting combination of diction. It is colloquial as well as sophisticated and urbane. Cite several examples of each type of diction. (Glossary: *Diction*)

Vocabulary

Refer to your dictionary to define the following words as they are used in this selection. Then use each word in a sentence of your own.

divulge (1)	vulgar (7)
extenuation (2)	paraphernalia (10)
lust (3)	commodious (11)
vintage (4)	cascading (14)

Suggested Writing Assignments

1. Baker's essay is a spoof on how not to buy an automobile. But how should a person really buy a new (or used) car? Write an essay in which you explain the process to follow to insure getting the car you want at a price you can afford. Be sure that you use transitions effectively to link the steps in the selection process you prescribe.

2. Write a short essay in which you describe the steps a person ought to take when making a major decision, such as determining where to go to school. Be sure to use transitions wherever necessary, both to make the sequence of your ideas clear and to give your essay coherence.

7

EFFECTIVE SENTENCES

Each of the following paragraphs describes the city of Vancouver. Although the content of both paragraphs is essentially the same, the first paragraph is written in sentences of nearly the same length and pattern and the second paragraph in sentences of varying length and pattern.

Water surrounds Vancouver on three sides. The snow-crowned Coast Mountains ring the city on the northeast. Vancouver has a floating quality of natural loveliness. There is a curved beach at English Bay. This beach is in the shape of a half moon. Residential high rises stand behind the beach. They are in pale tones of beige, blue, and ice-cream pink. Turn-of-the-century houses of painted wood frown upward at the glitter of office towers. Any urban glare is softened by folds of green lawns, flowers, fountains, and trees. Such landscaping appears to be unplanned. It links Vancouver to her ultimate treasure of greenness. That treasure is thousand-acre Stanley Park. Surrounding stretches of water dominate. They have image-evoking names like False Creek and Lost Lagoon. Sailboats and pleasure craft skim blithely across Burrard Inlet. Foreign freighters are out in English Bay. They await their turn to take on cargoes of grain.

Surrounded by water on three sides and ringed to the northeast by the snow-crowned Coast Mountains, Vancouver has a floating quality of natural loveliness. At English Bay, the half-moon curve of beach is backed by high rises in pale tones of beige, blue, and ice-cream pink. Turn-of-the-century houses of painted wood frown upward at the glitter of office towers. Yet any urban glare is quickly softened by folds of green lawns, flowers, fountains, and trees that in a seemingly unplanned fashion link Vancouver to her ultimate treasure of greenness—thousand-acre Stanley Park. And always it is the surrounding stretches of water that dominate, with their image-evoking names like False Creek and Lost Lagoon. Sailboats and pleasure craft skim blithely across Burrard Inlet, while out in English Bay foreign freighters await their turn to take on cargoes of grain.

The difference between these two paragraphs is dramatic. The first is monotonous because of the sameness of the sentences and because the ideas are not related to one another in a meaningful way. The second paragraph is much more interesting and readable; its sentences vary in length and are structured to clarify the relationships among the ideas. Sentence variety, an important aspect of all good writing, should not be used for its own sake, but rather to express ideas precisely and to emphasize the most important ideas within each sentence. Sentence variety includes the use of subordination, the periodic and loose sentence, the dramatically short sentence, the active and passive voice, and coordination.

SUBORDINATION, the process of giving one idea less emphasis than another in a sentence, is one of the most important characteristics of an effective sentence and a mature prose style. Writers subordinate ideas by introducing them either with subordinating conjunctions (*because, if, as though, while, when, after, in order that*) or with relative pronouns (*that, which, who, whomever, what*). Subordination not only deemphasizes some ideas, but also highlights others that the writer feels are more important.

Of course, there is nothing about an idea—*any* idea—that automatically makes it primary or secondary in importance. The writer decides what to emphasize, and he or she may choose to emphasize the less profound or noteworthy of two ideas. Consider, for example, the following sentence: "Jane was reading a novel the day that Mount St. Helens erupted." Everyone, including the author of the sentence, knows that the Mount St. Helens eruption is a more noteworthy event than Jane's reading a novel. But the sentence concerns Jane, not the volcano, and so her reading is stated in the main clause, while the eruption is subordinated in a dependent clause.

Generally, writers place the ideas they consider important in main clauses, and other ideas go into dependent clauses. For example:

> When she was thirty years old, she made her first solo flight across the Atlantic.
>
> When she made her first solo flight across the Atlantic, she was thirty years old.

The first sentence emphasizes the solo flight; in the second, the emphasis is on the pilot's age.

Another way to achieve emphasis is to place the most important words, phrases, and clauses at the beginning or end of a sentence. The ending is the most emphatic part of a sentence; the beginning is less emphatic; and the middle is the least emphatic of all. The two sentences about the pilot put the main clause at the end, achieving special emphasis. The same thing occurs in a much longer kind of sentence, called a PERIODIC SENTENCE. Here is an example from John Updike:

> On the afternoon of the first day of spring, when the gutters were still heaped high with Monday's snow but the sky itself had been swept clean, we put on our galoshes and walked up the sunny side of Fifth Avenue to Central Park.

By holding the main clause back, Updike keeps his readers in suspense, and so puts the most emphasis possible on his main idea.

A LOOSE SENTENCE, on the other hand, states its main idea at the beginning and then adds details in subsequent phrases and clauses. Rewritten as a loose sentence, Updike's sentence might read like this:

> We put on our galoshes and walked up the sunny side of Fifth Avenue to Central Park on the afternoon of the first day of spring, when the gutters were still heaped high with Monday's snow but the sky itself had been swept clean.

The main idea still gets plenty of emphasis, since it is contained in a main clause at the beginning of the sentence. Yet a loose sentence resembles the way people talk: It flows naturally and is easy to understand.

Another way to create emphasis is to use a DRAMATICALLY SHORT SENTENCE. Especially following a long and involved sentence, a short declarative sentence helps drive a point home. Here are two examples, the first from Edwin Newman and the second from David Wise:

> Meaning no disrespect, I suppose there is, if not general rejoicing, at least some sense of relief when the football season ends. It's a long season.

> The executive suite on the thirty-fifth floor of the Columbia Broadcasting System skyscraper in Manhattan is a tasteful blend of dark wood paneling, expensive abstract paintings, thick carpets, and pleasing colors. It has the quiet look of power.

Finally, since the subject of a sentence is automatically emphasized, writers may choose to use the ACTIVE VOICE when they want to emphasize the doer of an action, and the PASSIVE VOICE when they want to downplay or omit the doer completely. Here are two examples:

> High winds pushed our sailboat onto the rocks, where the force of the waves tore it to pieces.

> Our sailboat was pushed by high winds onto the rocks, where it was torn to pieces by the force of the waves.

The first sentence emphasizes the natural forces that destroyed the boat, while the second sentence focuses attention on the boat itself. The passive voice may be useful in placing emphasis, but it has important disadvantages. As the examples show, and as the terms suggest, active-voice verbs are more vigorous and vivid than the same verbs in the passive voice. Then, too, some writers use the passive voice to hide or evade responsibility. "It has been decided" conceals who did the deciding, whereas "I have decided" makes all clear. So the passive voice should be used only when necessary—as it is in this sentence.

Often, a writer wants to place equal emphasis on several facts or ideas. One way to do this is to give each its own sentence. For example:

> Tom Watson selected his club. He lined up his shot. He chipped the ball to within a foot of the pin.

But a long series of short, simple sentences quickly becomes tedious. Many writers would combine these three sentences by using COORDINATION. The coordinating conjunctions *and, but, or, nor, for, so,* and *yet* connect words, phrases, and clauses of equal importance:

> Tom Watson selected his club, lined up his shot, *and* chipped the ball to within a foot of the pin.

By coordinating three sentences into one, the writer not only makes the same words easier to read, but also shows that Watson's three actions are equally important parts of a single process.

When parts of a sentence are not only coordinated but also grammatically the same, they are *parallel.* Parallelism in a sentence is created by balancing a word with a word, a phrase with a phrase, or a clause with a clause. Parallelism is often used in speeches, for example in the last sentence of Lincoln's *Gettysburg Address* (p. 155). Here is another example, from the beginning of Mark Twain's *The Adventures of Huckleberry Finn:*

> Persons attempting to find a motive in this narrative will be prosecuted; persons attempting to find a moral in it will be banished; persons attempting to find a plot in it will be shot.

AN EYE-WITNESS ACCOUNT OF THE SAN FRANCISCO EARTHQUAKE

Jack London

Jack London (1876–1916) was born in San Francisco and attended school only until the age of fourteen. A prolific and popular fiction writer, he is perhaps best remembered for his novels The Call of the Wild *(1903),* The Sea Wolf *(1904), and* White Fang *(1906). London was working near San Francisco when the great earthquake hit that city in the early morning of April 16, 1906. Notice how, in this account of the quake's aftermath, London uses a variety of sentence structures to capture the feelings that this disaster evoked in him.*

The earthquake shook down in San Francisco hundreds of thousands of dollars' worth of walls and chimneys. But the conflagration that followed burned up hundreds of millions of dollars' worth of property. There is no estimating within hundreds of millions the actual damage wrought. Not in history has a modern imperial city been so completely destroyed. San Francisco is gone! Nothing remains of it but memories and a fringe of dwelling houses on its outskirts. Its industrial section is wiped out. Its social and residential section is wiped out. The factories and warehouses, the great stores and newspaper buildings, the hotels and the palaces of the nabobs, are all gone. Remains only the fringe of dwelling houses on the outskirts of what was once San Francisco.

Within an hour after the earthquake shock the smoke of San Francisco's burning was a lurid tower visible a hundred miles away. And for three days and nights this lurid tower swayed in the sky, reddening the sun, darkening the day, and filling the land with smoke.

On Wednesday morning at a quarter past five came the earthquake. A minute later the flames were leaping upward. In a dozen different quarters south of Market Street, in the working-class ghetto, and in the factories, fires started. There was no opposing the flames. There was no organization, no communication. All the cunning adjustments of a twentieth-century city had been smashed by the earthquake. The streets were humped into ridges and depressions and piled with debris of fallen walls. The steel rails were twisted into perpendicular and horizontal angles. The telephone and telegraph systems were disrupted. And the great water mains had burst. All the shrewd contrivances and safeguards of man had been thrown out of gear by thirty seconds' twitching of the earth crust.

By Wednesday afternoon, inside of twelve hours, half the   4
heart of the city was gone. At that time I watched the vast conflagration from out on the bay. It was dead calm. Not a flicker of wind stirred. Yet from every side wind was pouring in upon the city. East, west, north, and south, strong winds were blowing upon the doomed city. The heated air rising made an enormous suck. Thus did the fire of itself build its own colossal chimney through the atmosphere. Day and night, this dead calm continued, and yet, near to the flames, the wind was often half a gale, so mighty was the suck. . . .

Wednesday night saw the destruction of the very heart of the   5
city. Dynamite was lavishly used, and many of San Francisco's proudest structures were crumbled by man himself into ruins, but there was no withstanding the onrush of the flames. Time and again successful stands were made by the fire fighters, and every time the flames flanked around on either side, or came up from the rear, and turned to defeat the hard-won victory.

An enumeration of the buildings destroyed would be a direc-   6
tory of San Francisco. An enumeration of the buildings undestroyed would be a line and several addresses. An enumeration of the deeds of heroism would stock a library and bankrupt the Carnegie medal fund.* An enumeration of the dead—will never be made. All vestiges of them were destroyed by the flames. The number of the victims of the earthquake will never be known.

---

*Fund established by the philanthropist Andrew Carnegie in 1905 for the recognition of heroic deeds.

Questions for Study and Discussion

1. Why do you suppose London does not make one sentence out of his first two sentences? What effect does he gain by using two sentences?
2. If the third sentence in paragraph 3 were rewritten as follows, how would its impact differ from that of the original: "Fires started in a dozen different quarters south of Market Street, in the working-class ghetto, and in the factories"?
3. What is the effect of the short sentences "San Francisco is gone!" and "It was dead calm." in paragraphs 1 and 4?
4. Why do you suppose London uses the passive voice instead of the active voice in paragraph 3? (Glossary: *Voice*)
5. Point out examples of parallelism in paragraphs 1, 2, and 6. How does London add emphasis through the use of this rhetorical device? (Glossary: *Parallelism*)
6. In paragraph 4 London says that "the fire of itself [built] its own colossal chimney through the atmosphere." What does he mean?

Vocabulary

Refer to your dictionary to define the following words as they are used in this selection. Then use each word in a sentence of your own.

conflagration (1)	contrivances (3)
nabobs (1)	vestiges (6)
lurid (2)	

Suggested Writing Assignments

1. If you have ever been an eyewitness to a disaster, either natural or man-made, write an account similar to London's of its consequences. Give special attention to the variety of your sentences according to the advice provided in the introduction to "Effective Sentences."
2. Write a brief essay using one of the following sentences to focus and control the descriptive details you select. Place

the sentence in the essay wherever it will have the greatest emphasis.

It was a strange party.
He was nervous.
I was shocked.
Music filled the air.
Dirt was everywhere.

TERROR AT TINKER CREEK

Annie Dillard

Annie Dillard was born in Pittsburgh, and now makes her home in the Pacific Northwest. A poet, journalist, and contributing editor to Harper's *magazine, Dillard has written* Tickets for a Prayer Wheel *(1975) and* Holy the Firm *(1977). In 1974 she published* Pilgrim at Tinker Creek, *a fascinating collection of natural observations for which she was awarded the Pulitzer Prize for nonfiction. As you read the following selection from that work, notice how the varied structures of Dillard's sentences enhance her descriptions of her experience.*

A couple of summers ago I was walking along the edge of the island to see what I could see in the water, and mainly to scare frogs. Frogs have an inelegant way of taking off from invisible positions on the bank just ahead of your feet, in dire panic, emitting a froggy "Yike!" and splashing into the water. Incredibly, this amused me, and incredibly, it amuses me still. As I walked along the grassy edge of the island, I got better and better at seeing frogs both in and out of the water. I learned to recognize, slowing down, the difference in texture of the light reflected from mudbank, water, grass, or frog. Frogs were flying all around me. At the end of the island I noticed a small green frog. He was exactly half in and half out of the water, looking like a schematic diagram of an amphibian, and he didn't jump.

He didn't jump; I crept closer. At last I knelt on the island's winterkilled grass, lost, dumbstruck, staring at the frog in the creek just four feet away. He was a very small frog with wide, dull eyes. And just as I looked at him, he slowly crumpled and began to sag. The spirit vanished from his eyes as if snuffed. His skin emptied and drooped; his very skull seemed to collapse and settle like a kicked tent. He was shrinking before my eyes like a deflating football. I watched the taut, glistening skin on his shoulders ruck, and rumple, and fall. Soon, part of his skin, formless as a pricked balloon, lay in floating folds like bright scum on top of the water: it was a monstrous and terrifying thing. I gaped bewildered, appalled. An oval shadow hung in the water behind the drained frog; then the shadow glided away. The frog skin bag started to sink.

I had read about the giant water bug, but never seen one. "Giant water bug" is really the name of the creature, which is an enormous, heavy-bodied brown beetle. It eats insects, tadpoles, fish, and frogs. Its grasping forelegs are mighty and hooked inward. It seizes a victim with these legs, hugs it tight, and paralyzes it with enzymes injected during a vicious bite. That one bite is the only bite it ever takes. Through the puncture shoot the poisons that dissolve the victim's muscles and bones and organs—all but the skin—and through it the giant water bug sucks out the victim's body, reduced to a juice. This event is quite common in warm fresh water. The frog I saw was being sucked by a giant water bug. I had been kneeling on the island grass; when the unrecognizable flap of frog skin settled on the creek bottom, swaying, I stood up and brushed the knees of my pants. I couldn't catch my breath.

3

Questions for Study and Discussion

1. Why do you suppose that Dillard could not catch her breath after the experience she describes?
2. Paragraph 1 contains sentences that are varied in both length and structure, including loose sentences as well as periodic sentences, long ones as well as short. Identify two loose sentences and two periodic sentences, and compare the effects each one has on the narrative.
3. Can you recognize a relationship between kinds of sentences and the content they contain? In other words, does Dillard use loose sentences for certain kinds of information and periodic sentences for other kinds? Support your answer with examples from the selection.

4. The first sentence in paragraph 2 contains a semicolon. Would the sentence have a different sense if the two clauses were instead joined with a coordinating conjunction—for example, *and* or *so*? Would they be different if punctuated with a period? How?

5. A simile is a comparison introduced by *like* or *as*. For example, paragraph 2 contains the simile "formless as a pricked balloon." Identify two other similes in this selection, and explain what they contribute to the description.

6. Can you characterize the words Dillard uses to describe the water bug in paragraph 3? What does her choice of words indicate about her feeling about the bug? (Glossary: *Diction*)

Vocabulary

Refer to your dictionary to define the following words as they are used in this selection. Then use each word in a sentence of your own.

dire (1)   taut (2)
schematic (1)   appalled (2)
dumbstruck (2)   enzymes (3)

Suggested Writing Assignments

1. After watching the attack on the frog by the water bug, Annie Dillard says, in her last sentence, "I couldn't catch my breath." If you have ever had a similar response to an event, not necessarily tied to an event in nature, describe it in such a way that the reader understands it. At each stage of the writing process—writing a first draft, revising, and editing—you should pay particular attention to the variety of your sentences, making sure that they add emphasis and interest to your writing.

2. Without changing the meaning, rewrite the following paragraph using a variety of sentence structures to add interest and emphasis.

   The hunter crept through the leaves. The leaves had fallen. The leaves were dry. The hunter was tired. The hunter had a gun. The gun was new. The hunter saw a deer. The deer had antlers. A tree partly hid the antlers. The deer was beautiful. The hunter shot at the deer. The hunter missed. The shot frightened the deer. The deer bounded away.

SALVATION

Langston Hughes

Born in Joplin, Missouri, Langston Hughes (1902–1967), an important figure in the Harlem Renaissance, wrote poetry, fiction, and plays, and contributed a column to the New York Post. *He is best known for* The Weary Blues *(1926) and other books of poetry that express his racial pride, his familiarity with black traditions, and his understanding of jazz rhythms. As you read the following selection from his autobiography* The Big Sea *(1940), notice how Hughes varies the lengths and types of sentences he uses for the sake of emphasis.*

I was saved from sin when I was going on thirteen. But not really saved. It happened like this. There was a big revival at my Auntie Reed's church. Every night for weeks there had been much preaching, singing, praying, and shouting, and some very hardened sinners had been brought to Christ, and the membership of the church had grown by leaps and bounds. Then just before the revival ended, they held a special meeting for children, "to bring the young lambs to the fold." My aunt spoke of it for days ahead. That night I was escorted to the front row and placed on the mourners' bench with all the other young sinners, who had not yet been brought to Jesus. 1

My aunt told me that when you were saved you saw a light, and something happened to you inside! And Jesus came into your life! And God was with you from then on! She said you could see and hear and feel Jesus in your soul. I believed her. I have heard a great many old people say the same thing and it seemed to me they ought to know. So I sat there calmly in the hot, crowded church, waiting for Jesus to come to me. 2

The preacher preached a wonderful rhythmical sermon, all moans and shouts and lonely cries and dire pictures of hell, and then he sang a song about the ninety and nine safe in the 3 fold, but one little lamb was left out in the cold. Then he said: "Won't you come? Won't you come to Jesus? Young lambs, won't you come?" And he held out his arms to all us young sinners there on the mourners' bench. And the little girls cried. And some of them jumped up and went to Jesus right away. But most of us just sat there.

A great many old people came and knelt around us and   4
prayed, old women with jet-black faces and braided hair, old men with work-gnarled hands. And the church sang a song about the lower lights are burning, some poor sinners to be saved. And the whole building rocked with prayer and song.

Still I kept waiting to *see* Jesus.   5

Finally all the young people had gone to the altar and were   6
saved, but one boy and me. He was a rounder's son named Westley. Westley and I were surrounded by sisters and deacons praying. It was very hot in the church, and getting late now. Finally Westley said to me in a whisper: "God damn! I'm tired o' sitting here. Let's get up and be saved." So he got up and was saved.

Then I was left all alone on the mourners' bench. My aunt   7
came and knelt at my knees and cried, while prayers and songs swirled all around me in the little church. The whole congregation prayed for me alone, in a mighty wail of moans and voices. And I kept waiting serenely for Jesus, waiting, waiting—but he didn't come. I wanted to see him, but nothing happened to me. Nothing! I wanted something to happen to me, but nothing happened.

I heard the songs and the minister saying: "Why don't you   8
come? My dear child, why don't you come to Jesus? Jesus is waiting for you. He wants you. Why don't you come? Sister Reed, what is this child's name?"

"Langston," my aunt sobbed.   9

"Langston, why don't you come? Why don't you come and be   10
saved? Oh, Lamb of God! Why don't you come?"

Now it was really getting late. I began to be ashamed of my-   11
self, holding everything up so long. I began to wonder what God thought about Westley, who certainly hadn't seen Jesus either, but who was now sitting proudly on the platform, swinging his knickerbockered legs and grinning down at me, surrounded by deacons and old women on their knees praying. God had not

struck Westley dead for taking his name in vain or for lying in the temple. So I decided that maybe to save further trouble, I'd better lie, too, and say that Jesus had come, and get up and be saved.

So I got up.   12

Suddenly the whole room broke into a sea of shouting, as   13
they saw me rise. Waves of rejoicing swept the place. Women leaped in the air. My aunt threw her arms around me. The minister took me by the hand and led me to the platform.

When things quieted down, in a hushed silence, punctuated   14
by a few ecstatic "Amens," all the new young lambs were blessed in the name of God. Then joyous singing filled the room.

That night, for the last time in my life but one—for I was a   15
big boy twelve years old—I cried. I cried, in bed alone, and couldn't stop. I buried my head under the quilts, but my aunt heard me. She woke up and told my uncle I was crying because the Holy Ghost had come into my life, and because I had seen Jesus. But I was really crying because I couldn't bear to tell her that I had lied, that I had deceived everybody in the church, that I hadn't seen Jesus, and that now I didn't believe there was a Jesus any more, since he didn't come to help me.

Questions for Study and Discussion

1. Why does young Langston Hughes expect to be saved at the revival meeting? Once the children are in church, what appeals are made to them to encourage them to seek salvation?

2. What would be gained or lost if the essay began with the first two sentences combined as follows: "I was saved from sin when I was going on thirteen, but I was not really saved"?

3. Identify the coordinating conjunctions in paragraph 3. Rewrite the paragraph without them. Compare your paragraph with the original, and explain what Hughes gains by using coordinating conjunctions. (Glossary: *Coordination*)

4. Identify the subordinating conjunctions in paragraph 15. What is it about the ideas in this last paragraph that makes it necessary for him to use these subordinating conjunctions?

5. How do the short one-sentence paragraphs aid Hughes in telling his story?

6. How does Hughes's choice of words, or diction, help to establish a realistic atmosphere for a religious revival meeting?

Vocabulary

Refer to your dictionary to define the following words as they are used in this selection. Then use each word in a sentence of your own.

dire (3) punctuated (14)
gnarled (4) ecstatic (14)
vain (11)

Suggested Writing Assignments

1. Like the young Langston Hughes, we sometimes find ourselves in situations in which, for the sake of conformity, we do things we do not believe in. Consider one such experience you have had, and write an essay about it. What is it about human nature that makes us occasionally act in ways that contradict our inner feelings? As you write, pay particular attention to your sentence variety.

2. Reread the introduction to this chapter. Then review one of the essays that you have written, paying particular attention to sentence structure. Recast sentences as necessary in order to make your writing more interesting and effective.

II

THE
LANGUAGE
OF THE
ESSAY

8

DICTION AND TONE

DICTION

Diction refers to a writer's choice and use of words. Good diction is precise and appropriate—the words mean exactly what the writer intends, and the words are well suited to the writer's subject, purpose, and intended audience.

For careful writers it is not enough merely to come close to saying what they want to say; they select words that convey their exact meaning. Perhaps Mark Twain put this best when he said, "The difference between the right word and the almost right word is the difference between lightning and the lightning bug." Inaccurate, imprecise, or inappropriate diction not only fails to convey the writer's intended meaning but also may cause confusion and misunderstanding for the reader.

Connotation and Denotation

Both connotation and denotation refer to the meanings of words. Denotation is the dictionary meaning of a word, the literal meaning. Connotative meanings are the associations or emotional overtones that words have acquired gradually. For example, the word *home* denotes a place where someone lives, but it connotes warmth, security, family, comfort, affection, and other more private thoughts and images. The word *residence* also denotes a place where someone lives, but its connotations are colder and more formal.

Many words in English have synonyms, words with very similar denotations: for example, *mob, crowd, multitude,* and *bunch.* Deciding which to use depends largely on the connotations that each synonym has and the context in which the word is to be used. For example, you might say, "There was a crowd at the lecture," but not "There was a mob at the lecture." Good writers are sensitive to both the denotations and the connotations of words.

Abstract and Concrete Words

Abstract words name ideas, conditions, emotions—things nobody can touch, see, or hear. Some abstract words are *love, wisdom, cowardice, beauty, fear,* and *liberty.* People often disagree about abstract things. You may find a forest beautiful, while someone else might find it frightening, and neither of you would be wrong. Beauty and fear are abstract ideas; they exist in your mind, not in the forest along with the trees and the owls. Concrete words refer to things we can touch, see, hear, smell, and taste, such as *sandpaper, soda, birch trees, smog, cow, sailboat, rocking chair,* and *pancake.* If you disagree with someone on a concrete issue—say, you claim that the forest is mostly birch trees, while the other person says it is mostly pine—only one of you can be right, and both of you can be wrong; what kinds of trees grow in the forest is a concrete fact, not an abstract idea.

Good writing balances ideas and facts, and it also balances abstract and concrete diction. If the writing is too abstract, with too few concrete facts and details, it will be unconvincing and tiresome. If the writing is too concrete, devoid of ideas and emotions, it can seem pointless and dry.

General and Specific Words

General and *specific* do not necessarily refer to opposites. The same word can often be either general or specific, depending on the context: *Dessert* is more specific than *food,* but more general than *chocolate cream pie.* Being very specific is like being concrete: *chocolate cream pie* is something you can see and taste. Being general, on the other hand, is like being abstract. *Food, dessert,* and even *pie* are general classes of things that bring no particular taste or image to mind.

Good writing moves back and forth from the general to the specific. Without specific words, generalities can be unconvincing and even confusing: the writer's idea of "good food" may be very different from the reader's. But writing that does not relate specifics to each other by generalization often lacks focus and direction.

Clichés

Some words, phrases, and expressions have become trite through overuse. Let's assume your roommate has just returned from an evening out. You ask her "How was the concert?" She responds, "The concert was okay, but they had us *packed in* there *like sardines*. How was your evening?" And you reply, "Well, I finished my term paper, but the noise here is enough to *drive me crazy*. The dorm is a real *zoo*." At one time the italicized expressions were vivid and colorful, but through constant use they have grown stale and ineffective. The experienced writer always tries to avoid such clichés as *believe it or not, doomed to failure, hit the spot, let's face it, sneaking suspicion, step in the right direction,* and *went to great lengths.*

Jargon

Jargon, or technical language, is the special vocabulary of a trade or profession. Writers who use jargon do so with an awareness of their audience. If their audience is a group of coworkers or professionals, jargon may be used freely. If the audience is a more general one, jargon should be used sparingly and carefully so that readers can understand it. Jargon becomes inappropriate when it is overused, used out of context, or used pretentiously. For example, computer terms such as *input, output,* and *feedback* are sometimes used in place of *contribution, result,* and *response* in other fields, especially in business. If you think about it, the terms suggest that people are machines, receiving and processing information according to a program imposed by someone else.

Formal and Informal Diction

Diction is appropriate when it suits the occasion for which it is intended. If the situation is informal—a friendly letter, for example—the writing may be colloquial; that is, its words may be chosen to suggest the way people talk with each other. If, on the other hand, the situation is formal—a term paper or a research report, for example—then the words should reflect this formality. Informal writing tends to be characterized by slang, contractions, references to the reader, and concrete nouns. Formal writing tends to be impersonal, abstract, and free of contractions and references to the reader. Formal writing and informal writing are, of course, the extremes. Most writing falls between these two extremes and is a blend of those formal and informal elements that best fit the context.

TONE

Tone is the attitude a writer takes toward the subject and the audience. The tone may be friendly or hostile, serious or humorous, intimate or distant, enthusiastic or skeptical.

As you read the following paragraphs, notice how each writer has created a different tone and how that tone is supported by the diction—the writer's particular choice and use of words.

Nostalgic

My generation is special because of what we missed rather than what we got, because in a certain sense we are the first and the last. The first to take technology for granted. (What was a space shot to us, except an hour cut from Social Studies to gather before a TV in the gym as Cape Canaveral counted down?) The first to grow up with TV. My sister was 8 when we got our set, so to her it seemed magic and always somewhat foreign. She had known books already and would never really replace them. But for me, the TV set was, like the kitchen sink and the telephone, a fact of life.

Joyce Maynard, "An 18-Year-Old Looks Back on Life"

Angry

Cans. Beer cans. Glinting on the verges of a million miles of roadways, lying in scrub, grass, dirt, leaves, sand, mud, but never hidden. Piels, Rheingold, Ballantine, Schaefer, Schlitz, shining in the sun or picked by moon or the beams of headlights at night; washed by rain or flattened by wheels, but never dulled, never buried, never destroyed. Here is the mark of savages, the testament of wasters, the stain of prosperity.

Marya Mannes, "Wasteland"

Humorous

In perpetrating a revolution, there are two require-
ments: someone or something to revolt against and someone to actually show up and do the revolting. Dress is usually casual and both parties may be flexible about time and
place but if either faction fails to attend the whole enterprise is likely to come off badly. In the Chinese Revolution
of 1650 neither party showed up and the deposit on the hall
was forfeited.

Woody Allen,   "A Brief, Yet Helpful Guide to Civil Disobedience"

Resigned

I make my living humping cargo for Seaboard World
Airlines, one of the big international airlines at Kennedy
Airport. They handle strictly all cargo. I was once told that
one of the Rockefellers is the major stockholder for the airline, but I don't really think about that too much. I don't
get paid to think. The big thing is to beat that race with the
time clock every morning of your life so the airline will be
happy. The worst thing a man could ever do is to make suggestions about building a better airline. They pay people
$40,000 a year to come up with better ideas. It doesn't mat-
ter that these ideas never work; it's just that they get nervous when a guy from South Brooklyn or Ozone Park acts
like he has a brain.

Patrick Fenton, "Confessions of a Working Stiff"

Ironic

Once upon a time there was a small, beautiful, green and
graceful country called Vietnam. It needed to be saved. (In
later years no one could remember exactly what it needed
to be saved from, but that is another story.) For many years
Vietnam was in the process of being saved by France, but
the French eventually tired of their labors and left. Then
America took on the job. America was well equipped for
country-saving. It was the richest and most powerful nation on earth. It had, for example, nuclear explosives on
hand and ready to use equal to six tons of TNT for every
man, woman, and child in the world. It had huge and very
efficient factories, brilliant and dedicated scientists, and
most (but not everybody) would agree, it had good inten-

tions. Sadly, America had one fatal flaw—its inhabitants were in love with technology and thought it could do no wrong. A visitor to America during the time of this story would probably have guessed its outcome after seeing how its inhabitants were treating their own country. The air was mostly foul, the water putrid, and most of the land was either covered with concrete or garbage. But Americans were never much on introspection, and they didn't foresee the result of their loving embrace on the small country. They set out to save Vietnam with the same enthusiasm and determination their forefathers had displayed in conquering the frontier.

The Sierra Club, "A Fable for Our Times"

ON BEING 17, BRIGHT, AND UNABLE TO READ

David Raymond

When the following article appeared in The New York Times *in 1976, David Raymond was a high school student in Connecticut. In his essay he poignantly discusses his great difficulty in reading because of dyslexia and the many problems he experienced in school as a result. As you read, pay attention to the naturalness of the author's diction.*

One day a substitute teacher picked me to read aloud from the textbook. When I told her "No, thank you," she came unhinged. She thought I was acting smart, and told me so. I kept calm, and that got her madder and madder. We must have spent 10 minutes trying to solve the problem, and finally she got so red in the face I thought she'd blow up. She told me she'd see me after class.

Maybe someone like me was a new thing for that teacher. But she wasn't new to me. I've been through scenes like that all my life. You see, even though I'm 17 and a junior in high school, I can't read because I have dyslexia. I'm told I read "at a fourth-grade level," but from where I sit, that's not reading. You can't know what that means unless you've been there. It's not easy to tell how it feels when you can't read your homework assignments or the newspaper or a menu in a restaurant or even notes from your own friends.

My family began to suspect I was having problems almost from the first day I started school. My father says my early years in school were the worst years of his life. They weren't so good for me, either. As I look back on it now, I can't find the words to express how bad it really was. I wanted to die. I'd come home from school screaming, "I'm dumb. I'm dumb—I wish I were dead!"

I guess I couldn't read anything at all then—not even my own   4
name—and they tell me I didn't talk as good as other kids. But
what I remember about those days is that I couldn't throw a
ball where it was supposed to go, I couldn't learn to swim, and I
wouldn't learn to ride a bike, because no matter what anyone
told me, I knew I'd fail.

Sometimes my teachers would try to be encouraging. When I   5
couldn't read the words on the board they'd say, "Come on,
David, you know that word." Only I didn't. And it was embarrassing. I just felt dumb. And dumb was how the kids treated
me. They'd make fun of me every chance they got, asking me to
spell "cat" or something like that. Even if I knew how to spell
it, I wouldn't; they'd only give me another word. Anyway, it was
awful, because more than anything I wanted friends. On my
birthday when I blew out the candles I didn't wish I could learn
to read; what I wished for was that the kids would like me.

With the bad reports coming from school, and with me moan-   6
ing about wanting to die and how everybody hated me, my parents began looking for help. That's when the testing started.
The school tested me, the child-guidance center tested me, private psychiatrists tested me. Everybody knew something was
wrong—especially me.

It didn't help much when they stuck a fancy name onto it. I   7
couldn't pronounce it then—I was only in second grade—and I
was ashamed to talk about it. Now it rolls off my tongue, because I've been living with it for a lot of years—dyslexia.

All through elementary school it wasn't easy. I was always   8
having to do things that were "different," things the other kids
didn't have to do. I had to go to a child psychiatrist, for instance.

One summer my family forced me to go to a camp for chil-   9
dren with reading problems. I hated the idea, but the camp
turned out pretty good, and I had a good time. I met a lot of
kids who couldn't read and somehow that helped. The director
of the camp said I had a higher I.Q. than 90 percent of the population. I didn't believe him.

About the worst thing I had to do in fifth and sixth grade was   10
go to a special education class in another school in our town. A
bus picked me up, and I didn't like that at all. The bus also

picked up emotionally disturbed kids and retarded kids. It was like going to a school for the retarded. I always worried that someone I knew would see me on that bus. It was a relief to go to the regular junior high school.

Life began to change a little for me then, because I began to feel better about myself. I found the teachers cared; they had meetings about me and I worked harder for them for a while. I began to work on the potter's wheel, making vases and pots that the teachers said were pretty good. Also, I got a letter for being on the track team. I could always run pretty fast.

11

At high school the teachers are good and everyone is trying to help me. I've gotten honors some marking periods and I've won a letter on the cross-country team. Next quarter I think the school might hold a show of my pottery. I've got some friends. But there are still some embarrassing times. For instance, every time there is writing in the class, I get up and go to the special education room. Kids ask me where I go all the time. Sometimes I say, "to Mars."

12

Homework is a real problem. During free periods in school I go into the special ed room and staff members read assignments to me. When I get home my mother reads to me. Sometimes she reads an assignment into a tape recorder, and then I go into my room and listen to it. If we have a novel or something like that to read, she reads it out loud to me. Then I sit down with her and we do the assignment. She'll write, while I talk my answers to her. Lately I've taken to dictating into a tape recorder, and then someone—my father, a private tutor or my mother—types up what I've dictated. Whatever homework I do takes someone else's time, too. That makes me feel bad.

13

We had a big meeting in school the other day—eight of us, four from the guidance department, my private tutor, my parents and me. The subject was me. I said I wanted to go to college, and they told me about colleges that have facilities and staff to handle people like me. That's nice to hear.

14

As for what happens after college, I don't know and I'm worried about that. How can I make a living if I can't read? Who will hire me? How will I fill out the application form? The only thing that gives me any courage is the fact that I've learned about well-known people who couldn't read or had other prob-

15

lems and still made it. Like Albert Einstein, who didn't talk until he was 4 and flunked math. Like Leonardo da Vinci, who everyone seems to think had dyslexia.

I've told this story because maybe some teacher will read it   16
and go easy on a kid in the classroom who has what I've got. Or,
maybe some parent will stop nagging his kid, and stop calling
him lazy. Maybe he's not lazy or dumb. Maybe he just can't
read and doesn't know what's wrong. Maybe he's scared, like I
was.

Questions for Study and Discussion

1. What does Raymond say his purpose is in telling his story?
2. Would you characterize the diction in this selection as formal or informal? General or specific? Concrete or abstract?
   Is this diction appropriate considering Raymond's topic?
3. Raymond uses many colloquial and idiomatic expressions,
   such as "she got so red in the face I thought she'd blow up"
   and "she came unhinged." Identify other examples of such
   diction and tell how they affect the essay.
4. In the context of the essay, comment on the appropriateness
   of each of the following possible choices of diction. Which
   word is better in each case? Why?
   a. *selected* for *picked* (1)
   b. *experience* for *thing* (2)
   c. *speak as well* for *talk as good* (4)
   d. *negative* for *bad* (6)
   e. *important* for *big* (14)
   f. *failed* for *flunked* (15)
   g. *frightened* for *scared* (16)
5. How would you describe Raymond's tone in this essay?

Vocabulary

Refer to your dictionary to define the following words as they
are used in this selection. Then use each word in a sentence of
your own.

dyslexia (2)   psychiatrists (6)

Suggested Writing Assignments

1. Imagine that you are away at school. Recently you were caught in a radar speed trap—you were going 70 miles per hour in a 55-mile-per-hour zone—and have just lost your license; you will not be able to go home this coming weekend, as you had planned. Write two letters in which you explain why you will not be able to go home, one to your parents and the other to your best friend. Your audience is different in each case, so be sure to choose your diction accordingly.

2. Select an essay you have already completed in this course and rewrite it in a different tone. If the essay was originally formal or serious, lighten it so that it is now informal and humorous. Pay special attention to diction. Actually think in terms of a different reader as your audience—not your instructor but perhaps your classmates, your clergyman, your sister, or the state environmental protection board. Reshape your essay as necessary.

WHEN NOT TO CALL THE DOCTOR

Art Buchwald

*Art Buchwald, one of America's funniest and
most popular newspaper columnists, was born
in 1925 in Mt. Vernon, New York. Before finishing high school Buchwald joined the Marines; after serving in World War II, he attended the University of Southern California and left, before
graduating, to live in Paris. In Paris Buchwald
wrote a regular column for the Paris edition of
the* New York Herald Tribune, *and in 1962 he returned to the United States and started writing
his column from Washington, D.C., where he remains. Titled simply "Art Buchwald," the
column is syndicated to hundreds of newspapers
across the country. In the following essay, Buchwald focuses his satire on those who can't resist
diagnosing the illnesses of their friends and rela-
tives.*

Because medical costs are rising so fast, more and more
people are diagnosing their own illnesses or, worse still,
those of their friends. The government would do well to make a
study of how these nonprofessional diagnoses are affecting the
nation's health picture.

The other day I had a cold. It was just like the ones you see on
television. I was sneezing, coughing and looking mournfully at
my wife. I called my secretary at the office and said I wouldn't
be in because I felt lousy.

"You must have one of those 'eight-hour things' that's going
all around town," she said. "You'll feel perfectly well tomorrow."

Eight hours seemed to be a reasonable time to have a cold,
and I was looking forward to staying in bed, particularly since
the Yankees and Red Sox were playing a crucial game to get in
the American League playoffs.

My sister called, and I told her I had one of those "eight-hour things that's been going all around."

"Are you sure it's only an 'eight-hour thing'?" she asked. "It could be the '24-hour bug.' Harold had it last week. Do you have any fever?"

"A little—maybe 100."

"That's the '24-hour bug' for sure. Drink lots of fluids and take aspirin, and you'll be able to shake it off."

I really hadn't counted on staying in bed for 24 hours, but it's stupid to fight a bug.

My other sister called up 10 minutes later. "Edith says you've got a '24-hour bug.'"

"I don't know if it's a bug or just a cold."

"Is your nose red from blowing it?"

"Yah, sure it is. Why do you ask?"

"Then you don't have a '24-hour bug.' You have a '48-hour virus.'"

"My secretary said all I had was an 'eight-hour thing.' How come you moved it up to 48 hours?"

"The 'eight-hour thing' is entirely different. You feel funny but your nose doesn't get red when you blow it. The '24-hour bug' has all the symptoms of the 'eight-hour one,' except that you cough a lot. The '48-hour virus' makes you sneeze, cough and perspire while you're sleeping. You have to stay in bed for two days."

"But I can't stay in bed for two days!"

"Look," my sister said. "If you don't want medical advice, don't ask me."

I think I might have been all right except that my secretary told Healy I was home with the flu.

He called, of course. "I feel for you," he said. "You won't be able to shake it for two weeks. If it were a winter cold I'd say you'd be better in five, maybe six days. But you have an October cold. It's almost impossible to get rid of. You hear my voice? It's been like this since August."

"But suppose my cold goes away in 24 hours?"

"That's when it can become the most dangerous. You think it's gone away and then a week later you wake up and it's back with a vengeance. I'd rather have a two-week bout with a chest cold than a '24-hour bug' which sneaks up on you like a thief in the night."

Word travels fast in Washington, and Elfin of *Newsweek* was   23
terse and to the point. "Healy tells me you have an incurable
form of pneumonia."

"Either that," I said, "or an 'eight-hour thing' or a '24-hour   24
bug' or a '48-hour virus' or a two-week bout with the flu or a
simple cold. I'm waiting on another opinion right now."

"From whom?"   25

"My druggist. He says there's a lot of it going around."   26

"What's going around?"   27

"You name it, and he says he's never seen so much of it going   28
around."

Questions for Study and Discussion

1. What is Buchwald's tone in this essay? Give examples of
   how he has used diction to establish that tone.
2. What is Buchwald satirizing in this essay? (Glossary: *Satire*)
3. At what point in this essay do you first realize that Art
   Buchwald is being less than serious?
4. How do you think most readers would react to Buchwald's
   account of his bout with a common cold? Do you find the
   essay humorous? If so, why?

Vocabulary

Refer to your dictionary to define the following words as they
are used in this selection. Then use each word in a sentence of
your own.

diagnoses (1)   bout (22)
mournfully (2)   incurable (23)
vengeance (22)

Suggested Writing Assignments

1. Art Buchwald's essay shows him to have a real talent for
   taking an everyday occurrence, such as the common cold,

and making it the subject of a humorous essay. In his column Buchwald also finds humor in more serious contemporary events, especially those that deal with the president, Congress, and international affairs. Asked by a fan where he got his material, Buchwald replied that he got it all from the newspapers. Following Buchwald's practice, look through copies of your daily newspaper and select a topic worthy of satire. Then write a humorous essay inspired by what you have read in the newspaper.

2. Take a letter or memorandum that you have received from your college administration or some other bureaucratic body, and rewrite it so as to avoid the deadly dull diction and tone of most such correspondence. Your revision should convey all the necessary information contained in the original but should do so in a lively and entertaining way. Be sure, however, that your tone is appropriate for your audience and subject.

THE FLIGHT OF THE EAGLES

N. Scott Momaday

N. Scott Momaday, a professor of English at Stanford University, is a Kiowa Indian. He has based much of his writing on his Indian ancestry, particularly on his childhood experiences with his Kiowa grandmother. In 1969 he won the Pulitzer Prize for his novel House Made of Dawn *(1968). His other works include* The Way to Rainy Mountain *(1969),* Angle of Geese and Other Poems *(1974), and* The Gourd Dancer *(1976). In the following selection, taken from* House Made of Dawn, *Momaday closely observes the mating flight of a pair of golden eagles. Notice how his sensitive choice of verbs enables him to capture the beautiful and graceful movements of these birds.*

They were golden eagles, a male and a female, in their mating flight. They were cavorting, spinning and spiraling on the cold, clear columns of air, and they were beautiful. They swooped and hovered, leaning on the air, and swung close together, feinting and screaming with delight. The female was full-grown, and the span of her broad wings was greater than any man's height. There was a fine flourish to her motion; she was deceptively, incredibly fast, and her pivots and wheels were wide and full-blown. But her great weight was streamlined and perfectly controlled. She carried a rattlesnake; it hung shining from her feet, limp and curving out in the trail of her flight. Suddenly her wings and tail fanned, catching full on the wind, and for an instant she was still, widespread and spectral in the blue, while her mate flared past and away, turning around in the distance to look for her. Then she began to beat upward at an angle from the rim until she was small in the sky, and she let go of the snake. It fell slowly, writhing and rolling, floating out like a bit of silver thread against the wide back-drop of the land. She held still above, buoyed up on the cold current, her crop and hackles gleaming like copper in the sun. The male swerved and sailed. He was younger than she and a little more than half as large. He was quicker, tighter in his moves. He let the carrion drift by; then suddenly he gathered himself and stooped, sliding down in a blur of motion to the strike. He hit the snake in the head, with not the slightest de-flection of his course or speed, cracking its long body like a whip. Then he rolled and swung upward in a great pendulum arc, riding out his momentum. At the top of his glide he let go of the snake in turn, but the female did not go for it. Instead she soared out over the plain, nearly out of sight, like a mote reced-ing into the haze of the far mountain. The male followed.

Questions for Study and Discussion

1. What are the differences between the two eagles as Moma-day describes them?
2. In describing the mating flight of the golden eagles, Moma-day has tried to capture their actions accurately. Identify the strong verbs that he uses, and discuss how these verbs enhance his description. (Glossary: *Verb*)
3. Comment on the denotative and connotative meanings of the italicized words and phrases in the following excerpts:
   a. on the *cold, clear* columns of air
   b. feinting and screaming with *delight*
   c. a *fine flourish* to her motion
   d. her *pivots* and *wheels* were wide and full-blown
   e. her *crop* and *hackles* gleaming
4. Identify several examples of Momaday's use of concrete and specific diction. What effect does this diction have on you?
5. Identify the figures of speech that Momaday uses in this selection and tell how you think each one functions in the essay. (Glossary: *Figures of Speech*)

Vocabulary

Refer to your dictionary to define the following words as they are used in this selection. Then use each word in a sentence of your own.

cavorting   spectral
feinting

Suggested Writing Assignments

1. Select one of the following activities as the subject for a brief descriptive essay. Be sure to use strong verbs, as Momaday has done, in order to describe the action accurately and vividly.

   the movements of a dancer
   the actions of a kite
   the antics of a pet
   a traffic jam
   a violent storm

2. Accounts of natural events often rely on scientific data and are frequently presented in the third person. Carefully observe some natural event (fire, hurricane, birth of an animal, bird migration, etc.), and note significant details and facts about that occurrence. Then, using very carefully chosen diction, write an account of the event.

THE GETTYSBURG ADDRESS

Abraham Lincoln

*With the possible exception of "The Declaration
of Independence," perhaps no document of
American history is as famous as "The Gettysburg Address." Abraham Lincoln (1809–1865),
one of the most beloved of all presidents, delivered the address on the Gettysburg battlefield on
November 19, 1863. Although the address is only
three paragraphs long, its message is powerfully
stated. Lincoln's profound sentiments and careful diction make the address a nearly flawless
model of formal English prose.*

Four score and seven years ago our fathers brought forth
on this continent, a new nation, conceived in Liberty, and
dedicated to the proposition that all men are created equal.

Now we are engaged in a great civil war, testing whether that
nation, or any nation so conceived and so dedicated, can long
endure. We are met on a great battle-field of that war. We have
come to dedicate a portion of that field, as a final resting place
for those who here gave their lives that that nation might live.
It is altogether fitting and proper that we should do this.

But, in a larger sense, we can not dedicate—we can not
consecrate—we can not hallow—this ground. The brave men,
living and dead, who struggled here, have consecrated it, far
above our poor power to add or detract. The world will little
note, nor long remember what we say here, but it can never forget what they did here. It is for us the living, rather, to be dedicated here to the unfinished work which they who fought here
have thus far so nobly advanced. It is rather for us to be here
dedicated to the great task remaining before us—that from
these honored dead we take increased devotion to that cause
for which they gave the last full measure of devotion—that we
here highly resolve that these dead shall not have died in vain—

that this nation, under God, shall have a new birth of freedom—and that government of the people, by the people, for the people, shall not perish from the earth.

Questions for Study and Discussion

1. To what Civil War issue does Lincoln's opening sentence refer?
2. Lincoln's diction in the opening paragraph of "The Gettysburg Address" is calculated to achieve a certain effect on listeners and readers. Discuss the nature of this effect by comparing the opening paragraph to the following one: "Eighty-seven years ago our ancestors formed a new nation based on liberty and devoted to the notion that all men are created equal."
3. In an early draft of the address, the last sentence in paragraph 2 reads, "This we may, in all propriety, do." Why do you suppose Lincoln rewrote this sentence?
4. In the first sentence of paragraph 3, Lincoln uses the words *dedicate, consecrate,* and *hallow.* Do these words have the same denotative meaning? Why do you think Lincoln placed them in this particular order?
5. The tone of "The Gettysburg Address" can be described as reverential. Cite specific examples of Lincoln's diction that help to create this tone.

Vocabulary

Refer to your dictionary to define the following words as they are used in this selection. Then use each word in a sentence of your own.

proposition (1)   resolve (3)
detract (3)   vain (3)

Suggested Writing Assignments

1. Write two paragraphs in which you describe the same incident, person, scene, or thing. In the first paragraph, use formal language and in the second, informal language. Keep the factual content of the two paragraphs constant; vary only the language.

2. Write a letter to your school or local newspaper in which you express your displeasure with a recent occurrence or situation. Assume one of the following tones for your letter, making sure that it is appropriate for your particular subject, purpose, and audience.

   understanding
   forceful but rational
   sarcastic
   irate
   objective

NOBEL PRIZE ACCEPTANCE SPEECH

William Faulkner

William Faulkner (1897–1962), one of America's greatest writers, lived for most of his life in Oxford, Mississippi. He is best known for his novels Sartoris *(1929),* The Sound and the Fury *(1929),* As I Lay Dying *(1930),* Sanctuary *(1931),* Light in August *(1932), and* Absalom, Absalom! *(1936). In accepting the 1949 Nobel Prize for Literature, Faulkner made the following speech urging young writers to consider the power of words and to remember the durability of humankind.*

I feel that this award was not made to me as a man, but to my   1
work—a life's work in the agony and sweat of the human
spirit, not for glory and least of all for profit, but to create out
of the materials of the human spirit something which did not
exist before. So this award is only mine in trust. It will not be
difficult to find a dedication for the money part of it commen-
surate with the purpose and significance of its origin. But I
would like to do the same with the acclaim too, by using this
moment as a pinnacle from which I might be listened to by the
young men and women already dedicated to the same anguish
and travail, among whom is already that one who will some day
stand here where I am standing.

Our tragedy today is a general and universal physical fear so   2
long sustained by now that we can even bear it. There are no
longer problems of the spirit. There is only the question: When
will I be blown up? Because of this, the young man or woman
writing today has forgotten the problems of the human heart in
conflict with itself which alone can make good writing because
only that is worth writing about, worth the agony and the
sweat.

He must learn them again. He must teach himself that the   3
basest of all things is to be afraid; and, teaching himself that,

forget it forever, leaving no room in his workshop for anything but the old verities and truths of the heart, the old universal truths lacking which any story is ephemeral and doomed—love and honor and pity and pride and compassion and sacrifice. Until he does so, he labors under a curse. He writes not of love but of lust, of defeats in which nobody loses anything of value, of victories without hope and, worst of all, without pity or compassion. His griefs grieve on no universal bones, leaving no scars. He writes not of the heart but of the glands.

Until he relearns these things, he will write as though he   4 stood among and watched the end of man. I decline to accept the end of man. It is easy enough to say that man is immortal simply because he will endure: that when the last ding-dong of doom has clanged and faded from the last worthless rock hanging tideless in the last red and dying evening, that even then there will still be one more sound: that of his puny inexhaustible voice, still talking. I refuse to accept this. I believe that man will not merely endure: he will prevail. He is immortal, not because he alone among creatures has an inexhaustible voice, but because he has a soul, a spirit capable of compassion and sacrifice and endurance. The poet's, the writer's, duty is to write about these things. It is his privilege to help man endure by lifting his heart, by reminding him of the courage and honor and hope and pride and compassion and pity and sacrifice which have been the glory of his past. The poet's voice need not merely be the record of man, it can be one of the props, the pillars to help him endure and prevail.

Questions for Study and Discussion

1. What advice does Faulkner offer young writers? How would you interpret his last sentence?
2. Besides accepting the Nobel Prize, what is Faulkner's purpose in this speech? (Glossary: *Purpose*)
3. Pointing to specific examples in the speech, describe Faulkner's tone. Is it cynical? Ironic? Optimistic? Something else? How is his tone appropriate to his purpose?

4. Which particular words and phrases does Faulkner repeat
in his speech? How does this repetition strengthen his argument? How does it contribute to the general tone?

Vocabulary

Refer to your dictionary to define the following words as they
are used in this selection. Then use each word in a sentence of
your own.

commensurate (1)	verities (3)
pinnacle (1)	ephemeral (3)
travail (1)	inexhaustible (4)

Suggested Writing Assignments

1. Following Faulkner's model, compose a short speech in
which you state your view regarding an important contemporary issue. If you like, make a strong emotional appeal to
your audience, but be careful not to lose sight of your objective.

2. Paraphrase any paragraph of this essay, putting feelings
into your own words. Once you have "translated" each of
the thoughts, line for line, analyze the differences between
Faulkner's style and your own. What lessons in diction and
tone have you learned from this exercise?

9

Figurative Language

Figurative language is language used in an imaginative rather than a literal sense. Although it is most often associated with poetry, figurative language is used widely in our daily speech and in our writing. Prose writers have long known that figurative language not only brings freshness and color to writing, but also helps to clarify ideas.

Two of the most commonly used figures of speech are the simile and the metaphor. A *simile* is an explicit comparison between two essentially different ideas or things that uses the words *like* or *as* to link them.

> Canada geese sweep across the hills and valleys like a formation of strategic bombers.
>
> Benjamin B. Bachman

> I walked toward her and hailed her as a visitor to the moon might salute a survivor of a previous expedition.
>
> John Updike

A *metaphor*, on the other hand, makes an implicit comparison between dissimilar ideas or things without using *like* or *as*.

> She was very old and small and she walked slowly in the dark pine shadows, moving a little from side to side in her steps, with the balanced heaviness and lightness of a pendulum in a grandfather clock.
>
> Eudora Welty

> Charm is the ultimate weapon, the supreme seduction, against which there are few defenses.
>
> Laurie Lee

In order to take full advantage of the richness of a particular comparison, writers sometimes use several sentences or even a whole paragraph to develop a metaphor. Such a comparison is called an *extended metaphor*.

The point is that you have to strip down your writing before you can build it back up. You must know what the essential tools are and what job they were designed to do. If I may belabor the metaphor on carpentry, it is first necessary to be able to saw wood neatly and to drive nails. Later you can bevel the edges or add elegant finials, if that is your taste. But you can never forget that you are practicing a craft that is based on certain principles. If the nails are weak, your house will collapse. If your verbs are weak and your syntax is rickety, your sentences will fall apart.

William Zinsser

Another frequently used figure of speech is *personification*. In personification the writer attributes human qualities to animals or inanimate objects.

Blond October comes striding over the hills wearing a crimson shirt and faded green trousers.

Hal Borland

Indeed, haste can be the assassin of elegance.

T. H. White

In the preceding examples, the writers have, through the use of figurative language, both livened up their prose and given emphasis to their ideas. Keep in mind that figurative language should never be used merely to "dress up" writing; above all, it should help you to develop your ideas and to clarify your meaning for the reader.

THE MISSISSIPPI RIVER

Mark Twain

Mark Twain (1835–1910), born in Hannibal, Missouri, created Huckleberry Finn *(1884),* Tom Sawyer *(1876),* The Prince and the Pauper *(1882), and* A Connecticut Yankee in King Arthur's Court *(1889), among other classics. One of America's most popular writers, Twain is generally regarded as the most important practitioner of the realistic school of writing, a style that emphasized observable details. As you read the following passage, notice how Twain makes use of figurative language to describe two quite different ways of seeing the great Mississippi River.*

Now when I had mastered the language of this water and had come to know every trifling feature that bordered the great river as familiarly as I knew the letters of the alphabet, I had made a valuable acquisition. But I had lost something, too. I had lost something which could never be restored to me while I lived. All the grace, the beauty, the poetry, had gone out of the majestic river! I still kept in mind a certain wonderful sunset which I witnessed when steamboating was new to me. A broad expanse of the river was turned to blood; in the middle distance the red hue brightened into gold, through which a solitary log came floating, black and conspicuous; in one place a long, slanting mark lay sparkling upon the water; in another the surface was broken by boiling, tumbling rings that were as many-tinted as an opal; where the ruddy flush was faintest was a smooth spot that was covered with graceful circles and radiating lines, ever so delicately traced; the shore on our left was densely wooded, and the somber shadow that fell from this forest was broken in one place by a long, ruffled trail that shone like silver; and high above the forest wall a clean-

1

stemmed dead tree waved a single leafy bough that glowed like a flame in the unobstructed splendor that was flowing from the sun. There were graceful curves, reflected images, woody heights, soft distances, and over the whole scene, far and near, the dissolving lights drifted steadily, enriching it every passing moment with new marvels of coloring.

I stook like one bewitched. I drank it in, in a speechless rapture. The world was new to me and I had never seen anything like this at home. But as I have said, a day came when I began to cease from noting the glories and the charms which the moon and the sun and the twilight wrought upon the river's face; another day came when I ceased altogether to note them. Then, if that sunset scene had been repeated, I should have looked upon it without rapture and should have commented upon it inwardly after this fashion: "This sun means that we are going to have wind to-morrow; that floating log means that the river is rising, small thanks to it; that slanting mark on the water refers to a bluff reef which is going to kill somebody's steamboat one of these nights, if it keeps on stretching out like that; those tumbling 'boils' show a dissolving bar and a changing channel there; the lines and circles in the slick water over yonder are a warning that that troublesome place is shoaling up dangerously; that silver streak in the shadow of the forest is the 'break' from a new snag and he has located himself in the very best place he could have found to fish for steamboats; that tall dead tree, with a single living branch, is not going to last long, and then how is a body ever going to get through this blind place at night without the friendly old landmark?"

No, the romance and beauty were all gone from the river. All the value any feature of it had for me now was the amount of usefulness it could furnish toward compassing the safe piloting of a steamboat. Since those days, I have pitied doctors from my heart. What does the lovely flush in a beauty's cheek mean to a doctor but a "break" that ripples above some deadly disease? Are not all her visible charms sown thick with what are to him the signs and symbols of hidden decay? Does he ever see her beauty at all, or doesn't he simply view her professionally and comment upon her unwholesome condition all to himself? And doesn't he sometimes wonder whether he has gained most or lost most by learning his trade?

Questions for Study and Discussion

1. Twain's essay reveals that he has two attitudes towards the Mississippi River. What are those attitudes, and where are they presented in the essay? (Glossary: *Attitude*)
2. Twain uses a number of similes and metaphors in his essay. Identify three of each, and explain what is being compared in each case.
3. What is Twain's tone in this essay? (Glossary: *Tone*)
4. What effect do the italicized words have in each of the following quotations from this selection? How do these words contribute to Twain's description? (Glossary: *Connotation/Denotation*)

   a. ever so *delicately* traced (1)
   b. shadow that *fell* from the forest (1)
   c. *wrought* upon the river's face (2)
   d. show a *dissolving* bar (2)
   e. to get through this *blind* place at night (2)
   f. lovely *flush* in a beauty's cheek (3)
5. Reread Twain's conclusion. How effective do you find it? (Glossary: *Beginnings/Endings*)

Vocabulary

Refer to your dictionary to define the following words as they are used in this selection. Then use each word in a sentence of your own.

acquisition (1)	rapture (2)
hue (1)	romance (3)
opal (1)	

Suggested Writing Assignments

1. Write an essay modeled on Twain's in which you offer your two different views of a particular scene, event, or issue. Describe how you once regarded your subject, and then describe how you now view the subject. For example, you might wish to present the way you once viewed your home-

town or high school, and the way you now view it. Be sure to use at least one simile and one metaphor in your essay.

2. Write an essay describing one of the places listed below or any other place of your choice. Use at least one simile and one metaphor to clarify and enliven your description.

a factory
a place of worship
a fast-food restaurant
your dormitory
your college library
your favorite place on campus
your hometown

NOTES ON PUNCTUATION

Lewis Thomas

Lewis Thomas has had a distinguished career as a physician, administrator, researcher, teacher, and writer. In 1971 he started writing a series of essays for The New England Journal of Medicine, *many of which were collected in* The Lives of a Cell: Notes of a Biology Watcher *(1973). Recently, Thomas has published two other collections of essays,* Late Night Thoughts on Listening to Mahler's Ninth Symphony *(1983) and* The Youngest Science *(1983).* "Notes on Punctuation" *is taken from* The Medusa and the Snail, *a second collection of essays which appeared in 1979. In this selection Thomas discusses the meaning and practical value of various marks of punctuation and shows those punctuation marks at work. As you read the selection, note the figurative language Thomas uses to help clarify the meaning of punctuation.*

There are no precise rules about punctuation (Fowler lays out some general advice (as best he can under the complex circumstances of English prose (he points out, for example, that we possess only four stops (the comma, the semicolon, the colon and the period (the question mark and exclamation point are not, strictly speaking, stops; they are indicators of tone (oddly enough, the Greeks employed the semicolon for their question mark (it produces a strange sensation to read a Greek sentence which is a straightforward question: Why weepest thou; (instead of Why weepest thou? (and, of course, there are parentheses (which are surely a kind of punctuation making this whole matter much more complicated by having to count up the left-handed parentheses in order to be sure of closing with the right number (but if the parentheses were left out, with nothing to work with but the stops, we would have consid-

167

erably more flexibility in the deploying of layers of meaning than if we tried to separate all the clauses by physical barriers (and in the latter case, while we might have more precision and exactitude for our meaning, we would lose the essential flavor of language, which is its wonderful ambiguity)))))))))))).

The commas are the most useful and usable of all the stops. 2
It is highly important to put them in place as you go along. If you try to come back after doing a paragraph and stick them in the various spots that tempt you you will discover that they tend to swarm like minnows into all sorts of crevices whose existence you hadn't realized and before you know it the whole long sentence becomes immobilized and lashed up squirming in commas. Better to use them sparingly, and with affection, precisely when the need for each one arises, nicely, by itself.

I have grown fond of semicolons in recent years. The semico- 3
lon tells you that there is still some question about the preceding full sentence; something needs to be added; it reminds you sometimes of the Greek usage. It is almost always a greater pleasure to come across a semicolon than a period. The period tells you that is that; if you didn't get all the meaning you wanted or expected, anyway you got all the writer intended to parcel out and now you have to move along. But with a semicolon there you get a pleasant little feeling of expectancy; there is more to come; read on; it will get clearer.

Colons are a lot less attractive, for several reasons: firstly, 4
they give you the feeling of being rather ordered around, or at least having your nose pointed in a direction you might not be inclined to take if left to yourself, and, secondly, you suspect you're in for one of those sentences that will be labeling the points to be made: firstly, secondly and so forth, with the implication that you haven't sense enough to keep track of a sequence of notions without having them numbered. Also, many writers use this system loosely and incompletely, starting out with number one and number two as though counting off on their fingers but then going on and on without the succession of labels you've been led to expect, leaving you floundering about searching for the ninethly or seventeenthly that ought to be there but isn't.

Exclamation points are the most irritating of all. Look! they 5
say, look at what I just said! How amazing is my thought! It is

like being forced to watch someone else's small child jumping up and down crazily in the center of the living room shouting to attract attention. If a sentence really has something of importance to say, something quite remarkable, it doesn't need a mark to point it out. And if it is really, after all, a banal sentence needing more zing, the exclamation point simply emphasizes its banality!

Quotation marks should be used honestly and sparingly, when there is a genuine quotation at hand, and it is necessary to be very rigorous about the words enclosed by the marks. If something is to be quoted, the *exact* words must be used. If part of it must be left out because of space limitations, it is good manners to insert three dots to indicate the omission, but it is unethical to do this if it means connecting two thoughts which the original author did not intend to have tied together. Above all, quotation marks should not be used for ideas that you'd like to disown, things in the air so to speak. Nor should they be put in place around clichés; if you want to use a cliché you must take full responsibility for it yourself and not try to fob it off on anon., or on society. The most objectionable misuse of quotation marks, but one which illustrates the dangers of misuse in ordinary prose, is seen in advertising, especially in advertisements for small restaurants, for example "just around the corner," or "a good place to eat." No single, identifiable, citable person ever really said, for the record, "just around the corner," much less "a good place to eat," least likely of all for restaurants of the type that use this type of prose.

The dash is a handy device, informal and essentially playful, telling you that you're about to take off on a different tack but still in some way connected with the present course—only you have to remember that the dash is there, and either put a second dash at the end of the notion to let the reader know that he's back on course, or else end the sentence, as here, with a period.

The greatest danger in punctuation is for poetry. Here it is necessary to be as economical and parsimonious with commas and periods as with the words themselves, and any marks that seem to carry their own subtle meanings, like dashes and little rows of periods, even semicolons and question marks, should be left out altogether rather than inserted to clog up the thing with ambiguity. A single exclamation point in a poem, no matter what else the poem has to say, is enough to destroy the whole work.

The things I like best in T. S. Eliot's poetry, especially in the   9
Four Quartets, are the semicolons. You cannot hear them, but they are there, laying out the connections between the images and the ideas. Sometimes you get a glimpse of a semicolon coming, a few lines farther on, and it is like climbing a steep path through woods and seeing a wooden bench just at a bend in the road ahead, a place where you can expect to sit for a moment, catching your breath.

Commas can't do this sort of thing; they can only tell you how   10
the different parts of a complicated thought are to be fitted together, but you can't sit, not even take a breath, just because of a comma,

Questions for Study and Discussion

1. What point does Thomas make about punctuation in this essay?
2. Point out the four similes that Thomas uses in this selection. What is being compared in each? Why is each comparison appropriate?
3. In paragraph 5 Thomas personifies—attributes human qualities to—exclamation points. What other examples of personification can you find in the essay? Why is this figure of speech especially appropriate in this essay? How does it help Thomas to make his point?
4. Why do you suppose Thomas elected to use figurative language in an essay on punctuation?
5. While explaining the function of each mark of punctuation, Thomas writes in a manner that allows him to use that mark of punctuation. This is an example of illustration. When did you become aware of this strategy? Did it help you to better understand and appreciate the uses of punctuation? If so, how? (Glossary: *Illustration*)

Vocabulary

Refer to your dictionary to define the following words as they are used in this selection. Then use each word in a sentence of your own.

deploying (1)   floundering (4)
ambiguity (1)   banal (5)
parcel out (3)

Suggested Writing Assignments

1. Write a short essay in which you discuss a favorite subject (for example, movies, politics, traveling, nature, sports, cooking). Make use of figurative language—similes, metaphors, personification—as you describe the precise nature of your feelings about that subject.

2. Describe a memorable experience you have had—one which was especially impressive and influential in your life. Use similes and metaphors to help you capture the essence of that experience. If you like, select one of the following subjects for your description.

   an adventurous trip
   a family reunion
   meeting a famous person
   a death in the family
   a move to a new home

THE DEATH OF BENNY PARET

Norman Mailer

Norman Mailer, born in Long Branch, New Jersey, in 1923, graduated from Harvard University in 1943 with a degree in engineering. While at Harvard, he made the decision to become a writer and, with the publication of his first novel, The Naked and the Dead *(1948), based on his war experiences in the Pacific during World War II, Mailer established himself as a writer of note. Mailer's literary interests have ranged widely over the years, from novels to nonfiction and journalism; from politics, sports, feminism, and lunar exploration to popular culture, ancient Egyptian culture, and criminality. In this account of the welterweight championship fight between Benny Paret and Emile Griffith, we can experience what Mailer himself felt as he sat at ringside the fateful night of March 25, 1962, the night of Paret's last fight. As you read, notice the way Mailer uses figures of speech to evoke the scene for the reader.*

Paret was a Cuban, a proud club fighter who had become welterweight champion because of his unusual ability to take a punch. His style of fighting was to take three punches to the head in order to give back two. At the end of ten rounds, he would still be bouncing, his opponent would have a headache. But in the last two years, over the fifteen-round fights, he had started to take some bad maulings. 1

This fight had its turns. Griffith won most of the early rounds, but Paret knocked Griffith down in the sixth. Griffith had trouble getting up, but made it, came alive and was dominating Paret again before the round was over. Then Paret began to wilt. In the middle of the eighth round, after a clubbing punch had turned his back to Griffith, Paret walked three dis- 2 gusted steps away, showing his hindquarters. For a champion, he took much too long to turn back around. It was the first hint of weakness Paret had ever shown, and it must have inspired a particular shame, because he fought the rest of the fight as if he were seeking to demonstrate that he could take more punishment than any man alive. In the twelfth, Griffith caught him. Paret got trapped in a corner. Trying to duck away, his left arm and his head became tangled on the wrong side of the top rope. Griffith was in like a cat ready to rip the life out of a huge boxed rat. He hit him eighteen right hands in a row, an act which took perhaps three or four seconds, Griffith making a pent-up whimpering sound all the while he attacked, the right hand whipping like a piston rod which has broken through the crankcase, or like a baseball bat demolishing a pumpkin. I was sitting in the second row of that corner—they were not ten feet away from me, and like everybody else, I was hypnotized. I had never seen one man hit another so hard and so many times. Over the referee's face came a look of woe as if some spasm had passed its way through him, and then he leaped on Griffith to pull him away. It was the act of a brave man. Griffith was uncontrollable. His trainer leaped into the ring, his manager, his cut man, there were four people holding Griffith, but he was off on an orgy, he had left the Garden, he was back on a hoodlum's street. If he had been able to break loose from his handlers and the referee, he would have jumped Paret to the floor and whaled on him there.

And Paret? Paret died on his feet. As he took those eighteen punches something happened to everyone who was in psychic range of the event. Some part of his death reached out to us. One felt it hover in the air. He was still standing in the ropes, trapped as he had been before, he gave some little half-smile of regret, as if he were saying, "I didn't know I was going to die just yet," and then, his head leaning back but still erect, his death came to breathe about him. He began to pass away. As he passed, so his limbs descended beneath him, and he sank slowly to the floor. He went down more slowly than any fighter had ever gone down, he went down like a large ship which turns on end and slides second by second into its grave. As he went down, the sound of Griffith's punches echoed in the mind like a heavy ax in the distance chopping into a wet log.

Questions for Study and Discussion

1. Identify at least three similes in this essay. Why do you think Mailer felt the need to use figures of speech in describing Paret's death?
2. Explain how the first sentence of paragraph 2 functions in the context of that paragraph.
3. Mailer starts paragraph 3 with a question. What effect does this question have on you as a reader? (Glossary: *Rhetorical Question*)
4. Does Mailer place the blame for Paret's death on anyone? Explain.
5. Explain how Mailer personifies death in paragraph 3.

Vocabulary

Refer to your dictionary to define the following words as they are used in this selection. Then use each word in a sentence of your own.

wilt (2)   psychic (3)
spasm (2)   hover (3)

Suggested Writing Assignments

1. The death of Benny Paret was neither the first nor the last death to occur in professional boxing. Should boxing, therefore, be banned? Write an essay arguing for or against the continuation of professional boxing. As you write, use several figures of speech to enliven your essay.
2. Sports commentators and critics have pointed to the role fans have played in the promotion of violence in sports. If you feel that fans promote violent behavior, what do you suggest can be done, if anything, to alleviate the negative effect fans have? Using examples from your own experience in attending sporting events, write an essay explaining your position on this subject. Enrich your descriptions with figures of speech.

III

TYPES
OF
ESSAYS

10

ILLUSTRATION

Illustration is the use of examples to make ideas more concrete and to make generalizations more specific and detailed. Examples enable writers not just to tell but to show what they mean. For example, an essay about recently developed alternative sources of energy becomes clear and interesting with the use of some examples—say, solar energy or the heat from the earth's core. The more specific the example, the more effective it is. Along with general statements about solar energy, the writer might offer several examples of how the home building industry is installing solar collectors instead of conventional hot water systems, or building solar greenhouses to replace conventional central heating.

In an essay a writer uses examples to clarify or support the thesis; in a paragraph, to clarify or support the main idea. Sometimes a single striking example suffices; sometimes a whole series of related examples is necessary. The following paragraph presents a single extended example—an anecdote, or story—that illustrates the author's point about cultural differences:

> Whenever there is a great cultural distance between two people, there are bound to be problems arising from differences in behavior and expectations. An example is the American couple who consulted a psychiatrist about their marital problems. The husband was from New England and had been brought up by reserved parents who taught him to control his emotions and to respect the need for privacy. His wife was from an Italian family and had been brought up in close contact with all the members of her large family, who were extremely warm, volatile and demonstrative. When the husband came home after a hard day at the office, dragging his feet and longing for peace and quiet, his wife would rush to him and smother him. Clasping his hands, rubbing his brow, crooning over his

weary head, she never left him alone. But when the wife was upset or anxious about her day, the husband's response was to withdraw completely and leave her alone. No comforting, no affectionate embrace, no attention— just solitude. The woman became convinced her husband didn't love her and, in desperation, she consulted a psychiatrist. Their problem wasn't basically psychological but cultural.

Edward T. Hall

This single example is effective because it is *representative*— that is, essentially similar to other such problems he might have described and familiar to many readers. Hall tells the story with enough detail that readers can understand the couple's feelings and so better understand the point he is trying to make.

In contrast, Edwin Way Teale supports his topic sentence about country superstitions with eleven examples:

In the folklore of the country, numerous superstitions relate to winter weather. Back-country farmers examine their corn husks—the thicker the husk, the colder the winter. They watch the acorn crop—the more acorns, the more severe the season. They observe where white-faced hornets place their paper nests—the higher they are, the deeper will be the snow. They examine the size and shape and color of the spleens of butchered hogs for clues to the severity of the season. They keep track of the blooming of dogwood in the spring—the more abundant the blooms, the more bitter the cold in January. When chipmunks carry their tails high and squirrels have heavier fur and mice come into country houses early in the fall, the superstitious gird themselves for a long, hard winter. Without any scientific basis, a wider-than-usual black band on a woolly-bear caterpillar is accepted as a sign that winter will arrive early and stay late. Even the way a cat sits beside the stove carries its message to the credulous. According to a belief once widely held in the Ozarks, a cat sitting with its tail to the fire indicates very cold weather is on the way.

Edwin Way Teale

Teale uses numerous examples because he is writing about various superstitions. Also, putting all those strange beliefs

Illustration 179

side by side in a kind of catalogue makes the paragraph fun to read as well as informative.

Illustration is often found in effective writing; nearly every essay in this book contains one or more examples. Likewise this introduction has used examples to clarify its points about illustration.

REFEREE: ROUGHEST ROLE IN SPORTS

Bill Surface

Bill Surface was born in 1935 in Louisville, Kentucky, and attended the University of Kentucky. A sportswriter, Surface has not only written a number of books on baseball, but has also turned his attention to such topics as the Internal Revenue Service, cowboys, and thoroughbred racing. A frequent contributor to leading popular magazines, Surface wrote the following selection for Reader's Digest *in 1976. As you read, pay particular attention to the way Surface makes use of examples to illustrate the difficult task referees face.*

The scene: Boston Garden, tightly packed for the fifth game 1 in the 1976 National Basketball Association (NBA) championship series. A high-leaping Boston Celtic player swishes the ball through the basket, and the buzzer sounds to end the second overtime period—and the game. Bedlam erupts as the hometown fans cheer a Celtic victory over the Phoenix Suns.

But a sweat-drenched referee, Richie Powers, views the game 2 more precisely. The timekeeper, he notices, failed to stop the clock after the goal, so Powers rules that there is one second left in the game. When the clock starts again, the score is 112–110 in favor of Boston, but in that one second the Suns tie the game and send it into a third overtime period. Now, the hometown fans feel like killing Powers. One woman throws her purse at him and screams: "You ain't even human!"

"In this job," Powers retorts, "that helps." 3

Indeed, it takes a special breed of man to excel at the most 4 difficult job in all of professional basketball, baseball, football and hockey: officiating the game. Expertise is not enough. Simply no one in sports endures more pressure—and needs greater discipline—than the plucky, perceptive autocrats wearing "prison stripes" or "mortician's blue," depending on the sport.

Whether he's called referee, umpire or official, such a man   5
must be superbly skilled in his job in order to instantly interpret as many as 100 pages of complex rules. And an official often needs to outhustle the players to gain a strategic view of
every frenzied battle for the ball or puck to detect player viola-
tions.

An official also has to be something of a detective to notice   6
players' varied ruses to get opponents penalized for supposedly
fouling them. Referees often foil these plots swiftly—as when
hockey's Lloyd Gilmour simply ignored a crafty Chicago Black
Hawk who pretended that he had been tripped so viciously that
he somersaulted across the ice. The faker got up and fumed,
"What's it take to get a penalty on that killer?" Gilmour replied: "Better acting."

Far different techniques are needed to detect players who   7
conceal their violation more adroitly. Basketball players, for
example, will position their bodies to keep a referee from seeing when they clutch, rather than legally touch, opponents. But
referees learn through watching slow-motion films that the position of a player's arms or body tells, without fail, when he is
holding an opponent.

All officials need superior vision. Consider the baseball um-   8
pire's task. Bent in a fatiguing crouch behind the catcher, he
determines where the blurred, aspirin-sized image spinning
toward him at up to 100 m.p.h. unpredictably drops, rises or
curves. During 1/60 of a second, the umpire decides if the
slightest part of the ball crossed the plate while traveling on a
plane between the batter's armpits and knees. Even when the
ball misses the strike zone, an umpire must also judge if the
player—though he has drawn his bat back almost instantly—
has made a swing for a strike. Likewise, an umpire needs the
savvy to tell if the ball dropped suddenly because it had been il-
legally dampened with a pitcher's hair oil, saliva or perspira-
tion; or because a sharpened thumbnail had cut a hole in the
ball.

Referees must retain their composure while absorbing al-   9
most unbelievable psychological and verbal punishment. A referee, *always* working before unfriendly crowds which are apt
to jeer at the first sight of him, has orders to exude poise under
the most testing circumstances—no matter if pelted by ice,

frankfurters, and even bottles. Tougher yet, an official must resist both teams' attempts to unnerve him and gain more favorable decisions.

Still, a referee cannot be too rigid. Since league authorities rarely overrule his judgment, an official must also function as the sport's supreme court and thus deliberate if he, as the district judge, might have erred. Though never swayed by how loudly a fiery coach protests, a good official will change decisions when additional evidence appears.   10

Even when a referee's instant call is correct, he's still got to face the anger that smolders long, long after a game. Sometimes that anger takes on an ominous tone, as it did in the 1975 World Series. Umpire Larry Barnett's disputed ruling that a batter did not obstruct the catcher brought him a letter warning that if he did not make up a $10,000 bet loss, the sender would "put a .38-caliber bullet in your head." Yet, as one official reasons, "An umpire's really in trouble—not in making 'bad' calls—but when his decisions bring nice mail and nice smiles."   11

A referee must be strong physically and shrug off frequent pain. Occupational hazards include torn muscles, being cut by punches and spiked shoes when breaking up fights, being stunned by frozen pucks rocketing at 120 m.p.h. Baseballs, which often travel almost as fast as hockey pucks, have snapped the steel bars of umpires' face-masks, then knocked out teeth and broken jaws. In football, even an agile referee can be knocked down by gargantuan athletes charging full speed.   12

To get into superb shape, each sports official must report to pre-season training camps at a stipulated weight. There he stretches, sprints, lifts weights, does calisthenics and other exercises needed especially for his sport. Hockey's officials, for instance, must run a mile in no more than seven minutes, do 80 situps within two minutes, and skate in relay races for two hours. Then, to stretch and strengthen their leg muscles, they practice alternate squatting and standing on skates. Next comes the hand-wrestling needed to separate brawling players.   13

In an average pro-basketball game, a referee sprints some six miles on a hardwood court and loses up to ten pounds. Yet basketball's referees must satisfy a supervisor that their facial expression show "firmness and confidence"—and that their whis-   14

tle's short blast always has the requisite "sharp, crisp tone."
Baseball's umpires holler "ball" and "strike" from deep in
their chests to develop such a booming, authoritative voice that
they seldom can ever speak in a normal tone.

Pre-season study sessions are equally strenuous for football   15
officials. They plunge into a daily, 14-hour program that includes a 200-question rules examination and a concentrated
film study of all the major calls made by each of the 84 officials
during the previous season.

Referees have demonstrated their spunk long before they fi-   16
nally reach a major league. Combining a fondness for sports
and a need for extra income, most start officiating for as little
as $2 a game in small arenas. A "take-charge" referee may be
noticed by scouts as he doggedly advances to college games, to
umpiring schools or league try-out camps. Even so, the grittiest
ones who impress major leagues may wait for the few available
jobs that, like those in pro basketball and hockey, eventually
pay around $43,000 a season (plus another $8000 if selected for
championship playoffs).

Football's weekend referees—mostly coaches, teachers and   17
executives—wait still longer before they can hope to officiate
pro football for up to $575 a game ($1500 for the Super Bowl).
The National Football League (NFL) considers only men with
records proving that they have officiated for at least ten years
(including five years in college games) and have a lifelong dedication to the game. Nonetheless, of 150 such men found qualified to officiate, the NFL hires no more than six new ones each
season.

Referees in all sports are evaluated by scouts, supervisors   18
and often by wide-angle cameras focused on them. After poring
over films, the supervisors rate officials and notify them of the
conclusions. At season's end, usually from one to six officials in
each sport who are considered unsatisfactory are quietly dismissed.

Even the best referees find themselves under growing scru-   19
tiny. Television's slow-motion instant replays of close decisions
foster demands by angry fans that such cameras be used to
overrule, or even replace, officials. But in fact TV replays pin-
point only a few dozen of pro-football officials' 41,000 split-
second decisions during a season that are genuinely arguable

or wrong. As a result, many athletes are *against* cameras replacing referees. Instant replay, says one, eliminates a common alibi for the mistake that cost his team a victory: "The ref missed it."

The members of this exclusive breed of men are proud of their oft-scorned, but indispensable, role. Such pride was perhaps best characterized in a baseball game when umpire Nestor Chylak carefully brushed home plate, then "discovered" that he needed to be resupplied with baseballs—a kindly intended ploy to enable the catcher to shake off some pain caused by a wild pitch earlier. Minutes later, the ungrateful catcher grumbled loudly and waved his arms wildly over the final call ending the game. Chylak was loudly jeered on leaving the field. 20

"If it worth fighting off the world this way every day?" Chylak was asked later. He beamed, then said, "What other guy can walk away from a game feeling he's a winner—*every* time?" 21

Questions for Study and Discussion

1. What is Bill Surface's thesis, or main point, in this essay? Where is it stated? (Glossary: *Thesis*)
2. What effect do the examples have on you as a reader? Explain.
3. What examples does the author use to support the topic sentence of paragraph 6? of paragraphs 7 and 8?
4. Scan the essay, and pick out places where Surface has used dialogue in his essay. How does dialogue help him to get his points across? (Glossary: *Dialogue*)
5. How effective do you find the beginning and ending of Surface's essay? Explain. (Glossary: *Beginnings/Endings*)

Vocabulary

Refer to your dictionary to define the following words as they are used in this selection. Then use each word in a sentence of your own.

bedlam (1)   ruses (6)
plucky (4)   adroitly (7)

jeer (9)   spunk (16)
pelted (9)   ploy (20)
smolders (11)

Suggested Writing Assignments

1. In many ways the roles of our public servants are similar to the role of the referee: the potential for criticism and even abuse is great, while that for recognition is most often negligible. Write an essay, citing examples, in which you discuss the pressure that our firefighters, police officers, or rescue personnel live with each day. If you have a friend or relative who serves in one of these jobs, you might interview the person for first-hand experiences, or you may contact your local fire, police, or rescue stations for help. It is, of course, advisable to write or call first to set up an interview and to send a note of thanks afterwards for any help given.

2. Write an essay in which you compare and/or contrast a specific game or sporting event with life itself. Before you begin your actual essay, make an exhaustive list of the game's various features to use as examples, including the referee if there is one, to ensure the completeness of your analysis.

ONE ENVIRONMENT, MANY WORLDS

Judith and Herbert Kohl

Herbert Kohl is a teacher and the author of The
Open Classroom *(1970);* Thirty-Six Children
(1973); Reading, How To *(1974); and* On Teaching
*(1976). Also a teacher, Judith Kohl is a student of
animal behavior and archaeology. In the following selection from their book* The View from the
Oak *(1977), the Kohls give one extended example
as an illustration of their belief that no two creatures view their environment in exactly the same
way.*

Our dog Sandy is a golden retriever. He sits in front of our   1
house all day waiting for someone to come by and throw
him a stick. Chasing sticks or tennis balls and bringing them
back is the major activity in his life. If you pick up a stick or
ball to throw, he acts quite strangely. He looks at the way your
body is facing and as soon as you throw something, he runs in
the direction you seemed to throw it. He doesn't look at what
you threw. His head is down and he charges, all ears. If your
stick lands in a tree or on a roof, he acts puzzled and confused.
He runs to the sound of the falling stick and sometimes gets so
carried away that he will crash into a person or tree in the way
as he dashes to the place he hears the stick fall. As he gets close,
his nose takes over and smells the odor of your hand on the
stick.

Once we performed an experiment to see how sensitive   2
Sandy's nose really was. We were on a beach that was full of
driftwood. There was one particular pile that must have had
hundreds of sticks. We picked up one stick, walked away from
the pile and then threw it back into the pile. It was impossible
for us to tell with any certainty which stick we had originally
chosen. So many of them looked alike to us that the best we

could do was pick out seven sticks which resembled the one that had been thrown.

We tried the same thing with Sandy, only before throwing the stick we carved an X on it. Then we threw it, not once but a dozen times into the pile. Each time he brought back that stick. Once we pretended to throw the stick and he charged the driftwood pile without noticing that one of us still had the stick. He circled the pile over and over, dug out sticks, became agitated but wouldn't bring another stick. It wasn't the shape or the size or look of the stick that he used to pick it out from all the others. It was the smell we left on the stick.

It is hard to imagine, but for dogs every living creature has its own distinctive smell. Each person can be identified by the smell left on things. Each of us gives off a particular combination of chemicals. We can detect the smell of sweat, but even when we are not sweating, we are giving off smells that senses finer than ours can detect.

The noses of people have about five million cells that sense smell. Dogs' noses have anywhere from 125 to 300 million cells. Moreover, these cells are closer to the surface than are cells in our noses, and more active. It has been estimated that dogs such as Sandy have noses that are a million times more sensitive than ours. Clothes we haven't worn for weeks, places we've only touched lightly indicate our presence to dogs. Whenever Sandy is left alone in the house, on our return we find him surrounded by our sweaters, coats, handkerchiefs, shirts. He surrounds himself with our smell as if to convince himself that we still exist and will return.

His ears are also remarkable. He can hear sounds that humans can't and at distances which are astonishing. It is hard for us to know and understand that world. Most of us don't realize that no two people's hands smell the same. Our ears are not the tuned direction finders his are. It takes a major leap of the imagination to understand and feel the world the way he does, to construct a complicated way of dealing with reality using such finely tuned smell and hearing. Yet his world is no more or less real than ours. His world and ours fit together in some ways and overlap in places. We have the advantage of being able to imagine what his experience is like, though he probably doesn't think too much about how we see the world. From observing and trying to experience things through his ears and nose we can learn about hidden worlds around us and understand behavior that otherwise might seem strange or silly.

The environment is the world that all living things share. It is   7
what is—air, fire, wind, water, life, sometimes culture. The environment consists of all the things that act and are acted upon. Living creatures are born into the environment and are part of it too. Yet there is no creature who perceives all of what is and what happens. Sandy perceives things we can't, and we perceive and understand many things beyond his world. For a dog like Sandy a book isn't much different than a stick, whereas for us one stick is pretty much like every other stick. There is no one world experienced by all living creatures. Though we all live in the same environment, we make many worlds.

Questions for Study and Discussion

1. What point do the Kohls make in this essay, and where is it stated? (Glossary: *Thesis*)
2. What distinction do they make between the words *environment* and *world*?
3. Why do you suppose the authors use illustration to make their point?
4. How does the Kohls' use of examples give unity to their essay? (Glossary: *Unity*)

Vocabulary

Refer to your dictionary to define the following words as they are used in this selection. Then use each word in a sentence of your own.

agitated (3)   perceive (7)

Suggested Writing Assignments

1. Using the Kohls' statement "Though we all live in the same environment, we make many worlds" as your topic sentence, write an essay supporting this thesis with examples from your own experience. For instance, how is your world different from that of your parents, teachers, friends, or roommates?

2. Using one of the following statements as your main idea, write an essay illustrating your thesis with examples from personal experience or from your reading.

   People show their intelligence in many different ways.

   If things can go wrong, they probably will.

   Many toys on the market today promote sexual stereotypes.

   School teaches us as many undesirable things as good things.

   Clothes do/do not make the man/woman.

AT WAR WITH THE SYSTEM

Enid Nemy

Born in Winnipeg, Canada, Enid Nemy has had an active career in journalism. She worked as a reporter and an editor for Canadian newspapers before joining The New York Times *in 1963. At the* Times *she writes "New Yorkers, Etc.," an award-winning column devoted to New York City's people and events. Notice the author's use of examples in the following account of a professor's single-handed war with the business world.*

B usiness beware!   1
Do NOT trifle with Prof. David Klein.   2

Professor Klein looks like a nice, upper middle-class type.   3
Most of the time he is. Sometimes he's not. Nice, that is.

"I behave reasonably outrageously by current standards," he   4
admits without a hint of hedging or shilly-shallying.

Professor Klein has no middle-class hang-ups. He doesn't   5
care about his credit rating (although it's still impeccable); he
doesn't give a hoot whether business organizations and their
employees think he's cheap or crazy, or both, and he isn't a bit
abashed about making a scene, as long as the scene is quiet and
well-bred.

Professor Klein is at war with the system "and if more people   6
did what I do, business practices might improve," he said.

A distinguished looking man with a serious mien, twinkling   7
eyes and a Vandyke beard, Mr. Klein began his campaign three
or four years ago "when things began to deteriorate."

Take, for instance, one of his early experiences—a mere skir-   8
mish, but enough to whet the appetite.

The professor arrived at the Queen Elizabeth Hotel in Mon-   9
treal after a tiring air trip and was told that his confirmed res-

ervation could not be honored. There wasn't a room available. Sorry.

"I will give you three minutes to find me a room," he told the   10
clerk quietly but firmly. "After three minutes, I am going to undress in the lobby, put on my pajamas and go to sleep on one of the sofas."

He got a room. He also got a lot of cheers and pats on the   11
back from scores of other men waiting for overbooked rooms.

"But," Professor Klein recalled, a little sadly, "none of them   12
would go ahead and do the same thing. I think I made my point in a reasonable, courteous way, but I also took a no-nonsense approach."

More recently, Mr. Klein, who has a master's degree from Co-   13
lumbia University, and is a professor of social science and human development at Michigan State University, has had several run-ins with retail operations. As a result, he has evolved his own charge system. He bills the store for any time he spends clearing up errors they have made on his orders or his account.

The current Klein rate is $10 a letter, a reasonable fee, he   14
points out, when one considers not only his time but such expenses as photocopying checks that have already been cashed. Telephone calls are billed at $2 each. The fee scale is pre-inflation and is open to adjustment.

"I simply deduct the amount from my monthly charge ac-   15
count bill," he explained. "I add the total amount of time spent on letters and telephone calls when I'm billed incorrectly, or if orders come incomplete, or if merchandise is unsatisfactory.

"The complaint system has always struck me as terribly one-   16
sided," he continued. "The store has people to handle complaints, and these people not only get paid to handle them but the basic cost of the department is added to the merchandise. The customer is not only paying a higher cost for everything because of store errors, but he or she is also expected to spend time writing or telephoning to clear up something that should never have happened in the first place."

The last time Professor Klein was put in the position of clear-   17
ing up a complaint (one letter, three telephone calls) he deducted $15 from his bill at the end of the month. He knew what would happen, because he had had a similar reaction before.

A store representative telephoned, and the following conver-   18
sation ensued:

Professor Klein: "Miss X, are you being paid by your em-   19
ployer to make this call?"

Miss X: "Well, yes."   20

Professor Klein: "Well, I'm not, so you will understand why I   21
am not motivated to continue it. Goodbye."

Professor Klein figures that there are three courses of action   22
the store might take, and as far as he is concerned, it doesn't
matter which one they choose.

"If they want to sue me, fine," he said, cheerfully. "If they   23
want to cancel my charge account, fine. And if they want to cancel my debt and give me back a zero balance, fine. They have a
choice."

To date, the several stores that have encountered the Klein   24
method of retaliation have, eventually, deducted his "fee" from
the amount owed them.

"I do this as much as a matter of principle as a matter of   25
making money," the professor said.

"A lot of middle-class people live in terror of being consid-   26
ered cheap," he said. "I don't worry about that. A lot of my
solid middle-class friends say 'how do you dare do it . . . you'll
ruin your credit rating.' They think that the least little cross-
eyed look will ruin your credit rating. The fact is that a credit
rating isn't as delicate as all that."

Professor Klein has several other antisystem, antiannoyance   27
strategies. Among them are the following:

¶When buying an expensive item in a retail establishment   28
that honors credit cards, he will hold up both his credit card
and his checkbook and ask if the store will give him a three percent discount for cash. "They do," he said.

¶When unsolicited junk mail arrives, with a stamped reply   29
card or envelope enclosed, he returns the card or envelope with
his label stuck on it. The label reads: "This represents my effort
to discourage unsolicited junk mail by increasing its cost to the
sender." He had 1,000 labels printed for $1, but is somewhat
discouraged because the volume of unsolicited mail continues
unabated. "They can't read," he lamented.

¶He rarely pays cash for airline tickets because "if I put them   30
on my credit card, it usually takes three or four months for the

bill to arrive, and I can be earning interest on that money . . . no wonder Pan American is in trouble."

"One of the few nice things about being middle- or upper middle-class is that you have an enormous amount of clout," he said. "If people used it in the right way, they could make enormous changes in retailing, and in other practices." 31

Questions for Study and Discussion

1. What is Professor Klein's message to the American consumer?
2. Besides charging retailers for his services, what other "antisystem, antiannoyance strategies" does Klein suggest?
3. In paragraphs 9–12 Nemy recounts Klein's experiences at the Queen Elizabeth Hotel. What purpose does this example serve in the essay?
4. Consider the example presented in paragraphs 17–21. What is the relationship between this example and the material in paragraphs 13–16?

Vocabulary

Refer to your dictionary to define the following words as they are used in this selection. Then use each word in a sentence of your own.

hedging (4)   retaliation (24)
impeccable (5)   unsolicited (29)
ensued (18)   clout (31)

Suggested Writing Assignments

1. Is Professor Klein correct in saying "if more people did what I do, business practices might improve"? Think about your experience as a consumer. Write an essay in which you provide examples to support the following statement:

   As a customer, most of my experiences with the business community have been satisfactory/ unsatisfactory.

2. Using one of the following statements as your topic sentence, write an essay giving examples from personal experience or from reading to support your opinion.

Consumers have more power than they realize.

Most products do/do not measure up to the claims of their advertisements.

Religion is/is not alive and well.

Government works far better than its critics claim.

Being able to write well is more than a basic skill.

THIS IS PROGRESS?

Alan L. Otten

*After graduating from the Columbia University
School of Journalism, Alan Otten joined the staff
of* The Wall Street Journal, *where during the
seventies he wrote the weekly column "Politics
and People." In 1978 the* Journal *appointed Otten European Bureau Chief in London. In "This
Is Progress?" Otten provides an extensive array
of examples to support his view that progress is
not made without some unexpected side effects.*

A couple I know checked into one of the new Detroit hotels a   1
few months ago and, in due course, left a 7 a.m. wake-up
call.

Being an early riser, however, the husband was up long be-   2
fore 7, and decided he'd go down to breakfast and let his wife
sleep late. He dialed the hotel switchboard, explained the situation, and said he'd like to cancel the wake-up call.

"Sorry, sir," the answer came, "but we can't do that. It's in   3
the computer, and there's no way to get it out now."

Consider another story. A while back, a reporter phoned a   4
congressional committee and asked to speak to the staff director. Unfortunately, he was told, the staff director wouldn't be
in that morning; there'd been a power failure at his home. Well,
the reporter persisted, that was certainly too bad, but just why
did a power failure prevent him from coming to work?

"He can't get his car out of the garage," the secretary ex-   5
plained. "The garage doors are electrically controlled."

As these two anecdotes suggest, this is a column in praise of   6
progress: those wonderful advances in science and technology
that leave the world only slightly more snafued than before.

The balance sheet will eschew such common complaints as   7
the way the modern office grinds to a halt whenever the copying machine is out of order. Or the computerized magazine sub-

195

scription lists that take only four times longer than formerly to effect changes of address and which start mailing renewal notices six months before the subscription expires and then continue at weekly intervals.

Or the form letters that provide The New Yorker with so 8
many droll end-of-the-column items, like the letter that was sent to the "News Desk, Wall Street Journal," and led off, "Dear Mr. Desk . . . ." Or the new drugs, operations and health regimens that in due time are shown to be more dangerous than the illnesses.

Computers bulk centrally in many of the "this is progress?" 9
stories. For instance, a friend recently went to make a deposit at her local bank in upstate New York. The deposit couldn't be accepted, she was informed, "because it's raining too hard." Seems that when the rain gets beyond a certain intensity, the wires transmitting the message from the branch banks to the computer at the main bank in Albany send jumbled signals— and so branch-bank operations have to be suspended temporarily.

Every newspaper person knows that each technological advance 10
in the printing process somehow makes news deadlines earlier, rather than later as might logically be assumed. Computers, though, can foul things up in other ways, too. At a recent conference on press coverage of presidential campaigns, many participants suggested that the lengthy background stories prepared early in the campaign by the wire services or such special news services as those of The New York Times and Washington Post might be saved by subscribing papers and then used late in the campaign, when the public was more in the mood to pay attention.

"Are you kidding?" demanded a publisher present. "That 11
stuff now all comes in computerized, and it's erased at the end of the day. We don't save any copy any more."

Computers aren't the only villains, to be sure. Everyone has 12
observed bizarre scenes of a dozen people down on hands and knees searching the pavement or the grass or a tennis court for a lost contact lens. The other day, however, a colleague announced she was having trouble seeing out of one eye and was off to the optometrist's. About a half hour later, she was back,

giggling. The night before, she had apparently put one contact lens on top of another in the case where she kept an extra lens, and had that morning unwittingly put two lenses in one eye.

During last winter's snow storms, the Amtrak Metroliners   13 frequently had to be removed from service as snow clogged the motors so cleverly mounted underneath the new high-speed trains. (The cars are now beginning to be converted to a different motor-mounting scheme.) A number of high schools in this area have been built with windows that don't open; when the air conditioning fails on a hot spring or fall day, students are given the day off. Last fall, when the nation moved back to standard time, a young friend was appalled to find she was going to have to turn her time-and-date digital wristwatch ahead 30 days and 23 hours.

Still another acquaintance had his car battery go dead while   14 his power windows were rolled down—and then the rains came and poured in while he was parked alongside the highway waiting for help.

Society's rush to credit cards has its convenient aspects—but   15 also unpleasant ones. Just try to check into a hotel announcing that you prefer to pay cash rather than use a credit card. Scorn, suspicion, hostility, un-American, if not downright communistic.

Once upon a time, you could look up at the postmark on a letter and see exactly where and when it had been processed at   16 the post office.

Now, not only does the postmark deny you some or all of this   17 occasionally useful information, but it insists on selling you something instead: "National Guard Month—Gain Skills By Serving" or "Save Energy—Turn Off Lights."

And like most creations of American ingenuity, this, too, has   18 been exported to less fortunate lands. A letter from Belgium the other day carried the exhortatory postmark: *"Prévenez l'Hypertension. Evitez le Sel."** In case your French wasn't up to it, there was a drawing of a salt shaker.

---

*"Prevent high blood pressure. Avoid salt."

In all likelihood, corrective measures are being developed for   19
many of the problems described above, and helpful correspon-
dents will be writing in to tell me all about it. Yet I remain confident that new examples will come along to fill the gap. After
all, that's progress.

Questions for Study and Discussion

1. The title of this essay is "This Is Progress?" What does the
title relate about the main point of the essay? What is the
main point? What does the question mark in the title indicate about the author's attitude toward his thesis?
2. In paragraphs 1–5 Otten tells the story of a couple in a Detroit hotel and the story of the staff director of a congressional committee who could not get his car out of the garage.
Why do you think Otten opens with these anecdotes? Do you
think they serve as a good opening? Can you think of any
other way to begin this essay?
3. Otten provides many "this is progress?" examples. How
does he organize these examples? How does he introduce
his examples? How does he move from one example to another? (Glossary: *Organization* and *Transitions*)
4. How would you characterize Otten's tone in this essay?
What in the essay leads you to your conclusion? (Glossary:
Tone)

Vocabulary

Refer to your dictionary to define the following words as they
are used in this selection. Then use each word in a sentence of
your own.

anecdotes (6)   bizarre (12)
eschew (7)   unwittingly (12)
droll (8)   appalled (13)
regimens (8)

Suggested Writing Assignments

1. Do you agree or disagree with Otten's point of view in this essay? Write an essay explaining your position with examples from your own experience.

2. In paragraph 9 Otten says, "Computers bulk centrally in many of the 'this is progress?' stories." Indeed, as our world becomes increasingly computerized, we see more instances of both the benefits and the hazards of this new technology. Write an essay giving examples to illustrate how you feel about the way computers affect your life. First you might think about the following questions: Have you thought of how many ways computers touch your life? What has been your experience with computers? Have computers helped you? Aggravated you? Have they helped others but caused problems for you?

11

NARRATION

To *narrate* is to tell a story or to tell what happened. Whenever you relate an incident or use an anecdote to make a point, you use narration. In its broadest sense, narration is any account of an event or series of events. Although most often associated with fiction, narration is effective and useful in all kinds of writing.

Good narration has four essential features: a clear context, well-chosen details, a logical, often chronological organization, and an appropriate and consistent point of view. Consider, for example, the following paragraph from Willie Morris's "On a Commuter Train":

> One afternoon in late August, as the summer's sun streamed into the [railroad] car and made little jumping shadows on the windows, I sat gazing out at the tenement-dwellers, who were themselves looking out of their windows from the gray crumbling buildings along the tracks of upper Manhattan. As we crossed into the Bronx, the train unexpectedly slowed down for a few miles. Suddenly from out of my window I saw a large crowd near the tracks, held back by two policemen. Then, on the other side from my window, I saw a sight I would never be able to forget: a little boy almost severed in halves, lying at an incredible angle near the track. The ground was covered with blood, and the boy's eyes were opened wide, strained and disbelieving in his sudden oblivion. A policeman stood next to him, his arms folded, staring straight ahead at the windows of our train. In the orange glow of late afternoon the policemen, the crowd, the corpse of the boy were for a brief moment immobile, motionless, a small tableau to violence and death in the city. Behind me, in the next row of seats, there was a game of bridge. I heard one of the four men say as he looked out at the sight, "God, that's horrible." Another said, in a whisper, "Terrible, terrible." There was a momentary silence, punctuated only by the clicking

of the wheels on the track. Then, after the pause, I heard the first man say: "Two hearts."

Willie Morris

This paragraph contains all the elements of good narration. At the beginning Morris establishes a clear context for his narrative, telling when, where, and to whom the action happened. He has chosen details well, including enough detail so that we know what is happening but not so much that we become overwhelmed, confused, or bored. Morris organizes his narration logically, with a beginning that sets the scene, a middle that paints the picture, and an end that makes his point, all arranged chronologically. Finally, he tells the story from the first-person point of view: We experience the event directly through the writer's eyes and ears, as if we too had been on the scene of the action.

Morris could have told his story from the third-person point of view. In this point of view, the narrator is not a participant in the action, and does not use the pronoun *I*. In the following example, William Allen White narrates his daughter's fatal accident:

The last hour of her life was typical of its happiness. She came home from a day's work at school, topped off by a hard grind with the copy on the High School Annual, and felt that a ride would refresh her. She climbed into her khakis, chattering to her mother about the work she was doing, and hurried to get her horse and be out on the dirt roads for the country air and the radiant green fields of the spring. As she rode through the town on an easy gallop she kept waving at passers-by. She knew everyone in town. For a decade the little figure with the long pig-tail and the red hair ribbon has been familiar on the streets of Emporia, and she got in the way of speaking to those who nodded at her. She passed the Kerrs, walking the horse, in front of the Normal Library, and waved at them; passed another friend a few hundred feet further on, and waved at her. The horse was walking and, as she turned into North Merchant street she took off her cowboy hat, and the horse swung into a lope. She passed the Tripletts and waved her cowboy hat at them, still moving gaily north on Merchant street. A Gazette carrier passed—a High School boy friend—and she waved at him, but with her bridle hand: the horse veered quickly, plunged into the parking where the low-hanging limb faced her, and, while she still looked back waving, the blow came. But she did not fall from the horse; she slipped off, dazed a bit, staggered and fell in a faint. She never quite recovered consciousness.

William Allen White

SHAME

Dick Gregory

Dick Gregory, the well-known comedian, has long been active in the civil rights movement. During the 1960s Gregory was also an outspoken critic of America's involvement in Vietnam. In the following episode from his autobiography Nigger *(1964), he narrates the story of a childhood experience that taught him the meaning of shame. Through his use of authentic dialogue and vivid details, he dramatically re-creates this experience for his readers.*

I never learned hate at home, or shame. I had to go to school for that. I was about seven years old when I got my first big lesson. I was in love with a little girl named Helene Tucker, a light-complexioned little girl with pigtails and nice manners. She was always clean and she was smart in school. I think I went to school then mostly to look at her. I brushed my hair and even got me a little old handkerchief. It was a lady's handkerchief, but I didn't want Helene to see me wipe my nose on my hand. The pipes were frozen again, there was no water in the house, but I washed my socks and shirt every night. I'd get a pot, and go over to Mister Ben's grocery store, and stick my pot down into his soda machine. Scoop out some chopped ice. By evening the ice melted to water for washing. I got sick a lot that winter because the fire would go out at night before the clothes were dry. In the morning I'd put them on, wet or dry, because they were the only clothes I had.

Everybody's got a Helene Tucker, a symbol of everything you want. I loved her for her goodness, her cleanness, her popularity. She'd walk down my street and my brothers and sisters would yell, "Here comes Helene," and I'd rub my tennis sneakers on the back of my pants and wish my hair wasn't so nappy and the white folks' shirt fit me better. I'd run out on the street. If I knew my place and didn't come too close, she'd wink at me and say hello. That was a good feeling. Sometimes I'd follow her all the way home, and shovel the snow off her walk and try to make friends with her Momma and her aunts. I'd drop money on her stoop late at night on my way back from shining shoes in the taverns. And she had a Daddy, and he had a good job. He was a paper hanger.

I guess I would have gotten over Helene by summertime, but   3
something happened in that classroom that made her face hang in front of me for the next twenty-two years. When I played the drums in high school it was for Helene and when I broke track records in college it was for Helene and when I started standing behind microphones and heard applause I wished Helene could hear it, too. It wasn't until I was twenty-nine years old and married and making money that I finally got her out of my system. Helene was sitting in that classroom when I learned to be ashamed of myself.

It was on a Thursday. I was sitting in the back of the room,   4
in a seat with a chalk circle drawn around it. The idiot's seat, the troublemaker's seat.

The teacher thought I was stupid. Couldn't spell, couldn't   5
read, couldn't do arithmetic. Just stupid. Teachers were never interested in finding out that you couldn't concentrate because you were so hungry, because you hadn't had any breakfast. All you could think about was noontime, would it ever come? Maybe you could sneak into the cloakroom and steal a bite of some kid's lunch out of a coat pocket. A bite of something. Paste. You can't really make a meal of paste, or put it on bread for a sandwich, but sometimes I'd scoop a few spoonfuls out of the paste jar in the back of the room. Pregnant people get strange tastes. I was pregnant with poverty. Pregnant with dirt and pregnant with smells that made people turn away, pregnant with cold and pregnant with shoes that were never bought for me, pregnant with five other people in my bed and no Daddy in the next room, and pregnant with hunger. Paste doesn't taste too bad when you're hungry.

The teacher thought I was a troublemaker. All she saw from   6
the front of the room was a little black boy who squirmed in his idiot's seat and made noises and poked the kids around him. I guess she couldn't see a kid who made noises because he wanted someone to know he was there.

It was on a Thursday, the day before the Negro payday. The 7
eagle always flew on Friday. The teacher was asking each student how much his father would give to the Community Chest.
On Friday night, each kid would get the money from his father,
and on Monday he would bring it to the school. I decided I was
going to buy me a Daddy right then. I had money in my pocket
from shining shoes and selling papers, and whatever Helene
Tucker pledged for her Daddy I was going to top it. And I'd
hand the money right in. I wasn't going to wait until Monday to
buy me a Daddy.

I was shaking, scared to death. The teacher opened her book 8
and started calling out names alphabetically.

"Helene Tucker?" 9

"My daddy said he'd give two dollars and fifty cents." 10

"That's very nice, Helene. Very, very nice indeed." 11

That made me feel pretty good. It wouldn't take too much to 12
top that. I had almost three dollars in dimes and quarters in my
pocket. I stuck my hand in my pocket and held onto the money,
waiting for her to call my name. But the teacher closed her
book after she called everybody else in the class.

I stood up and raised my hand. 13

"What is it now?" 14

"You forgot me." 15

She turned toward the blackboard. "I don't have time to be 16
playing with you, Richard."

"My Daddy said he'd . . ." 17

"Sit down, Richard, you're disturbing the class." 18

"My Daddy said he'd give . . . fifteen dollars." 19

She turned around and looked mad. "We are collecting this 20
money for you and your kind, Richard Gregory. If your Daddy
can give fifteen dollars you have no business being on relief."

"I got it right now, I got it right now, my Daddy gave it to me 21
to turn in today, my Daddy said . . ."

"And furthermore," she said, looking right at me, her nos- 22
trils getting big and her lips getting thin and her eyes opening
wide, "we know you don't have a Daddy."

Helene Tucker turned around, her eyes full of tears. She felt 23
sorry for me. Then I couldn't see her too well because I was crying, too.

"Sit down, Richard." 24

And I always thought the teacher kind of liked me. She always picked me to wash the blackboard on Friday, after school. That was a big thrill, it made me feel important. If I didn't wash it, come Monday the school might not function right.   25

"Where are you going, Richard?"   26

I walked out of school that day, and for a long time I didn't go back very often. There was shame there.   27

Now there was shame everywhere. It seemed like the whole world had been inside that classroom, everyone had heard what the teacher had said, everyone had turned around and felt sorry for me. There was shame in going to the Worthy Boys Annual Christmas Dinner for you and your kind, because everybody knew what a worthy boy was. Why couldn't they just call it the Boys Annual Dinner; why'd they have to give it a name? There was shame in wearing the brown and orange and white plaid mackinaw the welfare gave to three thousand boys. Why'd it have to be the same for everybody so when you walked down the street the people could see you were on relief? It was a nice warm mackinaw and it had a hood, and my Momma beat me and called me a little rat when she found out I stuffed it in the bottom of a pail full of garbage way over on Cottage Street. There was shame in running over to Mister Ben's at the end of the day and asking for his rotten peaches, there was shame in asking Mrs. Simmons for a spoonful of sugar, there was shame in running out to meet the relief truck. I hated that truck, full of food for you and your kind. I ran into the house and hid when it came. And then I started to sneak through alleys, to take the long way home so the people going into White's Eat Shop wouldn't see me. Yeah, the whole world heard the teacher that day, we all know you don't have a Daddy.   28

Questions for Study and Discussion

1. What does Gregory mean by "shame"?
2. How do the first three paragraphs of the essay help to establish a context for the narrative that follows?
3. Why do you think Gregory narrates this episode in the first-

person point of view? What would be gained or lost if he instead wrote it in the third-person point of view?

4. Specific details can enhance the reader's understanding and appreciation of a narrative. Gregory's description of Helene Tucker's manners or the plaid of his mackinaw, for example, makes his account vivid and interesting. Cite several other specific details he gives, and consider how the narrative would be different without them.

5. Consider the diction of this essay. What effect does Gregory's repetition of the word *shame* have on you? Why do you think Gregory uses simple vocabulary to narrate this particular experience? (Glossary: *Diction*)

Vocabulary

Refer to your dictionary to define the following words as they are used in this selection. Then use each word in a sentence of your own.

nappy (2)   mackinaw (28)

Suggested Writing Assignments

1. Using Dick Gregory's essay as a model, write an essay narrating an experience that made you especially afraid, angry, surprised, embarrassed, or proud. Include sufficient detail so that your readers will know exactly what happened.

2. Most of us have had frustrating experiences with mechanical objects that seem to have perverse minds of their own. Write a brief narrative recounting one such experience with a vending machine, typewriter, television set, pay toilet, computer, pay telephone, or any other such machine. Be sure to establish a clear context for your narrative.

38 WHO SAW MURDER DIDN'T CALL POLICE

Martin Gansberg

Martin Gansberg was born in 1920 in Brooklyn, New York, and graduated from St. John's University. A long-time reporter, Gansberg wrote the following article for the New York Times *two weeks after the early morning events he so poignantly narrates. Once you've finished reading the essay, you will understand why it has been so often reprinted and why the name Kitty Genovese is still invoked whenever questions of public apathy arise.*

For more than half an hour 38 respectable, law-abiding citizens in Queens watched a killer stalk and stab a woman in three separate attacks in Kew Gardens.

Twice their chatter and the sudden glow of their bedroom lights interrupted him and frightened him off. Each time he returned, sought her out, and stabbed her again. Not one person telephoned the police during the assault; one witness called after the woman was dead.

That was two weeks ago today.

Still shocked is Assistant Chief Inspector Frederick M. Lussen, in charge of the borough's detectives and a veteran of 25 years of homicide investigations. He can give a matter-of-fact recitation on many murders. But the Kew Gardens slaying baffles him—not because it is a murder, but because the "good people" failed to call the police.

"As we have reconstructed the crime," he said, "the assailant had three chances to kill this woman during a 35-minute period. He returned twice to complete the job. If we had been called when he first attacked, the woman might not be dead now."

This is what the police say happened beginning at 3:20 A.M. in   6
the staid, middle-class, tree-lined Austin Street area:

Twenty-eight-year-old Catherine Genovese, who was called   7
Kitty by almost everyone in the neighborhood, was returning
home from her job as manager of a bar in Hollis. She parked
her red Fiat in a lot adjacent to the Kew Gardens Long Island
Rail Road Station, facing Mowbray Place. Like many residents
of the neighborhood, she had parked there day after day since
her arrival from Connecticut a year ago, although the railroad
frowns on the practice.

She turned off the lights of her car, locked the door, and   8
started to walk the 100 feet to the entrance of her apartment at
82–70 Austin Street, which is in a Tudor building, with stores
in the first floor and apartments on the second.

The entrance to the apartment is in the rear of the building   9
because the front is rented to retail stores. At night the quiet
neighborhood is shrouded in the slumbering darkness that
marks most residential areas.

Miss Genovese noticed a man at the far end of the lot, near a   10
seven-story apartment house at 82–40 Austin Street. She
halted. Then, nervously, she headed up Austin Street toward
Lefferts Boulevard, where there is a call box to the 102nd Police Precinct in nearby Richmond Hill.

She got as far as a street light in front of a bookstore before   11
the man grabbed her. She screamed. Lights went on in the 10-
story apartment house at 82–67 Austin Street, which faces the
bookstore. Windows slid open and voices punctuated the early-
morning stillness.

Miss Genovese screamed: "Oh, my God, he stabbed me!   12
Please help me! Please help me!"

From one of the upper windows in the apartment house, a   13
man called down: "Let that girl alone!"

The assailant looked up at him, shrugged, and walked down   14
Austin Street toward a white sedan parked a short distance
away. Miss Genovese struggled to her feet.

Lights went out. The killer returned to Miss Genovese, now   15
trying to make her way around the side of the building by the
parking lot to get to her apartment. The assailant stabbed her
again.

"I'm dying!" she shrieked. "I'm dying!"   16

Windows were opened again, and lights went on in many   17
apartments. The assailant got into his car and drove away. Miss
Genovese staggered to her feet. A city bus, O–10, the Lefferts
Boulevard line to Kennedy International Airport, passed. It
was 3:35 A.M.

The assailant returned. By then, Miss Genovese had crawled   18
to the back of the building, where the freshly painted brown
doors to the apartment house held out hope for safety. The
killer tried the first door; she wasn't there. At the second door,
82–62 Austin Street, he saw her slumped on the floor at the foot
of the stairs. He stabbed her a third time—fatally.

It was 3:50 by the time the police received their first call,   19
from a man who was a neighbor of Miss Genovese. In two minutes they were at the scene. The neighbor, a 70-year-old
woman, and another woman were the only persons on the
street. Nobody else came forward.

The man explained that he had called the police after much   20
deliberation. He had phoned a friend in Nassau County for advice and then he had crossed the roof of the building to the
apartment of the elderly woman to get her to make the call.

"I didn't want to get involved," he sheepishly told the police.   21

Six days later, the police arrested Winston Moseley, a 29-   22
year-old business-machine operator, and charged him with
homicide. Moseley had no previous record. He is married, has
two children and owns a home at 133–19 Sutter Avenue, South
Ozone Park, Queens. On Wednesday, a court committed him to
Kings County Hospital for psychiatric observation.

When questioned by the police, Moseley also said that he had   23
slain Mrs. Annie May Johnson, 24, of 146–12 133d Avenue, Ja-
maica, on Feb. 29 and Barbara Kralik, 15, of 174–17 140th Avenue, Springfield Gardens, last July. In the Kralik case, the police are holding Alvin L. Mitchell, who is said to have confessed
that slaying.

The police stressed how simple it would have been to have   24
gotten in touch with them. "A phone call," said one of the detectives, "would have done it." The police may be reached by dial-
ing "O" for operator or SPring 7-3100.

Today witnesses from the neighborhood, which is made up of   25
one-family homes in the $35,000 to $60,000 range with the ex-

ception of the two apartment houses near the railroad station, find it difficult to explain why they didn't call the police.

A housewife, knowingly if quite casually, said, "We thought   26
it was a lovers' quarrel." A husband and wife both said, "Frankly, we were afraid." They seemed aware of the fact that events might have been different. A distraught woman, wiping her hands in her apron, said, "I didn't want my husband to get involved."

One couple, now willing to talk about that night, said they   27
heard the first screams. The husband looked thoughtfully at the bookstore where the killer first grabbed Miss Genovese.

"We went to the window to see what was happening," he   28
said, "but the light from our bedroom made it difficult to see the street." The wife, still apprehensive, added: "I put out the light and we were able to see better."

Asked why they hadn't called the police, she shrugged and re-   29
plied: "I don't know."

A man peeked out from a slight opening in the doorway to his   30
apartment and rattled off an account of the killer's second attack. Why hadn't he called the police at the time? "I was tired," he said without emotion. "I went back to bed."

It was 4:25 A.M. when the ambulance arrived to take the body   31
of Miss Genovese. It drove off. "Then," a solemn police detective said, "the people came out."

Questions for Study and Discussion

1. What is the author's purpose in this selection? What are the advantages or disadvantages in using narration to accomplish this purpose? Explain. (Glossary: *Purpose*)
2. Where does the narrative actually begin? What is the function of the material that precedes the beginning of the narrative proper?
3. How would you describe Gansberg's tone? Is the tone appropriate for the story Gansberg narrates? Explain. (Glossary: *Tone*)
4. Gansberg uses dialogue throughout his essay. How many

people does he quote? What does he accomplish by using dialogue? (Glossary: *Dialogue*)

5. Why do you think Gansberg gives the addresses of the victims in paragraph 23?

6. Reflect on Gansberg's ending. What would be lost or gained by adding a paragraph that analyzed the meaning of the narrative for the reader? (Glossary: *Beginnings/Endings*)

Vocabulary

Refer to your dictionary to define the following words as they are used in this selection. Then use each word in a sentence of your own.

stalk (1)	shrouded (9)
recitation (4)	sheepishly (21)
assailant (5)	apprehensive (28)
staid (6)	

Suggested Writing Assignments

1. Gansberg's essay is about public apathy and fear. What is your own experience with the public? Modeling an essay after Gansberg's, narrate yet another event or series of events that you personally know about. Or, write a narration about public involvement, one that contradicts Gansberg's essay.

2. It is common when using narration to tell about firsthand experience and to tell the story in the first person. It is good practice, however, to try writing a narration about something you don't know about firsthand but must learn about, much the same as a newspaper reporter must do. For several days, be attentive to events occurring around you—in your neighborhood, school, community, region—events that would be an appropriate basis for a narrative essay. Interview the principal characters involved in your story, take detailed notes, and then write your narration.

HOW I DESIGNED AN A-BOMB
IN MY JUNIOR YEAR AT PRINCETON

John Aristotle Phillips and David Michaelis

*During his junior year at Princeton University,
John Aristotle Phillips developed the design for a
workable atomic bomb as a physics term paper.
He later collaborated with his classmate David
Michaelis on* Mushroom: The Story of the A-
Bomb Kid *(1978), an account of the project. In
the following selection, Phillips and Michaelis
tell the suspenseful story of the three months
leading up to the completion of Phillips's
paper—one that is now a U.S. government classified document.*

The first semester of my junior year at Princeton University
is a disaster, and my grades show it. D's and F's predominate, and a note from the dean puts me on academic probation.
Flunk one more course, and I'm out.

Fortunately, as the new semester gets under way, my courses
begin to interest me. Three hours a week, I attend one called
Nuclear Weapons Strategy and Arms Control in which three
professors lead 12 students through intense discussions of
counterforce capabilities and doomsday scenarios. The leader
is Hal Feiveson, renowned for his strong command of the subject matter. Assisting him are Marty Sherwin, an authority on
cold-war diplomacy, and Freeman Dyson, an eminent physicist.

One morning, Dyson opens a discussion of the atomic bomb:
"Let me describe what occurs when a 20-kiloton bomb is ex-
ploded, similar to the two dropped on Hiroshima and Nagasaki. First, the sky becomes illuminated by a brilliant white
light. Temperatures are so high around the point of explosion
that the atmosphere is actually made incandescent. To an observer standing six miles away the ball of fire appears brighter
than a hundred suns.

"As the fireball begins to spread up and out into a mush- 4
room-shaped cloud, temperatures spontaneously ignite all
flammable materials for miles around. Wood-frame houses
catch fire. Clothing bursts into flame, and people suffer intense
third-degree flash burns over their exposed flesh. The very high
temperatures also produce a shock wave and a variety of nuclear radiations capable of penetrating 20 inches of concrete.
The shock wave levels everything in the vicinity of ground zero;
hurricane-force winds then rush into the vacuum left by the ex-
panding shock wave and sweep up the rubble of masonry, glass
and steel, hurling it outward as lethal projectiles.

Silence falls over the room as the titanic proportions of the 5
destruction begin to sink in.

"It takes only 15 pounds of plutonium to fabricate a crude 6
atomic bomb," adds Hal Feiveson. "If breeder reactors come
into widespread use, there will be sufficient plutonium shipped
around the country each year to fashion thousands of bombs.
Much of it could be vulnerable to theft or hijacking."

The class discusses a possible scenario. A 200-pound ship- 7
ment disappears en route between a reprocessing facility and a
nuclear reactor. State and local police discover only an empty
truck and a dead driver. Two weeks later, a crude fission bomb
is detonated in Wall Street. Of the half-million people who
crowd the area during the regular business day, 100,000 are
killed outright. A terrorist group claims responsibility and
warns the President that if its extravagant political demands
are not met, there will be another explosion within a week.

"That's impossible," a student objects. "Terrorists don't 8
have the know-how to build a bomb."

"You have to be brilliant to design an A-bomb," says another. 9
"Besides, terrorists don't have access to the knowledge."

Impossible? Or is it? The specter of terrorists incinerating an 10
entire city with a homemade atomic bomb begins to haunt me.
I turn to John McPhee's book *The Curve of Binding Energy*, in
which former Los Alamos nuclear physicist Ted Taylor postu-
lates that a terrorist group could easily steal plutonium or ura-
nium from a nuclear reactor and then design a workable
atomic bomb with information available to the general public.
According to Taylor, all the ingredients—except plutonium—

are legally available at hardware stores and chemical-supply houses.

Suddenly, an idea comes to mind. Suppose an average—or below-average in my case—physics student could design a workable atomic bomb on paper? That would prove Taylor's point dramatically and show the federal government that stronger safeguards have to be placed on the storage of plutonium. If I could design a bomb, almost any intelligent person could. But I would have to do it in less than three months to turn it in as my junior independent project. I decide to ask Freeman Dyson to be my adviser.

"You understand," says Dyson, "my government security clearance will preclude me from giving you any more information than that which can be found in physics libraries? And that the law of 'no comment' governing scientists who have clearance to atomic secrets stipulates that, if asked a question about the design of a bomb, I can answer neither yes nor no?"

"Yes, sir," I reply. "I understand."

"Okay, then. I'll give you a list of textbooks outlining the general principles—and I wish you luck."

I'm tremendously excited as I charge over to the physics office to record my project, and can barely write down:

> John Aristotle Phillips
> Dr. Freeman Dyson, Adviser
> "How to Build Your Own
> Atomic Bomb"

A few days later, Dyson hands me a short list of books on nuclear-reactor technology, general nuclear physics and current atomic theory. "That's all?" I ask incredulously, having expected a bit more direction.

At subsequent meetings Dyson explains only the basic principles of nuclear physics, and his responses to my calculations grow opaque. If I ask about a particular design or figure, he will glance over what I've done and change the subject. At first, I think this is his way of telling me I am correct. To make sure, I hand him an incorrect figure. He reads it and changes the subject.

Over spring vacation, I go to Washington, D.C., to search for 18
records of the Los Alamos Project that were declassified between 1954 and 1964. I discover a copy of the literature given to
scientists who joined the project in the spring of 1943. This
text, *The Los Alamos Primer*, carefully outlines all the details
of atomic fissioning known to the world's most advanced scientists in the early '40s. A whole batch of copies costs me about
$25. I gather them together and go over to the bureaucrat at the
front desk. She looks at the titles, and then looks up at me.

"Oh, you want to build a bomb, too?" she asks matter-of- 19
factly.

I can't believe it. Do people go in there for bomb-building in- 20
formation every day? When I show the documents to Dyson, he
is visibly shaken. His reaction indicates to me that I actually
stand a chance of coming up with a workable design.

The material necessary to explode my bomb is plutonium- 21
239, a man-made, heavy isotope. Visualize an atomic bomb as a
marble inside a grapefruit inside a basketball inside a beach
ball. At the center of the bomb is the initiator, a marble-size
piece of metal. Around the initiator is a grapefruit-size ball of
plutonium-239. Wrapped around the plutonium is a three-inch
reflector shield made of beryllium. High explosives are placed
symmetrically around the beryllium shield. When these deto-
nate, an imploding shock wave is set off, compressing the
grapefruit-size ball of plutonium to the size of a plum. At this
moment, the process of atoms fissioning—or splitting apart—
begins.

There are many subtleties involved in the explosion of an 22
atomic bomb. Most of them center on the actual detonation of
the explosives surrounding the beryllium shield. The grouping
of these explosives is one of the most highly classified aspects
of the atomic bomb, and it poses the biggest problems for me as
I begin to design my bomb.

My base of operations is a small room on the second floor of 23
Ivy, my eating club. The conference table in the center of the
room is covered with books, calculators, design paper, notes.
My sleeping bag is rolled out on the floor. As the next three
weeks go by, I stop going to classes altogether and work day
and night. The other members at Ivy begin referring to me as

The Hobo because of my unshaven face and disheveled appearance. I develop a terrible case of bloodshot eyes. Sleep comes rarely.

I approach every problem from a terrorist's point of view. 24
The bomb must be inexpensive to construct, simple in design, and small enough to sit unnoticed in the trunk of a car or an abandoned U-Haul trailer.

As the days and nights flow by, linked together by cups of 25
coffee and bologna sandwiches, I scan government documents for gaps indicating an area of knowledge that is still classified. Essentially, I am putting together a huge jigsaw puzzle. The edge pieces are in place and various areas are getting filled in, but pieces are missing. Whenever the outline of one shows up, I grab my coffee Thermos and sit down to devise the solution that will fill the gap.

With only two weeks left, the puzzle is nearly complete, but 26
two pieces are still missing: which explosives to use, and how to arrange them around the plutonium.

During the next week I read that a high-explosive blanket 27
around the beryllium shield might work. But after spending an entire night calculating, I conclude that it is not enough to guarantee a successful implosion wave. Seven days before the design is due, I'm still deadlocked.

The alarm clock falls off the table and breaks. I take this as a 28
sign to do something drastic, and I start all over at the beginning. Occasionally I find errors in my old calculations, and I correct them. I lose sense of time.

With less than 24 hours to go, I run through a series of new 29
calculations, mathematically figuring the arrangement of the explosives around the plutonium. If my equations are correct, my bomb might be just as effective as the Hiroshima and Nagasaki bombs. But I can't be sure until I know the exact nature of the explosives I will use.

Next morning, with my paper due at 5 p.m., I call the Du Pont 30
Company from a pay phone and ask for the head of the chemical-explosives division, a man I'll call S. F. Graves. If he gives me even the smallest lead, I'll be able to figure the rest out by myself. Otherwise, I'm finished.

"Hello, Mr. Graves. My name is John Phillips. I'm a student 31 at Princeton, doing work on a physics project. I'd like to get some advice, if that's possible."

"What can I do for you?"　32

"Well," I stammer, "I'm doing research on the shaping of ex-　33
plosive products that create a very high density in a spherically shaped metal. Can you suggest a Du Pont product that would fit in this category?"

"Of course," he says, in a helpful manner.　34

I don't think he suspects, but I decide to try a bluff: "One of　35
my professors told me that a simple explosive blanket would work in the high-density situation."

"No, no. Explosive blankets went out with the Stone Age. We　36
sell [he names the product] to do the job in similar density-problem situations to the one you're talking about."

When I hang up the phone, I let out a whoop. Mr. Graves has　37
given me just the information I need. Now, if my calculations are correct with respect to the new information, all I have to do is complete my paper by five.

Five minutes to five, I race over to the physics building and　38
bound up the stairs. Inside the office, everybody stops talking and stares at me. I haven't shaved in over a week.

"Is your razor broken, young man?" asks one of the depart-　39
ment secretaries.

"I came to hand in my project," I explain. "I didn't have time　40
to shave. Sorry."

A week later, I return to the physics department to pick up　41
my project. One thought has persisted: If I didn't guess cor-rectly about the implosion wave, or if I made a mistake some-where in the graphs, I'll be finished at Princeton.

A secretary points to the papers. I flip through them, but　42
don't find mine. I look carefully; my paper is not there.

Trying to remain calm, I ask her if all the papers have been　43
graded.

"Yes, of course," she says.　44

Slowly I return to my room. The absence of my paper can　45
only mean that I blew it.

In the middle of the week, I go back to the physics-depart-　46
ment office, hoping to catch the chairman for a few minutes. The secretary looks up, then freezes.

"Aren't you John Phillips?" she asks.　47

"Yes," I reply. 48

"Aren't you the boy who designed the atomic bomb?" 49

"Yes, and my paper wasn't . . ." 50

She takes a deep breath. "The question has been raised by 51
the department whether your paper should be classified by the
U.S. government."

"What? Classified?" 52

She takes my limp hand, shaking it vigorously. "Congratula- 53
tions," she says, all smiles. "You got one of the only A's in the
department. Dr. Wigner wants to see you right away. He says
it's a fine piece of work. And Dr. Dyson has been looking for
you everywhere."

For a second I don't say anything. Then the madness of the 54
situation hits me. A small air bubble of giddiness rises in my
throat. Here I have put on paper the plan for a device capable
of killing thousands of people, and all I was worrying about
was flunking out.

Questions for Study and Discussion

1. Phillips tells how he first decided to try to design an atomic
   bomb and how he actually accomplished that task. Having
   read the essay, would you be able to build an atomic bomb?
   If not, what do you think is Phillips's purpose in telling his
   story?

2. In paragraphs 3 and 4 Professor Dyson describes what happens when an atomic bomb is detonated. Why does Dyson
   give this description to the class? Why do you suppose Phillips recounts Dyson's description for the reader?

3. Why does Phillips use the present tense throughout the
   narration? What would have been gained or lost had he told
   his story in the past tense?

4. Phillips's narrative spans the spring semester of his junior
   year at Princeton. How does he keep the reader informed of
   the passage of time?

5. Identify two analogies that Phillips uses in the essay. Explain why each analogy is effective. (Glossary: *Analogy*)

Vocabulary

Refer to your dictionary to define the following words as they are used in this selection. Then use each word in a sentence of your own.

scenarios (2)   fabricate (6)
eminent (2)   stipulates (12)
lethal (4)   opaque (17)
spontaneously (4)   disheveled (23)

Suggested Writing Assignments

1. Many political leaders have taken the position that the only way to assure peace is to build up our war machine. Write an argument that agrees or disagrees with this belief.

2. Write an essay in which you narrate an experience that occurred over an extended period of time—for example, applying for admission to college. Before you start to write, make a list of the essential events that you will include. Because your narrative may cover several months, be sure to indicate clearly the passage of time.

MOMMA, THE DENTIST, AND ME

Maya Angelou

*Maya Angelou is perhaps best known as the au-
thor of* I Know Why the Caged Bird Sings *(1970),
the first of four books in the series which constitutes her autobiography. Starting with her beginnings in St. Louis in 1928, Angelou presents a life
story of joyful triumph over hardships that
tested her courage and threatened her spirit.
Trained as a dancer, Angelou has also published
three books of poetry, acted in the television series "Roots," and, at the request of Martin
Luther King, Jr., served as a coordinator of the
Southern Christian Leadership Conference. In
the following excerpt from* I Know Why the
Caged Bird Sings, *Angelou narrates what happened, and what might have happened, when
her grandmother, the "Momma" of the story,
takes her to the local dentist.*

The angel of the candy counter had found me out at last,   1
and was exacting excruciating penance for all the stolen
Milky Ways, Mounds, Mr. Goodbars and Hersheys with Al-
monds. I had two cavities that were rotten to the gums. The
pain was beyond the bailiwick of crushed aspirins or oil of
cloves. Only one thing could help me, so I prayed earnestly that
I'd be allowed to sit under the house and have the building collapse on my left jaw. Since there was no Negro dentist in
Stamps, nor doctor either, for that matter, Momma had dealt
with previous toothaches by pulling them out (a string tied to
the tooth with the other end looped over her fist), pain killers
and prayer. In this particular instance the medicine had proved
ineffective; there wasn't enough enamel left to hook a string on,
and the prayers were being ignored because the Balancing Angel was blocking their passage.

I lived a few days and nights in blinding pain, not so much   2
toying with as seriously considering the idea of jumping in the

well, and Momma decided I had to be taken to a dentist. The nearest Negro dentist was in Texarkana, twenty-five miles away, and I was certain that I'd be dead long before we reached half the distance. Momma said we'd go to Dr. Lincoln, right in Stamps, and he'd take care of me. She said he owed her a favor.

I knew there were a number of whitefolks in town that owed her favors. Bailey and I had seen the books which showed how she had lent money to Blacks and whites alike during the Depression, and most still owed her. But I couldn't aptly remember seeing Dr. Lincoln's name, nor had I ever heard of a Negro's going to him as a patient. However, Momma said we were going, and put water on the stove for our baths. I had never been to a doctor, so she told me that after the bath (which would make my mouth feel better) I had to put on freshly starched and ironed underclothes from inside out. The ache failed to respond to the bath, and I knew then that the pain was more serious than that which anyone had ever suffered.

Before we left the Store, she ordered me to brush my teeth and then wash my mouth with Listerine. The idea of even opening my clamped jaws increased the pain, but upon her explanation that when you go to a doctor you have to clean yourself all over, but most especially the part that's to be examined, I screwed up my courage and unlocked my teeth. The cool air in my mouth and the jarring of my molars dislodged what little remained of my reason. I had frozen to the pain, my family nearly had to tie me down to take the toothbrush away. It was no small effort to get me started on the road to the dentist. Momma spoke to all the passers-by, but didn't stop to chat. She explained over her shoulder that we were going to the doctor and she'd "pass the time of day" on our way home.

Until we reached the pond the pain was my world, an aura that haloed me for three feet around. Crossing the bridge into whitefolks' country, pieces of sanity pushed themselves forward. I had to stop moaning and start walking straight. The white towel, which was drawn under my chin and tied over my head, had to be arranged. If one was dying, it had to be done in style if the dying took place in whitefolks' part of town.

On the other side of the bridge the ache seemed to lessen as if a whitebreeze blew off the whitefolks and cushioned everything in their neighborhood—including my jaw. The gravel road was smoother, the stones smaller and the tree branches hung down around the path and nearly covered us. If the pain didn't diminish then, the familiar yet strange sights hypnotized me into believing that it had.

But my head continued to throb with the measured insistence of a bass drum, and how could a toothache pass the calaboose, hear the songs of the prisoners, their blues and laughter, and not be changed? How could one or two or even a mouthful of angry tooth roots meet a wagonload of powhitetrash children, endure their idiotic snobbery and not feel less important? 7

Behind the building which housed the dentist's office ran a small path used by servants and those tradespeople who catered to the butcher and Stamps' one restaurant. Momma and I followed that lane to the backstairs of Dentist Lincoln's office. The sun was bright and gave the day a hard reality as we climbed up the steps to the second floor. 8

Momma knocked on the back door and a young white girl opened it to show surprise at seeing us there. Momma said she wanted to see Dentist Lincoln and to tell him Annie was there. The girl closed the door firmly. Now the humiliation of hearing Momma describe herself as if she had no last name to the young white girl was equal to the physical pain. It seemed terribly unfair to have a toothache and a headache and have to bear at the same time the heavy burden of Blackness. 9

It was always possible that the teeth would quiet down and maybe drop out of their own accord. Momma said we would wait. We leaned in the harsh sunlight on the shaky railings of the dentist's back porch for over an hour. 10

He opened the door and looked at Momma. "Well, Annie, what can I do for you?" 11

He didn't see the towel around my jaw or notice my swollen face. 12

Momma said, "Dentist Lincoln. It's my grandbaby here. She got two rotten teeth that's giving her a fit." 13

She waited for him to acknowledge the truth of her statement. He made no comment, orally or facially. 14

"She had this toothache purt' near four days now, and today I said, 'Young lady, you going to the Dentist.'" 15

"Annie?" 16

"Yes, sir, Dentist Lincoln." 17

He was choosing words the way people hunt for shells. "An- 18
nie, you know I don't treat nigra, colored people."

"I know, Dentist Lincoln. But this here is just my little grand- 19
baby, and she ain't gone be no trouble to you . . ."

"Annie, everybody has a policy. In this world you have to 20
have a policy. Now, my policy is I don't treat colored people."

The sun had baked the oil out of Momma's skin and melted 21
the Vaseline in her hair. She shone greasily as she leaned out of
the dentist's shadow.

"Seem like to me, Dentist Lincoln, you might look after her, 22
she ain't nothing but a little mite. And seems like maybe you
owe me a favor or two."

He reddened slightly. "Favor or no favor. The money has all 23
been repaid to you and that's the end of it. Sorry, Annie." He
had his hand on the doorknob. "Sorry." His voice was a bit
kinder on the second "Sorry," as if he really was.

Momma said, "I wouldn't press on you like this for myself 24
but I can't take No. Not for my grandbaby. When you come to
borrow my money you didn't have to beg. You asked me, and I
lent it. Now, it wasn't my policy. I ain't no moneylender, but
you stood to lose this building and I tried to help you out."

"It's been paid, and raising your voice won't make me change 25
my mind. My policy . . ." He let go of the door and stepped
nearer Momma. The three of us were crowded on the small
landing. "Annie, my policy is I'd rather stick my hand in a dog's
mouth than in a nigger's."

He had never once looked at me. He turned his back and went 26
through the door into the cool beyond. Momma backed up inside herself for a few minutes. I forgot everything except her
face which was almost a new one to me. She leaned over and
took the doorknob, and in her everyday soft voice she said,
"Sister, go on downstairs. Wait for me. I'll be there directly."

Under the most common of circumstances I knew it did no 27
good to argue with Momma. So I walked down the steep stairs,
afraid to look back and afraid not to do so. I turned as the door
slammed, and she was gone.

Momma walked in that room as if she owned it. She shoved 28
that silly nurse aside with one hand and strode into the dentist's
office. He was sitting in his chair, sharpening his mean instru-
ments and putting extra sting into his medicines. Her eyes were
blazing like live coals and her arms had doubled themselves in

length. He looked up at her just before she caught him by the collar of his white jacket.

"*Stand up when you see a lady, you contemptuous scoundrel.*" 29 *Her tongue had thinned and the words rolled off well enunciated. Enunciated and sharp like little claps of thunder.*

The dentist had no choice but to stand at R.O.T.C. attention. 30 *His head dropped after a minute and his voice was humble. "Yes, ma'am, Mrs. Henderson."*

"*You knave, do you think you acted like a gentleman, speak-* 31 *ing to me like that in front of my granddaughter?" She didn't shake him, although she had the power. She simply held him upright.*

"*No, ma'am, Mrs. Henderson.*" 32

"*No, ma'am, Mrs. Henderson, what?*" *Then she did give him* 33 *the tiniest of shakes, but because of her strength the action set his head and arms to shaking loose on the ends of his body. He stuttered much worse than Uncle Willie. "No, ma'am, Mrs. Henderson, I'm sorry."*

With just an edge of her disgust showing, Momma slung him 34 *back in his dentist's chair. "Sorry is as sorry does, and you're about the sorriest dentist I ever laid my eyes on." (She could afford to slip into the vernacular because she had such eloquent command of English.)*

"*I didn't ask you to apologize in front of Marguerite, because I* 35 *don't want her to know my power, but I order you, now and herewith. Leave Stamps by sundown."*

"*Mrs. Henderson, I can't get my equipment . . .*" *He was shak-* 36 *ing terribly now.*

"*Now, that brings me to my second order. You will never* 37 *again practice dentistry. Never! When you get settled in your next place, you will be a vegetarian caring for dogs with the mange, cats with the cholera and cows with the epizootic. Is that clear?"*

The saliva ran down his chin and his eyes filled with tears. 38 "*Yes, ma'am. Thank you for not killing me. Thank you, Mrs. Henderson."*

Momma pulled herself back from being ten feet tall with 39 *eight-foot arms and said, "You're welcome for nothing, you varlet, I wouldn't waste a killing on the likes of you."*

On her way out she waved her handkerchief at the nurse and 40 *turned her into a crocus sack of chicken feed.*

Momma looked tired when she came down the stairs, but   41
who wouldn't be tired if they had gone through what she had.
She came close to me and adjusted the towel under my jaw (I
had forgotten the toothache; I only knew that she made her
hands gentle in order not to awaken the pain). She took my
hand. Her voice never changed. "Come on, Sister."

I reckoned we were going home where she would concoct a   42
brew to eliminate the pain and maybe give me new teeth too.
New teeth that would grow overnight out of my gums. She led
me toward the drugstore, which was in the opposite direction
from the Store. "I'm taking you to Dentist Baker in Texarkana."

I was glad after all that I had bathed and put on Mum   43
and Cashmere Bouquet talcum powder. It was a wonderful surprise. My toothache had quieted to solemn pain, Momma had
obliterated the evil white man, and we were going on a trip to
Texarkana, just the two of us.

On the Greyhound she took an inside seat in the back, and I   44
sat beside her. I was so proud of being her granddaughter and
sure that some of her magic must have come down to me. She
asked if I was scared. I only shook my head and leaned over on
her cool brown upper arm. There was no chance that a dentist,
especially a Negro dentist, would dare hurt me then. Not with
Momma there. The trip was uneventful, except that she put her
arm around me, which was very unusual for Momma to do.

The dentist showed me the medicine and the needle before he   45
deadened my gums, but if he hadn't I wouldn't have worried.
Momma stood right behind him. Her arms were folded and she
checked on everything he did. The teeth were extracted and she
bought me an ice cream cone from the side window of a drug
counter. The trip back to Stamps was quiet, except that I had to
spit into a very small empty snuff can which she had gotten for
me and it was difficult with the bus humping and jerking on
our country roads.

At home, I was given a warm salt solution, and when I   46
washed out my mouth I showed Bailey the empty holes, where
the clotted blood sat like filling in a pie crust. He said I was
quite brave, and that was my cue to reveal our confrontation
with the peckerwood dentist and Momma's incredible powers.

I had to admit that I didn't hear the conversation, but what   47 else could she have said than what I said she said? What else done? He agreed with my analysis in a lukewarm way, and I happily (after all, I'd been sick) flounced into the Store. Momma was preparing our evening meal and Uncle Willie leaned on the door sill. She gave her version.

"Dentist Lincoln got right uppity. Said he'd rather put his   48
hand in a dog's mouth. And when I reminded him of the favor, he brushed it off like a piece of lint. Well, I sent Sister downstairs and went inside. I hadn't never been in his office before, but I found the door to where he takes out teeth, and him and the nurse was in there thick as thieves. I just stood there till he caught sight of me." Crash bang the pots on the stove. "He jumped just like he was sitting on a pin. He said, 'Annie, I done tole you, I ain't gonna mess around in no niggah's mouth.' I said, 'Somebody's got to do it then,' and he said, 'Take her to Texarkana to the colored dentist' and that's when I said, 'If you paid me my money I could afford to take her.' He said, 'It's all been paid.' I tole him everything but the interest been paid. He said ' 'Twasn't no interest.' I said ' 'Tis now. I'll take ten dollars as payment in full.' You know, Willie, it wasn't no right thing to do, 'cause I lent that money without thinking about it.

"He tole that little snippity nurse of his'n to give me ten dol-   49
lars and make me sign a 'paid in full' receipt. She gave it to me and I signed the papers. Even though by rights he was paid up before, I figger, he gonna be that kind of nasty, he gonna have to pay for it."

Momma and her son laughed and laughed over the white   50
man's evilness and her retributive sin.

I preferred, much preferred, my version.   51

Questions for Study and Discussion

1. What is Angelou's purpose in narrating the story she tells? (Glossary: *Purpose*)
2. Compare and contrast the content and style of the interaction between Momma and the dentist that is given in italics with the one given at the end of the narrative. (Glossary: *Comparison and Contrast*)

3. Angelou tells her story chronologically and in the first person. What are the advantages of the first person narrative?

4. Identify three similes that Angelou uses in her narrative. Explain how each simile serves her purposes. (Glossary: *Figures of Speech*)

5. How does Angelou describe the pain she feels? Why is it essential that Angelou's description be carefully drawn? (Glossary: *Description*)

Vocabulary

Refer to your dictionary to define the following words as they are used in this selection. Then use each word in a sentence of your own.

bailiwick (1)	varlet (39)
calaboose (7)	concoct (42)
mite (22)	snippety (49)
vernacular (34)	retributive (50)

Suggested Writing Assignments

1. One of Angelou's themes in "Momma, the Dentist, and Me" is that cruelty, whether racial, social, professional, or personal, is very difficult to endure and leaves a lasting impression on a person. Think of a situation where an unthinking or insensitive person made you feel inferior for reasons beyond your control. Prewrite by listing the sequence of events in your narrative before you draft it. You may find it helpful to reread the introduction to this section before you begin working.

2. Write a narrative in which, like Angelou, you give two versions of an actual event—one the way you thought or wished it happened and the other the way events actually took place.

12

DESCRIPTION

To describe is to create a verbal picture. A person, a place, a thing—even an idea or a state of mind—can be made vividly concrete through description. Here, for example, is Thomas Mann's brief description of a delicatessen:

> It was a narrow room, with a rather high ceiling, and crowded from floor to ceiling with goodies. There were rows and rows of hams and sausages of all shapes and colors—white, yellow, red, and black; fat and lean and round and long—rows of canned preserves, cocoa and tea, bright translucent glass bottles of honey, marmalade, and jam; round bottles and slender bottles, filled with liqueurs and punch—all these things crowded every inch of the shelves from top to bottom.

Writing any description requires, first of all, that the writer gather many details about a subject, relying not only on what the eyes see but on the other sense impressions—touch, taste, smell, hearing—as well. From this catalogue of details the writer selects those which will most effectively create a *dominant impression*—the single quality, mood, or atmosphere that the writer wishes to emphasize. Consider, for example, the details that Mary McCarthy uses to evoke the dominant impression in the following passage from *Memories of a Catholic Girlhood:*

> Whenever we children came to stay at my grandmother's house, we were put to sleep in the sewing room, a bleak, shabby, utilitarian rectangle, more office than bedroom, more attic than office, that played to the hierarchy of chambers the role of poor relation. It was a room without pride: the old sewing machine, some cast-off chairs, a shadeless lamp, rolls of wrapping paper, piles of cardboard boxes that might someday come in handy, papers of pins, and remnants of a material united with the iron folding cots put out for our use and the bare floor boards to

give an impression of intense and ruthless temporality. Thin white spreads, of the kind used in hospitals and charity institutions, and naked blinds at the windows reminded us of our orphaned condition and of the ephemeral character of our visit; there was nothing here to encourage us to consider this our home.

The dominant impression that McCarthy creates is one of clutter, bleakness, and shabbiness. There is nothing in the sewing room that suggests permanence or warmth.

Writers must also carefully plan the order in which to present their descriptive details. The pattern of organization must fit the subject of the description logically and naturally, and must also be easy to follow. For example, visual details can be arranged spatially—from left to right, top to bottom, near to far, or in any other logical order. Other patterns include smallest to largest, softest to loudest, least significant to most significant, most unusual to least unusual. McCarthy suggests a jumble of junk not only by her choice of details but by the apparently random order in which she presents them.

How much detail is enough? There is no fixed answer. A good description includes enough vivid details to create a dominant impression and to bring a scene to life, but not so many that readers are distracted, confused, or bored. In an essay that is purely descriptive, there is room for much detail. Usually, however, writers use description to create the setting for a story, to illustrate ideas, to help clarify a definition or a comparison, or to make the complexities of a process more understandable. Such descriptions should be kept short, and should include just enough detail to make them clear and helpful.

SUBWAY STATION

Gilbert Highet

Gilbert Highet (1906–1978) was born in Scotland and became a naturalized United States citizen in 1951. A prolific writer and translator, Highet was for many years a professor of classics at Columbia University. The following selection is taken from his book Talents and Geniuses *(1957). Notice the author's keen eye for detail as he describes the unseemly world of a subway station.*

Standing in a subway station, I began to appreciate the place—almost to enjoy it. First of all, I looked at the lighting: a row of meager electric bulbs, unscreened, yellow, and coated with filth, stretched toward the black mouth of the tunnel, as though it were a bolt hole in an abandoned coal mine. Then I lingered, with zest, on the walls and ceiling: lavatory tiles which had been white about fifty years ago, and were now encrusted with soot, coated with the remains of a dirty liquid which might be either atmospheric humidity mingled with smog or the result of a perfunctory attempt to clean them with cold water; and, above them, gloomy vaulting from which dingy paint was peeling off like scabs from an old wound, sick black paint leaving a leprous white undersurface. Beneath my feet, the floor was a nauseating dark brown with black stains upon it which might be stale oil or dry chewing gum or some worse defilement; it looked like the hallway of a condemned slum building. Then my eye traveled to the tracks, where two lines of glittering steel—the only positively clean objects in the whole place—ran out of darkness into darkness above an unspeakable mass of congealed oil, puddles of dubious liquid, and a mishmash of old cigarette packets, mutilated and filthy newspapers, and the débris that filtered down from the street above through a barred grating in the roof. As I looked up toward the sunlight, I could see more débris sifting slowly downward, and making an abominable pattern in the slanting beam of dirt-laden sunlight. I was going on to relish more features of this unique scene: such as the advertisement posters on the walls—here a text from the Bible, there a half-naked girl, here a woman wearing a hat consisting of a hen sitting on a nest full of eggs, and there a pair of girl's legs walking up the keys of a cash register—all scribbled over with unknown names and well-known obscenities in black crayon and red lipstick; but then my train came in at last, I boarded it, and began to read. The experience was over for the time.

Questions for Study and Discussion

1. What dominant impression of the subway station does Highet create in his description? (Glossary: *Dominant Impression*)
2. To present a clearly focused dominant impression, a writer must be selective in the use of details. Make a list of those details that help create Highet's dominant impression.
3. Highet uses a spatial organization in his essay. Trace the order in which he describes the various elements of the subway station. (Glossary: *Organization*)
4. What similes and metaphors can you find in Highet's description? How do they help to make the description vivid? (Glossary: *Figures of Speech*)

Vocabulary

Refer to your dictionary to define the following words as they are used in this selection. Then use each word in a sentence of your own.

meager	congealed
zest	dubious
defilement	unique

Suggested Writing Assignments

1. If you are familar with a subway station, write a lengthy one-paragraph description of it just as Highet has done. Once you have completed your description, compare and contrast your description with Highet's. How does the dominant impression you have created differ from the one Highet has created?

2. Write a short essay in which you describe one of the following places, or another place of your choice. Arrange the details of your description from top to bottom, left to right, near to far, or according to some other spatial organization.

   an airport terminal
   a pizza parlor
   a locker room
   a barbershop or beauty salon
   a bookstore
   a campus dining hall

THE SOUNDS OF THE CITY

James Tuite

James Tuite has had a long career at The New York Times, *where he once served as sports editor. As a free-lance writer he has contributed to all of the major sports magazines and has written* Snowmobiles and Snowmobiling *(1973) and* How to Enjoy Sports on TV *(1976). The following selection is a model of how a place can be described by using a sense other than sight. Tuite describes New York City by its sounds, which for him comprise the very life of the city.*

New York is a city of sounds: muted sounds and shrill sounds; shattering sounds and soothing sounds; urgent sounds and aimless sounds. The cliff dwellers of Manhattan—who would be racked by the silence of the lonely woods—do not hear these sounds because they are constant and eternally urban.

The visitor to the city can hear them, though, just as some animals can hear a high-pitched whistle inaudible to humans. To the casual caller to Manhattan, lying restive and sleepless in a hotel twenty or thirty floors above the street, they tell a story as fascinating as life itself. And back of the sounds broods the silence.

Night in midtown is the noise of tinseled honky-tonk and violence. Thin strains of music, usually the firm beat of rock 'n' roll or the frenzied outbursts of the discotheque, rise from ground level. This is the cacophony, the discordance of youth, and it comes on strongest when nights are hot and young blood restless.

Somewhere in the canyons below there is shrill laughter or raucous shouting. A bottle shatters against concrete. The whine of a police siren slices through the night, moving ever

234

closer, until an eerie Doppler effect* brings it to a guttural halt.

There are few sounds so exciting in Manhattan as those of fire apparatus dashing through the night. At the outset there is the tentative hint of the first-due company bullying his way through midtown traffic. Now a fire whistle from the opposite direction affirms that trouble is, indeed, afoot. In seconds, other sirens converging from other streets help the skytop listener focus on the scene of excitement.

But he can only hear and not see, and imagination takes flight. Are the flames and smoke gushing from windows not far away? Are victims trapped there, crying out for help? Is it a conflagration, or only a trash-basket fire? Or, perhaps, it is merely a false alarm.

The questions go unanswered and the urgency of the moment dissolves. Now the mind and the ear detect the snarling, arrogant bickering of automobile horns. People in a hurry. Taxicabs blaring, insisting on their checkered priority.

Even the taxi horns dwindle down to a precocious few in the gray and pink moments of dawn. Suddenly there is another sound, a morning sound that taunts the memory for recognition. The growl of a predatory monster? No, just garbage trucks that have begun a day of scavenging.

Trash cans rattle outside restaurants. Metallic jaws on sanitation trucks gulp and masticate the residue of daily living, then digest it with a satisfied groan of gears. The sounds of the new day are businesslike. The growl of buses, so scattered and distant at night, becomes a demanding part of the traffic bedlam. An occasional jet or helicopter injects an exclamation point from an unexpected quarter. When the wind is right, the vibrant bellow of an ocean liner can be heard.

The sounds of the day are as jarring as the glare of a sun that outlines the canyons of midtown in drab relief. A pneumatic drill frays countless nerves with its rat-a-tat-tat, for dig they must to perpetuate the city's dizzy motion. After each screech

*The drop in pitch that occurs as a source of sound quickly passes by a listener.

of brakes there is a moment of suspension, of waiting for the thud or crash that never seems to follow.

The whistles of traffic policemen and hotel doormen chirp from all sides, like birds calling for their mates across a frenzied aviary. And all of these sounds are adult sounds, for childish laughter has no place in these canyons.   11

Night falls again, the cycle is complete, but there is no surcease from sound. For the beautiful dreamers, perhaps, the "sounds of the rude world heard in the day, lulled by the moonlight have all passed away," but this is not so in the city.   12

Too many New Yorkers accept the sounds about them as bland parts of everyday existence. They seldom stop to listen to the sounds, to think about them, to be appalled or enchanted by them. In the big city, sounds are life.   13

Questions for Study and Discussion

1. What is Tuite's purpose in describing the sounds of New York City? (Glossary: *Purpose*)
2. How does Tuite organize his essay? Do you think that the organization is effective? (Glossary: *Organization*)
3. Tuite describes "raucous shouting" and the "screech of brakes." Make a list of the various other sounds that he describes in his essay. How do the varied adjectives and verbs Tuite uses to capture the essence of each sound enhance his description? (Glossary: *Diction*)
4. Locate several metaphors and similes in the essay. What picture of the city does each one give you? (Glossary: *Figures of Speech*)
5. What dominant impression of New York City does Tuite create in this essay? (Glossary: *Dominant Impression*)

Vocabulary

Refer to your dictionary to define the following words as they are used in this selection. Then use each word in a sentence of your own.

muted (1)   precocious (8)
inaudible (2)   taunts (8)
restive (2)   vibrant (9)
raucous (4)   perpetuate (10)
tentative (5)

Suggested Writing Assignments

1. In a short composition describe a city or another place that you know well. Try to capture as many sights, sounds, and smells as you can to depict the place you describe. Your goal should be to create a single dominant impression of the place, as Tuite does in his essay.

2. Describe an inanimate object familiar to you so as to bring out its character and make it interesting to a reader. First determine your purpose for describing the object. For example, suppose your family has had a dining table ever since you can remember. Think of what that table has been a part of over the years—the birthday parties, the fights, the holiday meals, the sad times, the intimate times, the long hours of studying and doing homework. Probably such a table would be worth describing for the way it has figured prominently in the history of your family. Next make an exhaustive list of the object's physical features; then write your descriptive essay.

UNFORGETTABLE MISS BESSIE

Carl T. Rowan

Carl T. Rowan is a former ambassador to Finland and was director of the United States Information Agency. Born in 1925 in Ravenscroft, Tennessee, he received degrees from Oberlin College and the University of Minnesota. Once a columnist for the Minneapolis Tribune *and the* Chicago Sun-Times, *Rowan is now a syndicated columnist and a* Reader's Digest *roving editor. In the following essay, Rowan describes his former high school teacher whose lessons went far beyond the subjects she taught.*

She was only about five feet tall and probably never 1
weighed more than 110 pounds, but Miss Bessie was a
towering presence in the classroom. She was the only woman
tough enough to make me read *Beowulf* and think for a few
foolish days that I liked it. From 1938 to 1942, when I attended
Bernard High School in McMinnville, Tenn., she taught me English, history, civics—and a lot more than I realized.

I shall never forget the day she scolded me into reading 2
Beowulf.

"But Miss Bessie," I complained, "I ain't much interested 3
in it."

Her large brown eyes became daggerish slits. "Boy," she 4
said, "how dare you say 'ain't' to me! I've taught you better
than that."

"Miss Bessie," I pleaded, "I'm trying to make first-string end 5
on the football team, and if I go around saying 'it isn't' and
'they aren't,' the guys are gonna laugh me off the squad."

"Boy," she responded, "you'll play football because you have 6
guts. But do you know what *really* takes guts? Refusing to
lower your standards to those of the crowd. It takes guts to say
you've got to live and be somebody fifty years after all the football games are over."

I started saying "it isn't" and "they aren't," and I still made ₇ first-string end—and class valedictorian—without losing my buddies' respect.

During her remarkable 44-year career, Mrs. Bessie Taylor ₈ Gwynn taught hundreds of economically deprived black youngsters—including my mother, my brother, my sisters and me. I remember her now with gratitude and affection—especially in this era when Americans are so wrought-up about a "rising tide of mediocrity" in public education and the problems of finding competent, caring teachers. Miss Bessie was an example of an informed, dedicated teacher, a blessing to children and an asset to the nation.

Born in 1895, in poverty, she grew up in Athens, Ala., where ₉ there was no public school for blacks. She attended Trinity School, a private institution for blacks run by the American Missionary Association, and in 1911 graduated from the Normal School (a "super" high school) at Fisk University in Nashville. Mrs. Gwynn, the essence of pride and privacy, never talked about her years in Athens; only in the months before her death did she reveal that she had never attended Fisk University itself because she could not afford the four-year course.

At Normal School she learned a lot about Shakespeare, but ₁₀ most of all about the profound importance of education—especially, for a people trying to move up from slavery. "What you put in your head, boy," she once said, "can never be pulled out by the Ku Klux Klan, the Congress or anybody."

Miss Bessie's bearing of dignity told anyone who met her ₁₁ that she was "educated" in the best sense of the word. There was never a discipline problem in her classes. We didn't dare mess with a woman who knew about the Battle of Hastings, the Magna Charta and the Bill of Rights—and who could also play the piano.

This frail-looking woman could make sense of Shakespeare, ₁₂ Milton, Voltaire, and bring to life Booker T. Washington and W. E. B. DuBois. Believing that it was important to know who the officials were that spent taxpayers' money and made public policy, she made us memorize the names of everyone on the Supreme Court and in the President's Cabinet. It could be embarrassing to be unprepared when Miss Bessie said, "Get up and tell the class who Frances Perkins is and what you think about her."

Miss Bessie knew that my family, like so many others during   13
the Depression, couldn't afford to subscribe to a newspaper.
She knew we didn't even own a radio. Still, she prodded me to
"look out for your future and find some way to keep up with
what's going on in the world." So I became a delivery boy for
the Chattanooga *Times*. I rarely made a dollar a week, but I got
to read a newspaper every day.

Miss Bessie noticed things that had nothing to do with   14
schoolwork, but were vital to a youngster's development. Once
a few classmates made fun of my frayed, hand-me-down overcoat, calling me "Strings." As I was leaving school, Miss Bessie
patted me on the back of that old overcoat and said, "Carl,
never fret about what you *don't* have. Just make the most of
what you *do* have—a brain."

Among the things that I did not have was electricity in the lit-   15
tle frame house that my father had built for $400 with his
World War I bonus. But because of her inspiration, I spent
many hours squinting beside a kerosene lamp reading Shakespeare and Thoreau, Samuel Pepys and William Cullen Bryant.

No one in my family had ever graduated from high school, so   16
there was no tradition of commitment to learning for me to
lean on. Like millions of youngsters in today's ghettos and barrios, I needed the push and stimulation of a teacher who truly
cared. Miss Bessie gave plenty of both, as she immersed me in a
wonderful world of similes, metaphors and even onomato-
poeia. She led me to believe that I could write sonnets as well
as Shakespeare, or iambic-pentameter verse to put Alexander
Pope to shame.

In those days the McMinnville school system was rigidly   17
"Jim Crow," and poor black children had to struggle to put
anything in their heads. Our high school was only slightly
larger than the once-typical little red schoolhouse, and its library was outrageously inadequate—so small, I like to say,
that if two students were in it and one wanted to turn a page,
the other one had to step outside.

Negroes, as we were called then, were not allowed in the   18
town library, except to mop floors or dust tables. But through
one of those secret Old South arrangements between whites of
conscience and blacks of stature, Miss Bessie kept getting
books smuggled out of the white library. That is how she intro-

duced me to the Brontës, Byron, Coleridge, Keats and Tenny-
son. "If you don't read, you can't write, and if you can't write,
you might as well stop dreaming," Miss Bessie once told me.
So I read whatever Miss Bessie told me to, and tried to re-   19
member the things she insisted that I store away. Forty-five
years later, I can still recite her "truths to live by," such as
Henry Wadsworth Longfellow's lines from "The Ladder of St.
Augustine":

> The heights by great men reached and kept
> Were not attained by sudden flight.
> But they, while their companions slept,
> Were toiling upward in the night.

Years later, her inspiration, prodding, anger, cajoling and al-   20
most osmotic infusion of learning finally led to that lovely day
when Miss Bessie dropped me a note saying, "I'm so proud to
read your column in the Nashville *Tennessean*."
Miss Bessie was a spry 80 when I went back to McMinnville   21
and visited her in a senior citizens' apartment building. Pointing out proudly that her building was racially integrated, she
reached for two glasses and a pint of bourbon. I was momentar-
ily shocked, because it would have been scandalous in the
1930s and '40s for word to get out that a teacher drank, and nobody had ever raised a rumor that Miss Bessie did.
I felt a new sense of equality as she lifted her glass to mine.   22
Then she revealed a softness and compassion that I had never
known as a student.
"I've never forgotten that examination day," she said, "when   23
Buster Martin held up seven fingers, obviously asking you for
help with question number seven, 'Name a common carrier.' I
can still picture you looking at your exam paper and humming
a few bars of 'Chattanooga Choo Choo.' I was so tickled, I
couldn't punish either of you."
Miss Bessie was telling me, with bourbon-laced grace, that I   24
never fooled her for a moment.
When Miss Bessie died in 1980, at age 85, hundreds of her   25
former students mourned. They knew the measure of a great
teacher: love and motivation. Her wisdom and influence had
rippled out across generations.

Some of her students who might normally have been doomed   26
to poverty went on to become doctors, dentists and college professors. Many, guided by Miss Bessie's example, became
public-school teachers.

"The memory of Miss Bessie and how she conducted her   27
classroom did more for me than anything I learned in college,"
recalls Gladys Wood of Knoxville, Tenn., a highly respected English teacher who spent 43 years in the state's school system.
"So many times, when I faced a difficult classroom problem, I
asked myself, *How would Miss Bessie deal with this?* And I'd remember that she would handle it with laughter and love."

No child can get all the necessary support at home, and mil-   28
lions of poor children get *no* support at all. This is what makes
a wise, educated, warm-hearted teacher like Miss Bessie so vital to the minds, hearts and souls of this country's children.

Questions for Study and Discussion

1. Throughout the essay Rowan offers details of Miss Bessie's
   physical appearance. What specific details does he give, and
   in what context does he give them? Did Miss Bessie's physical characteristics match the quality of her character? Explain.

2. How would you sum up the character of Miss Bessie? Make
   a list of the key words that Rowan uses that you feel best
   describe her.

3. At what point in the essay does Rowan give us the details
   of Miss Bessie's background? Why do you suppose he
   delays giving us this important information? (Glossary:
   Beginnings/Endings)

4. How does dialogue serve Rowan's purposes? (Glossary:
   Dialogue)

5. Does Miss Bessie's drinking influence your opinion of her?
   Explain. Why do you think Rowan included this part of her
   behavior in his essay?

Vocabulary

Refer to your dictionary to define the following words as they are used in this selection. Then use each word in a sentence of your own.

civics (1)   cajoling (20)
barrios (16)   osmotic (20)
conscience (18)   measure (25)

Suggested Writing Assignments

1. Think of all the teachers you have had, and write a description of the one that has had the greatest influence on you. Remember to give some consideration to the balance you want to achieve between physical attributes and personality traits.

2. In paragraph 18 Rowan writes the following: " 'If you don't read, you can't write, and if you can't write, you might as well stop dreaming,' Miss Bessie once told me." Write an essay in which you explore this theme which, in essence, is also the theme of *Models for Writers*.

MY FRIEND, ALBERT EINSTEIN

Banesh Hoffmann

A mathematician, Banesh Hoffmann has served on the faculties of the University of Rochester, the Institute for Advanced Study at Princeton University, and Queens College. Hoffmann is the author of The Strange Story of the Quantum *(1947) and* The Tyranny of Testing *(1962) and co-author with Albert Einstein of an article on the theory of relativity. In the following selection, Hoffmann describes the kind of man he found Einstein to be.*

He was one of the greatest scientists the world has ever known, yet if I had to convey the essence of Albert Einstein in a single word, I would choose *simplicity*. Perhaps an anecdote will help. Once, caught in a downpour, he took off his hat and held it under his coat. Asked why, he explained, with admirable logic, that the rain would damage the hat, but his hair would be none the worse for its wetting. This knack for going instinctively to the heart of a matter was the secret of his major scientific discoveries—this and his extraordinary feeling for beauty.

I first met Albert Einstein in 1935, at the famous Institute for Advanced Study in Princeton, N.J. He had been among the first to be invited to the Institute, and was offered *carte blanche* as to salary. To the director's dismay, Einstein asked for an impossible sum: it was far too *small*. The director had to plead with him to accept a larger salary.

I was in awe of Einstein, and hesitated before approaching him about some ideas I had been working on. When I finally knocked on his door, a gentle voice said, "Come"—with a rising inflection that made the single word both a welcome and a question. I entered his office and found him seated at a table, calculating and smoking his pipe. Dressed in ill-fitting clothes, his hair characteristically awry, he smiled a warm welcome. His utter naturalness at once set me at ease.

As I began to explain my ideas, he asked me to write the equations on the blackboard so he could see how they developed. Then came the staggering—and altogether endearing—request: "Please go slowly. I do not understand things quickly." This from Einstein! He said it gently, and I laughed. From then on, all vestiges of fear were gone.

Einstein was born in 1879 in the German city of Ulm. He had been no infant prodigy; indeed, he was so late in learning to speak that his parents feared he was a dullard. In school, though his teachers saw no special talent in him, the signs were already there. He taught himself calculus, for example, and his teachers seemed a little afraid of him because he asked questions they could not answer. At the age of 16, he asked himself whether a light wave would seem stationary if one ran abreast of it. From that innocent question would arise, ten years later, his theory of relativity.

Einstein failed his entrance examinations at the Swiss Federal Polytechnic School, in Zurich, but was admitted a year later. There he went beyond his regular work to study the masterworks of physics on his own. Rejected when he applied for academic positions, he ultimately found work, in 1902, as a patent examiner in Berne, and there in 1905 his genius burst into fabulous flower.

Among the extraordinary things he produced in that memorable year were his theory of relativity, with its famous offshoot, $E=mc^2$ (energy equals mass times the speed of light squared), and his quantum theory of light. These two theories were not only revolutionary, but seemingly contradictory: the former was intimately linked to the theory that light consists of waves, while the latter said it consists somehow of particles. Yet this unknown young man boldly proposed both at once— and he was right in both cases, though how he could have been is far too complex a story to tell here.

Collaborating with Einstein was an unforgettable experience. In 1937, the Polish physicist Leopold Infeld and I asked if we could work with him. He was pleased with the proposal, since he had an idea about gravitation waiting to be worked out in detail. Thus we got to know not merely the man and the friend, but also the professional.

The intensity and depth of his concentration were fantastic.   9
When battling a recalcitrant problem, he worried it as an animal worries its prey. Often, when we found ourselves up against a seemingly insuperable difficulty, he would stand up, put his pipe on the table, and say in his quaint English, "I will a little tink" (he could not pronounce "th"). Then he would pace up and down, twirling a lock of his long, graying hair around his forefinger.

A dreamy, faraway and yet inward look would come over his   10
face. There was no appearance of concentration, no furrowing of the brow—only a placid inner communion. The minutes would pass, and then suddenly Einstein would stop pacing as his face relaxed into a gentle smile. He had found the solution to the problem. Sometimes it was so simple that Infeld and I could have kicked ourselves for not having thought of it. But the magic had been performed invisibly in the depths of Einstein's mind, by a process we could not fathom.

Although Einstein felt no need for religious ritual and be-   11
longed to no formal religious group, he was the most deeply religious man I have known. He once said to me, "Ideas come from God," and one could hear the capital "G" in the reverence with which he pronounced the word. On the marble fireplace in the mathematics building at Princeton University is carved, in the original German, what one might call his scientific credo: "God is subtle, but he is not malicious." By this Einstein meant that scientists could expect to find their task difficult, but not hopeless: the Universe was a Universe of law, and God was not confusing us with deliberate paradoxes and contradictions.

Einstein was an accomplished amateur musician. We used to   12
play duets, he on the violin, I at the piano. One day he surprised me by saying Mozart was the greatest composer of all. Beethoven "created" his music, but the music of Mozart was of such purity and beauty one felt he had merely "found" it—that it had always existed as part of the inner beauty of the Universe, waiting to be revealed.

It was this very Mozartean simplicity that most character-   13
ized Einstein's methods. His 1905 theory of relativity, for example, was built on just two simple assumptions. One is the so-

called principle of relativity, which means, roughly speaking, that we cannot tell whether we are at rest or moving smoothly. The other assumption is that the speed of light is the same no matter what the speed of the object that produces it. You can see how reasonable this is if you think of agitating a stick in a lake to create waves. Whether you wiggle the stick from a stationary pier, or from a rushing speedboat, the waves, once generated, are on their own, and their speed has nothing to do with that of the stick.

Each of these assumptions, by itself, was so plausible as to seem primitively obvious. But together they were in such violent conflict that a lesser man would have dropped one or the other and fled in panic. Einstein daringly kept both—and by so doing he revolutionized physics. For he demonstrated they could, after all, exist peacefully side by side, provided we gave up cherished beliefs about the nature of time. 14

Science is like a house of cards, with concepts like time and space at the lowest level. Tampering with time brought most of the house tumbling down, and it was this that made Einstein's work so important—and controversial. At a conference in Princeton in honor of his 70th birthday, one of the speakers, a Nobel Prize-winner, tried to convey the magical quality of Einstein's achievement. Words failed him, and with a shrug of helplessness he pointed to his wristwatch, and said in tones of awed amazement, "It all came from this." His very ineloquence made this the most eloquent tribute I have heard to Einstein's genius. 15

We think of Einstein as one concerned only with the deepest aspects of science. But he saw scientific principles in everyday things to which most of us would give barely a second thought. He once asked me if I had ever wondered why a man's feet will sink into either dry or completely submerged sand, while sand that is merely damp provides a firm surface. When I could not answer, he offered a simple explanation. 16

It depends, he pointed out, on *surface tension*, the elastic-skin effect of a liquid surface. This is what holds a drop together, or causes two small raindrops on a windowpane to pull into one big drop the moment their surfaces touch. 17

When sand is damp, Einstein explained, there are tiny amounts of water between grains. The surface tensions of these 18 tiny amounts of water pull all the grains together, and friction then makes them hard to budge. When the sand is dry, there is obviously no water between grains. If the sand is fully immersed, there is water between grains, but no water *surface* to pull them together.

This is not as important as relativity; yet there is no telling what seeming trifle will lead an Einstein to a major discovery. And the puzzle of the sand does give us an inkling of the power and elegance of his mind. 19

Einstein's work, performed quietly with pencil and paper, seemed remote from the turmoil of everyday life. But his ideas were so revolutionary they caused violent controversy and irrational anger. Indeed, in order to be able to award him a belated Nobel Prize, the selection committee had to avoid mentioning relativity, and pretend the prize was awarded primarily for his work on the quantum theory. 20

Political events upset the serenity of his life even more. When the Nazis came to power in Germany, his theories were officially declared false because they had been formulated by a Jew. His property was confiscated, and it is said a price was put on his head. 21

When scientists in the United States, fearful that the Nazis might develop an atomic bomb, sought to alert American authorities to the danger, they were scarcely heeded. In desperation, they drafted a letter which Einstein signed and sent directly to President Roosevelt. It was this act that led to the fateful decision to go all-out on the production of an atomic bomb—an endeavor in which Einstein took no active part. When he heard of the agony and destruction that his $E = mc^2$ had wrought, he was dismayed beyond measure, and from then on there was a look of ineffable sadness in his eyes. 22

There was something elusively whimsical about Einstein. It is illustrated by my favorite anecdote about him. In his first year in Princeton, on Christmas Eve, so the story goes, some children sang carols outside his house. Having finished, they knocked on his door and explained they were collecting money to buy Christmas presents. Einstein listened, then said, "Wait a moment." He put on his scarf and overcoat, and took his violin from its case. Then, joining the children as they went from door 23 to door, he accompanied their singing of "Silent Night" on his violin.

How shall I sum up what it meant to have known Einstein 24 and his works? Like the Nobel Prize-winner who pointed helplessly at his watch, I can find no adequate words. It was akin to the revelation of great art that lets one see what was formerly hidden. And when, for example, I walk on the sand of a lonely beach, I am reminded of his ceaseless search for cosmic simplicity—and the scene takes on a deeper, sadder beauty.

Questions for Study and Discussion

1. Hoffmann feels that the word *simplicity* captures the essence of Albert Einstein. What character traits does Hoffmann describe in order to substantiate this impression of the man?

2. Make a list of the details of Einstein's physical features. From these details, can you tell what Einstein looked like?

3. Hoffmann uses a number of anecdotes to develop his description of Einstein. In what ways are such anecdotes preferable to mere statements regarding Einstein's character? Refer to several examples to illustrate your opinion.

4. Why do you suppose Hoffmann begins his essay where he does instead of the sentence "Einstein was born in 1879 in the German city of Ulm"? (Glossary: *Beginnings/Endings*)

Vocabulary

Refer to your dictionary to define the following words as they are used in this selection. Then use each word in a sentence of your own.

anecdote (1)	fathom (10)
awry (3)	credo (11)
vestiges (4)	trifle (19)
prodigy (5)	ineffable (22)
recalcitrant (9)	

Suggested Writing Assignments

1. Write a descriptive essay on a person you know well, perhaps a friend or a relative. Before writing, be sure that you establish a purpose for your description. Remember that your reader will not know that person; therefore, try to show what makes your subject different from other people.

2. In his essay Hoffmann reveals something of himself—his beliefs, his tastes, his intelligence, his values. Write an essay in which you argue that every writer, to a lesser or greater degree, reveals something of himself or herself in writing about any subject. Choose whatever examples you wish to make your point. You might, however, decide to use Carl Rowan and his essay on Miss Bessie as your primary example. Finally, you might wish to emphasize the significance of the self-revealing qualities of writing.

13

PROCESS ANALYSIS

When you give directions for getting to your house, tell how to make ice cream, or explain how a president is elected, you are using *process analysis.*

Process analysis usually arranges a series of events in order and relates them to one another, as narration and cause and effect do, but it has different emphases. Whereas narration tells mainly *what* happens and cause and effect focuses on *why* it happens, process analysis tries to explain—in detail—*how* it happens.

There are two types of process analysis: directional and informational. The *directional* type provides instructions on how to do something. These instructions can be as brief as the directions printed on a label for making instant coffee or as complex as the directions in a manual for building a home computer. The purpose of directional process analysis is simple: to give the reader directions to follow that lead to the desired results.

Consider the directions for constructing an Astro Tube, a cylindrical airfoil made out of a sheet of heavy writing paper, on p. 252.

The *informational* type of process analysis, on the other hand, tells how something works, how something is made, or how something occurred. You would use informational process analysis if you wanted to explain how the human heart functions, how an atomic bomb works, how hailstones are formed, how you selected the college you are attending, or how the polio vaccine was developed. Rather than giving specific directions, informational process analysis explains and informs.

Clarity is crucial for successful process analysis. The most effective way to explain a process is to divide it into steps and to present those steps in a clear (usually chronological) sequence. Transitional words and phrases such as *first, next,* and *in conclusion* help to connect steps to one another. Naturally,

251

you must be sure that no step is omitted or out of order. Also, you may sometimes have to explain *why* a certain step is necessary, especially if it is not obvious. With intricate, abstract, or particularly difficult steps, you might use analogy or comparison to clarify the steps for your reader.

Start with an 8.5-inch by 11-inch sheet of heavy writing paper. (Never use newspaper in making paper models because it isn't strongly bonded and can't hold a crease.) Follow these numbered steps, corresponding to the illustrations.

1. With the long side of the sheet toward you, fold up one third of the paper.

2. Fold the doubled section in half.

3. Fold the section in half once more and crease well.

4. Unfold preceding crease.

5. Curve the ends together to form a tube, as shown in the illustration.

6. Insert the right end inside the left end between the single outer layer and the doubled layers. Overlap the ends about an inch and a half. (This makes a tube for right-handers, to be used with an underhand throw. For an overhand tube, or an underhand version to be thrown by a lefty, reverse the directions, and insert the left end inside the right end at this step.)

7. Hold the tube at the seam with one hand, where shown by the dot in the illustration, and turn the rim inward along the crease made in step 3. Start turning in at the seam and roll the rim under, moving around the circumference in a circular manner. Then round out the rim.

8. Fold the fin to the left, as shown, then raise it so that it's perpendicular to the tube. Be careful not to tear the paper at the front.

9. Hold the tube from above, near the rim. Hold it between the thumb and fingers.

The rim end should be forward, with the fin on the bottom. Throw the tube underhanded, with a motion like throwing a bowling ball, letting it spin off the fingers as it is released. The tube will float through the air, spinning as it goes. Indoor flights of 30 feet or more are easy. With practice you can achieve remarkable accuracy.

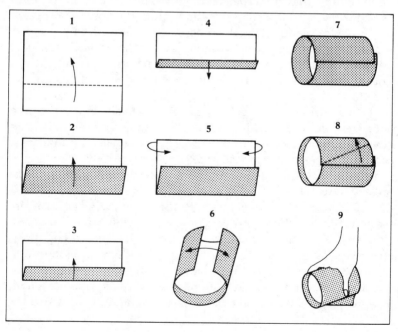

How to Build a Fire in a Fireplace

Bernard Gladstone

Bernard Gladstone is a free-lance writer who specializes in do-it-yourself building and home maintenance. As home improvement editor of The New York Times *for over ten years, he has written useful articles about common household problems, new home products, and the use of new and old tools. In the following selection from his book* The New York Times Complete Manual of Home Repair *(1980), Gladstone gives directions for building a fire in a fireplace.*

Though "experts" differ as to the best technique to follow when building a fire, one generally accepted method consists of first laying a generous amount of crumpled newspaper on the hearth between the andirons. Kindling wood is then spread generously over this layer of newspaper and one of the thickest logs is placed across the back of the andirons. This should be as close to the back of the fireplace as possible, but not quite touching it. A second log is then placed an inch or so in front of this, and a few additional sticks of kindling are laid across these two. A third log is then placed on top to form a sort of pyramid with air space between all logs so that flames can lick freely up between them.   1

A mistake frequently made is in building the fire too far forward so that the rear wall of the fireplace does not get properly heated. A heated back wall helps increase the draft and tends to suck smoke and flames rearward with less chance of sparks or smoke spurting out into the room.   2

Another common mistake often made by the inexperienced fire-tender is to try to build a fire with only one or two logs, instead of using at least three. A single log is difficult to ignite properly, and even two logs do not provide an efficient bed with adequate fuel-burning capacity.   3

Use of too many logs, on the other hand, is also a common 4
fault and can prove hazardous. Building too big a fire can create more smoke and draft than the chimney can safely handle,
increasing the possibility of sparks or smoke being thrown out
into the room. For best results, the homeowner should start
with three medium-size logs as described above, then add additional logs as needed if the fire is to be kept burning.

Questions for Study and Discussion

1. What type of process analysis is used in this essay, directional or informational? Why is this type of process analysis especially appropriate to the author's purpose?
2. Make a list of the steps Gladstone describes for building a
fire in a fireplace.
3. What is the purpose of paragraphs 2, 3, and 4 in this process
analysis?
4. Identify the transitional words that Gladstone uses in paragraph 1 to indicate the sequence of steps involved in making
a fire. (Glossary: *Transitions*)

Vocabulary

Refer to your dictionary to define the following words as they
are used in this selection. Then use each word in a sentence of
your own.

hearth (1)   kindling (1)
andirons (1)

Suggested Writing Assignments

1. Most do-it-yourself jobs require that you follow a set process in order to achieve the best results. Write a process
essay in which you provide directions for doing one of the
following household activities:

prune shrubbery
apply driveway sealer

    paint a room
    clean windows
    do laundry
    care for a lawn
    wash a car
    bake bread or chocolate chip cookies
    change a flat tire
    give a home permanent

2. Write an essay in which you give directions or advice for finding a summer job or part-time employment during the school year. In what ways is looking for such jobs different from looking for permanent positions?

HOW TO SURVIVE A HOTEL FIRE

R. H. Kauffman

*R. H. Kauffman, born in Portland, Oregon, in
1941, is a captain in the Los Angeles Fire Department. He is best known, however, as the author
of a booklet entitled* Caution: Hotels Could Be
Hazardous to Your Health, *which has over 44
million copies in print. As you read the following
selection, an excerpt from his booklet, notice
how clearly Kauffman has presented the steps
you should follow and those you should avoid if
you are caught in a hotel fire.*

As a firefighter, I have seen many people die in hotel fires. 1
Most could have saved themselves had they been prepared. There are *over 10,000 hotel fires per year* in the United
States. In 1979, the latest year for which figures are available,
there were 11,500 such fires, resulting in 140 deaths and 1225
injuries.

Contrary to what you have seen in the movies, fire is not 2
likely to chase you down and burn you to death. It's the by-
products of fire—smoke and panic—that are almost always the
causes of death.

For example, a man wakes up at 2:30 A.M. to the smell of 3
smoke. He pulls on his pants and runs into the hallway—to be
greeted by heavy smoke. He has no idea where the exit is, so he
runs first to the right. No exit. Where is it? Panic sets in. He's
coughing and gagging now; his eyes hurt. He can't see his way
back to his room. His chest hurts; he needs oxygen desperately.
He runs in the other direction, completely disoriented. At 2:50
A.M. we find him . . . dead of smoke inhalation.

Remember, the presence of smoke doesn't necessarily mean 4
that the hotel will burn down. Air-conditioning and air-
exchange systems will sometimes pick up smoke from one
room and carry it to other rooms or floors.

Smoke, because it is warmer than air, will start accumulat- 5
ing at the ceiling and work its way down. The fresh air you

256

should breathe is near the floor. What's more, smoke is extremely irritating to the eyes. Your eyes will take only so much irritation, then they will close and you won't be able to open them.

Your other enemy, panic—a contagious, overpowering terror—can make you do things that could kill you. The man in the foregoing example would not have died if he had known what to do. Had he found out beforehand where the exit was—four doors down on the left—he could have gotten down on his hands and knees close to the floor, where the air is fresher. Then, even if he couldn't keep his eyes open, he could have felt the wall as he crawled, counting doors. 6

Here are my rules for surviving hotel fires: 7

Know where the exits are. As soon as you drop your luggage in your room, turn around and go back into the hallway to check for an exit. If two share a room, both should locate the exit. Open the exit door. Are there stairs or another door beyond? As you return to your room, count the doors you pass. Is there anything in the hallway that would be in your way—an ice machine, maybe? This procedure takes very little time and, to be effective, it must become a habit. 8

Become familiar with your room. See if your bathroom has an exhaust fan. In an emergency you can turn it on to help remove smoke. Check the window. If it opens, look outside. Do you see any ledges? How high up are you? 9

Leave the hotel at the first sign of smoke. If something awakens you during the night, investigate it before you go back to sleep. In a hotel fire near Los Angeles airport, one of the guests was awakened by people yelling but went back to bed thinking it was a party. He nearly died in bed. 10

Always take your key. Don't lock yourself out of your room. You may find conditions elsewhere unbearable. Get in the habit of putting the key in the same place. The night stand, close to the bed, is an excellent spot. 11

Stay on your hands and knees. If you do wake up to smoke, grab your key from the night stand, roll off the bed and crawl toward the door. Even if you could tolerate the smoke when standing, don't. Save your eyes and lungs for as long as possible. Five feet up, the air may already be full of carbon monoxide. If the door isn't hot, open it slowly and check the hallway. 12

Should you decide to leave, close the door behind you. Most 13 doors take hours to burn. They are excellent fire shields, so close every one you go through.

Make your way to the exit. Stay against the wall closest to the 14
exit, counting doors as you pass.

Don't use the elevator. Elevator shafts extend through all 15
floors of a building, and easily fill with smoke and carbon monoxide. Smoke, heat, and fire do odd things to elevator controls.
Several years ago a group of firemen used an elevator in re-
sponding to a fire on a 20th floor. They pushed No. 18, but the
elevator shot past the 18th floor and opened on the 20th—to an
inferno that killed the firemen.

If you can't go down, go up. When you reach the exit stairwell 16
and begin to descend, hang on to the handrail as you go. People
may be running and they could knock you down.

Sometimes smoke gets into the stairwell. If it's a tall build- 17
ing, the smoke may not rise very high before it cools and becomes heavy, or "stacked." You could enter the stairwell on the
23rd floor and find it clear, then as you descend, encounter
smoke. Do not try to run through it; people die that way. Turn
around and walk up.

When you reach the roof, prop open the door. (This is the 18
only time to leave a door open.) Any smoke in the stairwell can
now vent itself. Find the windward side of the building (the side
that the wind is blowing *from*) and wait until the firefighters
reach you. Don't panic if you can't get out onto the roof because
the door is locked. Many people have survived by staying put in
the stairwell until the firefighters arrived. Again, don't try to
run through the smoke.

Look before you leap. If you're on the ground floor, of course, 19
just open the window and climb out. From the next floor you
might make it with only a sprained ankle, but you must jump
out far enough to clear the building. Many people hit window-
sills and ledges on the way down, and cartwheel to the ground.
If you're any higher than the third floor, chances are you won't
survive the fall. You would probably be better off staying inside, and fighting the fire.

If you can't leave your room, fight the fire. If your door is too 20
hot to open or the hallway is completely filled with smoke,
don't panic. First, open the window to help vent any smoke in
your room. (Don't break the window; if there is smoke outside,
you may need to close it.)

If your phone is still working, call the fire department. (Do not assume it has been notified. Incredibly enough, some hotels will not call the fire department until they verify whether there is really a fire and try to put it out themselves.) 21

Flip on the bathroom fan. Fill the tub with water. Wet some sheets or towels, and stuff them into the cracks around your door to keep out smoke. Fill your ice bucket or wastebasket with water from the bathtub and douse the door and walls to keep them cool. If possible, put your mattress up against the door and secure it with the dresser. Keep everything wet. A wet towel tied around your nose and mouth can be an effective filter of smoke particles. Swing a wet towel around the room; it will help clear the smoke. If there is fire outside the window, remove the drapes, move away as much combustible material as you can, and throw water around the window. Use your common sense, and keep fighting until help arrives. 22

Questions for Study and Discussion

1. What are the two by-products of fire that Kauffman says are most often the cause of death?

2. What is the relationship between paragraph 2 and paragraphs 3–6?

3. At what point in the essay does Kauffman begin to give directions or use directional process? Can any steps in this process be reordered? What would be the effect of any suggested changes?

4. What is Kauffman's tone in this essay? How, specifically, has he established his tone? Is the tone appropriate for his material? Explain. (Glossary: *Tone*)

Vocabulary

Refer to your dictionary to define the following words as they are used in this selection. Then use each word in a sentence of your own.

disoriented (3)	inferno (15)
unbearable (11)	incredibly (21)
carbon monoxide (12)	

Suggested Writing Assignments

1. Knowing what to do and what not to do in a potentially dangerous situation can be lifesaving information. Frequently such information is process oriented. Write an essay in which you explain the process to follow if you observe one of the following situations:

   a heart attack

   a drowning

   an automobile accident

   a house fire

   a choking episode

   a farm machinery accident

   a mugging

   an accidental poisoning

2. In order to give another person directions about how to do something, you yourself need a thorough understanding of the process. Analyze one of the following activities by listing materials you would need and the steps you would follow in completing it:

   studying for an exam

   determining miles per gallon for an automobile

   getting from where your writing class meets to where you
       normally have lunch

   preparing for a week-long camping trip

   writing an essay

   buying a used car

   beginning an exercise program

Now write an essay in which you give directions for successfully performing the task.

HOW THE BODY RESPONDS TO STRESS

Robert L. Veninga and James P. Spradley

*Robert L. Veninga, born in 1941 in Milwaukee,
Wisconsin, is professor of health education at
the University of Minnesota. Coauthor James P.
Spradley, born in 1933 in Baker, Oregon, was De-
Witt Wallace Professor of Anthropology at Ma-
calester College, St. Paul, Minnesota, at the time
of his death in 1982. Together Veninga and
Spradley wrote* The Work/Stress Connection:
How to Cope with Job Burnout, *from which the
following selection was taken. As you read, pay
special attention to the four processes in the human body's response to stress.*

One of the most remarkable discoveries of modern science   1
is that human beings have a general response to all forms
of stress. Your body switches on the stress response whether
you suffer from third-degree burns or receive an eviction notice. The pattern follows a similar course and it has a single
goal: *to bring relief from the stress.* The stress response has
evolved over millions of years and gives us, along with other
mammals, a definite survival advantage.

During an earlier period of human existence, many daily   2
stresses posed a direct threat to survival. One's life depended
on an appropriate response executed with the greatest speed.
The vast majority of strategies used by the earliest humans for
dealing with threat depended on *muscular activity.* Like our
primate ancestors before them, early hunter-gatherers depended exclusively on immediately available natural resources. They roamed about within a specific territory, chasing
game animals, moving with wet and dry seasons to sources of
food and water, fighting off predators, and protecting themselves against severe weather. The ability to use physical
strength, speed, agility, and stamina was an important selective advantage. Through the long process of evolution, human

beings came to share with other mammals this generalized stress response. It seeks to bring relief from stress *by means of vigorous muscular activity.*

Dr. Walter Cannon, an American physiologist, initiated the study of this stress response during the 1920s. Scientific research since then has supported the general outline of his theory, although we now know far more about the biochemical nature of this response pattern. Dr. Cannon called it the "fight-or-flight" response. He argued that it played an important role in survival. "If fear always paralyzed it would result in danger of destruction," he wrote. "But fear and aggressive feeling, as anticipatory responses to critical situations, make ready for action and thereby they have had great survival values."

The stress response actually involves four closely related processes. It begins when your body undergoes a rapid *mobilization*, a preparation for muscular activity. Consider the stress response of Ron Dorsey, a patrolman on the graveyard shift of a large city police department. On a cold night in January 1979, shortly after three o'clock, a call came over his radio. "Burglary in process at Sixteen hundred Grand Avenue." "That's mine!" he shouted to himself and at the same instant felt his heart begin to pound. Tense with fear, even though he had been on the force for six years, Ron sped to the address, an apartment building a few blocks away. As he skidded into the snow-covered alley behind the building, he saw a dark figure rush out the back door, dash across the alley, and run between two houses. "Stop or I'll shoot!" Ron yelled as he jumped from his car and started after the person. "I had no intention of shooting," Ron admitted later, "but I wanted to scare that guy into stopping." And stop he did, hands high in the air. In a moment Ron had him pushed up against the side of the house, frisked him for weapons, and then walked him back to his patrol car where he radioed for help. Less than four minutes had passed since Ron had first heard the call.

Like all of us under stress, Ron was keenly aware of his feelings, thoughts, and actions—what we call the behavioral aspects of the stress response. However, hidden from view, a host of endocrine and automatic-nervous-system functions had also taken place. A dramatic biochemical change had coursed through Ron's body. Hundreds of scientific studies have confirmed that the human body, anticipating the necessity of fight or flight, begins to mobilize almost instantly. And this happens whether you're chasing a criminal, denied a promotion, working under unrealistic deadlines, or ground down by an autocratic boss. . . .

It all starts in the hypothalamus, a tiny bundle of nerve cells   6
at the center of the brain. Messages race from that command post and spread the alarm throughout the nervous system. Muscles tense. Blood vessels constrict. The tiny capillaries under the skin shut down altogether. The pituitary gland sends out two hormones that move through the bloodstream to stimulate the thyroid and adrenal glands. Thyroid hormones increase the energy supply you need to cope physically with the stress. The adrenals send some thirty additional hormones to nearly every organ in the body. This automatic stress response causes the pulse rate to shoot up; blood pressure soars. The stomach and intestines stop all the busy activity of digestion. Hearing and smell become more acute. Hundreds of other physical changes occur without us even knowing it.

The second process, one which starts immediately, is a sharp   7
increase in energy consumption. The alarm reaction that puts the entire body in a state of readiness burns up considerable energy. That's why, in the aftermath of an auto accident or other sudden stress, even people who suffered no injuries will feel completely drained. It also helps to explain why people can sometimes perform feats of exceptional strength in stress situations. Ron Dorsey's body began to burn up energy at a rapid rate the moment he received the call. His feelings of lassitude from several hours of dull routine disappeared with the changes in body chemistry.

Dr. Hans Selye, the pioneering endocrinologist and father of   8
stress research, believes that under stress we use up a special fuel source, what he calls "adaptation energy." This energy provides power to mobilize the body; it also appears to give us strength for the fight-or-flight reaction. The way our body consumes this adaptation energy is critical to our understanding of job burnout. After four decades of stress research, Dr. Selye concluded that each human being has a finite amount of adaptation energy available at the time we encounter stress. After

burning up part or all that is available, we need an opportunity to replenish the available supply by removing ourselves from the stress. When stress continues for a prolonged period, the available adaptation energy burns up and exhaustion sets in.

The third process that makes up part of our stress response 9 is the *muscular action involved in fight or flight.* All the mobilization and energy consumption has this end in sight: taking some vigorous action to eliminate or escape the stress. The fight-or-flight adaptation worked well for early human beings, and it works well for us today, but only in certain situations. Taking quick and skillful action enabled Ron Dorsey to apprehend a suspected criminal. His stress response could hardly have been designed to carry out its job more efficiently. If you've ever had to jump out of the way of an oncoming automobile, swerve or hit your brakes to avoid a collision, stay up all night with a sick child, or rush someone to a hospital emergency room, you know the value of the fight-or-flight response.

Finally, the stress response ends with the *return of the body* 10 *to a state of equilibrium.* Within a few hours Ron was back on the street, cruising in his patrol car. He felt tired but relaxed. That morning Ron went to bed early and slept for nine hours. He woke up feeling great. His adaptation energy had been renewed. Once again he was prepared to respond calmly to emergency situations. During the next few days, his body would continue to build up the supply of adaptation energy. Fortunately, nature has designed these relatively stable periods, including sleep, to restore our adaptation-energy level, leaving us prepared for future stress.

Questions for Study and Discussion

1. What type of process analysis is this essay, directional or informational? How do you know?
2. What is the authors' purpose in this essay? (Glossary: *Purpose*)
3. How have the authors organized their essay? (Glossary: *Organization*) You may find it helpful to outline the essay in answering this question. How have the authors indicated

that they are beginning a new section of the essay? Explain. (Glossary: *Transitions*)

4. Do you find that the essay has helped you understand the way you feel in certain situations? Explain.

5. How have the authors made what is a rather technical subject more understandable for the average reader? Explain. (Glossary: *Illustration*)

Vocabulary

Refer to your dictionary to define the following words as they are used in this selection. Then use each word in a sentence of your own.

primate (2)   capillaries (6)
agility (2)   lassitude (7)
biochemical (3)   burnout (8)

Suggested Writing Assignments

1. Using Veninga and Spradley's essay as a model, write an essay in which you explain a recurring natural process—for example, the flowering of a tree, the formation of tides, a particular human reflex action, the spawning of salmon, or the formation of a hurricane.

2. Write an informational process analysis explaining how one of the following works:

   a checking account
   cell division
   an automobile engine
   the human eye
   economic supply and demand
   a microwave oven

14

DEFINITION

To communicate precisely what you want to say, you will frequently need to *define* key words. Your reader needs to know just what you mean when you use unfamiliar words, such as *accouterment*, or words that are open to various interpretations, such as *liberal*, or words that, while generally familiar, are used in a particular sense. Failure to define important terms, or to define them accurately, confuses readers and hampers communication.

There are three basic ways to define a word; each is useful in its own way. The first method is to give a *synonym*, a word that has nearly the same meaning as the word you wish to define: *face* for *countenance, nervousness* for *anxiety.* No two words ever have *exactly* the same meaning, but you can, nevertheless, pair an unfamiliar word with a familiar one and thereby clarify your meaning.

Another way to define a word quickly, often within a single sentence, is to give a *formal definition*; that is, to place the term to be defined in a general class and then to distinguish it from other members of that class by describing its particular characteristics. For example:

WORD	CLASS	CHARACTERISTICS
A *watch*	is *a mechanical device*	*for telling time* and is usually *carried* or *worn.*
Semantics	is an *area of linguistics*	*concerned with the study of the meaning of words.*

The third method is known as *extended definition*. While some extended definitions require only a single paragraph, more often than not you will need several paragraphs or even an entire essay to define a new or difficult term or to rescue a controversial word from misconceptions and associations that may obscure its meaning.

One controversial term that illustrates the need for extended definition is *obscene*. What is obscene? Books that are banned in one school system are considered perfectly acceptable in another. Movies that are shown in one town cannot be shown in a neighboring town. Clearly, the meaning of *obscene* has been clouded by contrasting personal opinions as well as by conflicting social norms. Therefore, if you use the term *obscene* (and especially if you tackle the issue of obscenity itself), you must be careful to define clearly and thoroughly what you mean by that term—that is, you have to give an extended definition. There are a number of methods you might use to develop such a definition. You could define *obscene* by explaining what it does not mean. You could also make your meaning clear by narrating an experience, by comparing and contrasting it to related terms such as *pornographic* or *exotic*, by citing specific examples, or by classifying the various types of obscenity.

A JERK

Sydney J. Harris

Since 1944 Sydney J. Harris has written for the Chicago Daily News *the syndicated column "Strictly Personal," in which he has considered virtually every aspect of contemporary American life. In the following essay from his book* Last Things First *(1961), Harris defines the term* jerk *by differentiating it from other similar slang terms.*

I don't know whether history repeats itself, but biography certainly does. The other day, Michael came in and asked me what a "jerk" was—the same question Carolyn put to me a dozen years ago.

At that time, I fluffed her off with some inane answer, such as "A jerk isn't a very nice person," but both of us knew it was an unsatisfactory reply. When she went to bed, I began trying to work up a suitable definition.

It is a marvelously apt word, of course. Until it was coined, not more than 25 years ago, there was really no single word in English to describe the kind of person who is a jerk—"boob" and "simp" were too old hat, and besides they really didn't fit, for they could be lovable, and a jerk never is.

Thinking it over, I decided that a jerk is basically a person without insight. He is not necessarily a fool or a dope, because some extremely clever persons can be jerks. In fact, it has little to do with intelligence as we commonly think of it; it is, rather, a kind of subtle but persuasive aroma emanating from the inner part of the personality.

I know a college president who can be described only as a jerk. He is not an unintelligent man, nor unlearned, nor even unschooled in the social amenities. Yet he is a jerk *cum laude*, because of a fatal flaw in his nature—he is totally incapable of looking into the mirror of his soul and shuddering at what he sees there.

Jerks don't want to admit their faults.

268

A jerk, then, is a man (or woman) who is utterly unable to see himself as he appears to others. He has no grace, he is tactless without meaning to be, he is a bore even to his best friends, he is an egotist without charm. All of us are egotists to some extent, but most of us—unlike the jerk—are perfectly and horribly aware of it when we make asses of ourselves. The jerk never knows. 6

Questions for Study and Discussion

1. What, according to Harris, is a jerk?
2. Jerks, boobs, simps, fools, and dopes are all in the same class. How does Harris differentiate a jerk from a boob or a simp on the one hand, and a fool or a dope on the other?
3. In paragraph 5 Harris presents the example of the college president. How does this example support his definition?

Vocabulary

Refer to your dictionary to define the following words as they are used in this selection. Then use each word in a sentence of your own.

inane (2)   emanating (4)
apt (3)   amenities (5)
coined (3)   tactless (6)

Suggested Writing Assignments

1. Write one or two paragraphs in which you give your own definition of *jerk* or another slang term of your choice.
2. Every generation develops its own slang, which generally enlivens the speech and writing of those who use it. Ironically, however, no generation can arrive at a consensus definition of even its most popular slang terms—for example, *nimrod, air-head, flag*. Select a slang term that you use frequently, and write an essay in which you define the term. Read your definition aloud in class. Do the other members of your class agree with your definition?

WHAT IS FREEDOM?

Jerald M. Jellison and John H. Harvey

Jerald M. Jellison, professor of psychology at the University of Southern California, specializes in theories of human social behavior. John H. Harvey, professor of social psychology at Vanderbilt University, recently coedited a collection of studies in social behavior. In this selection from Psychology Today, *Jellison and Harvey use an illustrative story to help them define* freedom, *an important but elusive concept.*

The pipe under your kitchen sink springs a leak and you call in a plumber. A few days later you get a bill for $40. At the bottom is a note saying that if you don't pay within 30 days, there'll be a 10 percent service charge of $4. You feel trapped, with no desirable alternative. You pay $40 now or $44 later. 1

Now make two small changes in the script. The plumber sends you a bill for $44, but the note says that if you pay within 30 days you'll get a special $4 discount. Now you feel pretty good. You have two alternatives, one of which will save you $4. 2

In fact, your choices are the same in both cases—pay $40 now or $44 later—but your feelings about them are different. This illustrates a subject we've been studying for several years: What makes people feel free and why does feeling free make them happy? One factor we've studied is that individuals feel freer when they can choose between positive alternatives (delaying payment or saving $4) rather than between negative ones (paying immediately or paying $4 more). 3

Choosing between negative alternatives often seems like no choice at all. Take the case of a woman trying to decide whether to stay married to her inconsiderate, incompetent husband, or get a divorce. She doesn't want to stay with him, but she feels divorce is a sign of failure and will stigmatize her socially. Or think of the decision faced by many young men a few 4

270

years ago, when they were forced to choose between leaving their country and family or being sent to Vietnam.

When we face decisions involving only alternatives we see as negatives, we feel so little freedom that we twist and turn searching for another choice with some positive characteristics. 5

Freedom is a popular word. Individuals talk about how they feel free with one person and not with another, or how their bosses encourage or discourage freedom on the job. We hear about civil wars and revolutions being fought for greater freedom, with both sides righteously making the claim. The feeling of freedom is so important that people say they're ready to die for it, and supposedly have. 6

Still, most people have trouble coming up with a precise definition of freedom. They give answers describing specific situations—"Freedom means doing what I want to do, not what the Government wants me to do," or "Freedom means not having my mother tell me when to come home from a party"—rather than a general definition covering many situations. The idea they seem to be expressing is that freedom is associated with making decisions, and that other people sometimes limit the number of alternatives from which they can select. 7

Questions for Study and Discussion

1. What general definition of *freedom* do Jellison and Harvey present? Where in the essay is that definition given?

2. When, according to Jellison and Harvey, do individuals feel free?

3. Explain how Jellison and Harvey use examples to develop their definition of *freedom*. (You may find it helpful to outline the essay paragraph by paragraph.)

4. Paragraph 5 is pivotal in this essay. Explain why it is so important. (It might be helpful to consider the essay without paragraph 5.)

5. The authors' tone in this essay is informal, almost conversa-

tional. Cite examples of diction and sentence structure to show how they establish and maintain this tone. (Glossary: *Tone*)

Vocabulary

Refer to your dictionary to define the following words as they are used in this selection. Then use each word in a sentence of your own.

script (2)   stigmatize (4)
incompetent (4)   righteously (6)

Suggested Writing Assignments

1. Write an essay of your own defining freedom. You may wish to consult the work of others, writers and philosophers, for example, or draw exclusively on personal observations and experiences.
2. Write a short essay in which you define one of the following abstract terms. Begin your essay with an illustrative example as Jellison and Harvey do in their essay.

   charm
   friendship
   hatred
   leadership
   trust
   commitment
   religion
   love

THE BARRIO

Robert Ramirez

*Robert Ramirez has worked as a cameraman, re-
porter, anchorman, and producer for the news
team at KGBT-TV in Edinburg, Texas. Presently,
he works in the Latin American division of the
Northern Trust Bank in Chicago. In the following essay, Ramirez discusses those distinctive
characteristics that, when taken together, define
the district called the* barrio.

The train, its metal wheels squealing as they spin along the   1
silvery tracks, rolls slower now. Through the gaps between the cars blinks a streetlamp, and this pulsing light on a
barrio streetcorner beats slower, like a weary heartbeat, until
the train shudders to a halt, the light goes out, and the barrio is
deep asleep.

Throughout Aztlán (the Nahuatl term meaning "land to the   2
north"), trains grumble along the edges of a sleeping people.
From Lower California, through the blistering Southwest,
down the Rio Grande to the muddy Gulf, the darkness and mystery of dreams engulf communities fenced off by railroads, ca-
nals, and expressways. Paradoxical communities, isolated
from the rest of the town by concrete columned monuments of
progress, and yet stranded in the past. They are surrounded by
change. It eludes their reach, in their own backyards, and the
people, unable and unwilling to see the future, or even touch
the present, perpetuate the past.

Leaning from the expressway or jolting across the tracks,   3
one enters a different physical world permeated by a different
attitude. The physical dimensions are impressive. It is a large
section of town which extends for fifteen blocks north and
south along the tracks, and then advances eastward, thinning
into nothingness beyond the city limits. Within the invisible
(yet sensible) walls of the barrio, are many, many people living

273

in too few houses. The homes, however, are much more numerous than on the outside.

Members of the barrio describe the entire area as their home. 4 It is a home, but it is more than this. The barrio is a refuge from the harshness and the coldness of the Anglo world. It is a forced refuge. The leprous people are isolated from the rest of the community and contained in their section of town. The stoical pariahs of the barrio accept their fate, and from the angry seeds of rejection grow the flowers of closeness between outcasts, not the thorns of bitterness and the mad desire to flee. There is no want to escape, for the feeling of the barrio is known only to its inhabitants, and the material needs of life can also be found here.

The *tortillería* [tortilla factory] fires up its machinery three 5 times a day, producing steaming, round, flat slices of barrio bread. In the winter, the warmth of the tortilla factory is a wool *sarape* [blanket] in the chilly morning hours, but in the summer, it unbearably toasts every noontime customer.

The *panadería* [bakery] sends its sweet messenger aroma 6 down the dimly lit street, announcing the arrival of fresh, hot sugary *pan dulce* [sweet rolls].

The small corner grocery serves the meal-to-meal needs of 7 customers, and the owner, a part of the neighborhood, willingly gives credit to people unable to pay cash for foodstuffs.

The barbershop is a living room with hydraulic chairs, radio, 8 and television, where old friends meet and speak of life as their salted hair falls aimlessly about them.

The pool hall is a junior level country club where 'chucos 9 [young men], strangers in their own land, get together to shoot pool and rap, while veterans, unaware of the cracking, popping balls on the green felt, complacently play dominoes beneath rudely hung *Playboy* foldouts.

The *cantina* [canteen or snackbar] is the night spot of the bar- 10 rio. It is the country club and the den where the rites of puberty are enacted. Here the young become men. It is in the taverns that a young dude shows his *machismo* through the quantity of beer he can hold, the stories of *rucas* [women] he has had, and his willingness and ability to defend his image against hardened and scarred old lions.

No, there is no frantic wish to flee. It would be absurd to 11
leave the familiar and nervously step into the strange and cold
Anglo community when the needs of the Chicano can be met in
the barrio.

The barrio is closeness. From the family living unit, familial 12
relationships stretch out to immediate neighbors, down the
block, around the corner, and to all parts of the barrio. The
feeling of family, a rare and treasurable sentiment, pervades
and accounts for the inability of the people to leave. The barrio
is this attitude manifested on the countenances of the people,
on the faces of their homes, and in the gaiety of their gardens.

The color-splashed homes arrest your eyes, arouse your curi- 13
osity, and make you wonder what life scenes are being played
out in them. The flimsy, brightly colored, wood-frame houses ignore no neon-brilliant color. Houses trimmed in orange, char-
treuse, lime-green, yellow, and mixtures of these and other
hues beckon the beholder to reflect on the peculiarity of each
home. Passing through this land is refreshing like Brubeck,*
not narcoticizing like revolting rows of similar houses, which
neither offend nor please.

In the evenings, the porches and front yards are occupied 14
with men calmly talking over the noise of children playing
baseball in the unpaved extension of the living room, while the
women cook supper or gossip with female neighbors as they
water the *jardines* [gardens]. The gardens mutely echo the ex-
pressive verses of the colorful houses. The denseness of multi-
colored plants and trees gives the house the appearance of an
oasis or a tropical island hideaway, sheltered from the rest of
the world.

Fences are common in the barrio, but they are fences and not 15
the walls of the Anglo community. On the western side of town,
the high wooden fences between houses are thick, impenetra-
ble walls, built to keep the neighbors at bay. In the barrio, the
fences may be rusty, wire contraptions or thick green shrubs.
In either case you can see through them and feel no sense of in-
trusion when you cross them.

---

*Dave Brubeck, pianist, composer, and conductor of "cool" modern jazz.

Many lower-income families of the barrio manage to main- 16
tain a comfortable standard of living through the communal
action of family members who contribute their wages to the
head of the family. Economic need creates interdependence
and closeness. Small barefooted boys sell papers on cool, dark
Sunday mornings, deny themselves pleasantries, and give their
earnings to *mamá*. The older the child, the greater the responsibility to help the head of the household provide for the rest of
the family.

There are those, too, who for a number of reasons have not 17
achieved a relative sense of financial security. Perhaps it
results from too many children too soon, but it is the homes of
these people and their situation that numbs rather than
charms. Their houses, aged and bent, oozing children, are fissures in the horn of plenty. Their wooden homes may have
brick-pattern asbestos tile on the outer walls, but the tile is not
convincing.

Unable to pay city taxes or incapable of influencing the city 18
to live up to its duty to serve all the citizens, the poorer barrio
families remain trapped in the nineteenth century and survive
as best they can. The backyards have well-worn paths to the
outhouses, which sit near the alley. Running water is considered a luxury in some parts of the barrio. Decent drainage is
usually unknown, and when it rains, the water stands for days,
an incubator of health hazards and an avoidable nuisance.
Streets, costly to pave, remain rough, rocky trails. Tires do not
last long, and the constant rattling and shaking grind away a
car's life and spread dust through screen windows.

The houses and their *jardines*, the jollity of the people in an 19
adverse world, the brightly feathered alarm clock pecking
away at supper and cautiously eyeing the children playing
nearby, produce a mystifying sensation at finding the noble
savage alive in the twentieth century. It is easy to look at the
positive qualities of life in the barrio, and look at them with a
distantly envious feeling. One wishes to experience the feelings
of the barrio and not the hardships. Remembering the illness,
the hunger, the feeling of time running out on you, the walls,
both real and imagined, reflecting on living in the past, one
finds his envy becoming more elusive, until it has vanished altogether.

Back now beyond the tracks, the train creaks and groans, the   20
cars jostle each other down the track, and as the light begins its
pulsing, the barrio, with all its meanings, greets a new dawn
with yawns and restless stretchings.

Questions for Study and Discussion

1. What is a barrio? How does it serve the needs of its inhabitants?
2. Ramirez relies heavily on description in his definition of the
   word *barrio*, describing the physical appearance of the barrio as well as the feelings that the inhabitants have for the
   barrio. Briefly summarize the important physical details
   and emotional associations he provides, and comment on
   their contribution to his definition.
3. In defining *barrio* Ramirez also uses the words *home, refuge, family, closeness,* and *neighborhood*. What connotations do these words have? Do they add a particular element to the definition? Are they essential to Ramirez's
   definition, or just helpful? (Glossary: *Connotation/
   Denotation*)
4. Identify three similes or metaphors that Ramirez uses in
   this essay. In what ways is each appropriate and effective?
   (Glossary: *Figures of Speech*)
5. Explain Ramirez's use of the imagery of walls and fences to
   develop his theme of cultural isolation. What might this
   imagery be symbolic of? (Glossary: *Symbol*)
6. For what audience is Ramirez writing? What evidence do
   you find in the essay to support your answer? (Glossary:
   Audience)

Vocabulary

Refer to your dictionary to define the following words as they
are used in this selection. Then use each word in a sentence of
your own.

paradoxical (2)   aroma (6)
eludes (2)   countenances (12)
permeated (3)   fissures (17)
stoical (4)   elusive (19)

Suggested Writing Assignments

1. Many experiences in our lives are much more meaningful than their formal definitions would ever indicate. The connotations of language can be rich. Think for a moment what it means to have a home; to be a leader; what politics, fear, bravery, and anxiety are really all about; and what constitutes a family or a Thanksgiving dinner. Select one of these topics or choose one of your own, and write an extended definition that gets at the essence of your subject.

2. Write a brief essay in which you draw upon personal experiences and observations in order to define one of the following concepts:

    honesty
    conflict of interest
    integrity
    sincerity
    perseverance
    commitment

15

DIVISION AND CLASSIFICATION

To divide is to separate a class of things or ideas into categories, whereas to classify is to group separate things or ideas into those categories. The two processes can operate separately but often go together. Division and classification can be a useful organizational strategy in writing. Here, for example, is a passage about levers in which the writer first discusses generally how levers work and then, in the second paragraph, uses division to establish three categories of levers and classification to group individual levers into those categories:

> Every lever has one fixed point called the "fulcrum" and is acted upon by two forces—the "effort" (exertion of hand muscles) and the "weight" (object's resistance). Levers work according to a simple formula: the effort (how hard you push or pull) multiplied by its distance from the fulcrum (effort arm) equals the weight multiplied by its distance from the fulcrum (weight arm). Thus two pounds of effort exerted at a distance of four feet from the fulcrum will raise eight pounds located one foot from the fulcrum.
> There are three types of levers, conventionally called "first kind," "second kind," and "third kind." Levers of the first kind have the fulcrum located between the effort and the weight. Examples are a pump handle, an oar, a crowbar, a weighing balance, a pair of scissors, and a pair of pliers. Levers of the second kind have the weight in the middle and magnify the effort. Examples are the handcar crank and doors. Levers of the third kind, such as a power shovel or a baseball batter's forearm, have the effort in the middle and always magnify the distance.

In writing, division and classification are affected directly by the writer's practical purpose. That purpose—what the writer wants to explain or prove—determines the class of things or ideas being divided and classified. For instance, a writer might divide television programs according to their audiences—adults, families, or children—and then classify individual programs into each of these categories in order to show how much emphasis the television stations place on reaching each audience. A different purpose would require different categories. A writer concerned about the prevalence of violence in television programming would first divide television programs into those which include fights and murders, and those which do not, and would then classify a large sample of programs into those categories. Other writers with different purposes might divide television programs differently—by the day and time of broadcast, for example, or by the number of women featured in prominent roles—and then classify individual programs accordingly.

The following guidelines can help you in using division and classification in your writing:

1. *Identify a clear purpose, and be sure that your principle of division is appropriate to that purpose.* To determine the makeup of a student body, for example, you might consider the following principles of division: college or program, major, class level, sex. It would not be helpful to divide students on the basis of their toothpaste unless you had a purpose and thus a reason for doing so.

2. *Divide your subject into categories that are mutually exclusive.* An item can belong to only one category. For example, it would be unsatisfactory to divide students as men, women, and athletes.

3. *Make your division and classification complete.* Your categories should account for all items in a subject class. In dividing students on the basis of geographic origin, for example, it would be inappropriate to consider only home states, for such a division would not account for foreign students. Then, for your classification to be complete, every student must be placed in one of the established categories.

4. *Be sure to state clearly the conclusion that your division and classification lead you to draw.* For example, a study of the student body might lead to the conclusion that 45 percent of the male athletes with athletic scholarships come from west of the Mississippi.

CHILDREN'S INSULTS

Peter Farb

From his undergraduate years at Vanderbilt University on, Peter Farb (1929–1980) had an intense interest in language and its role in human behavior. Farb was a consultant to the Smithsonian Institution, a curator of the Riverside Museum in New York City, and a visiting lecturer in English at Yale. In this essay, taken from Word Play: What Happens When People Talk *(1973), Farb classifies the names children use to insult one another.*

The insults spoken by adults are usually more subtle than the simple name-calling used by children, but children's insults make obvious some of the verbal strategies people carry into adult life. Most parents engage in wishful thinking when they regard name-calling as good-natured fun which their children will soon grow out of. Name-calling is not good-natured and children do not grow out of it; as adults they merely become more expert in its use. Nor is it true that "sticks and stones may break my bones, but names will never hurt me." Names can hurt very much because children seek out the victim's true weakness, then jab exactly where the skin is thinnest. Name-calling can have major impact on a child's feelings about his identity, and it can sometimes be devastating to his psychological development.

Almost all examples of name-calling by children fall into four categories:

1. Names based on physical peculiarities, such as deformities, use of eyeglasses, racial characteristics, and so forth. A child may be called *Flattop* because he was born with a misshapen skull—or, for obvious reasons, *Fat Lips, Gimpy, Four Eyes, Peanuts, Fatso, Kinky,* and so on.
2. Names based on a pun or parody of the child's own name.

Children with last names like Fitts, McClure, and Farb usually find them converted to *Shits, Manure,* and *Fart.*

3. Names based on social relationships. Examples are *Baby* used by a sibling rival or *Chicken Shit* for someone whose courage is questioned by his social group.

4. Names based on mental traits—such as *Clunkhead, Dummy, Jerk,* and *Smartass.*

These four categories were listed in order of decreasing offensiveness to the victims. Children regard names based on physical peculiarities as the most cutting, whereas names based on mental traits are, surprisingly, not usually regarded as very offensive. Most children are very vulnerable to names that play upon the child's rightful name—no doubt because one's name is a precious possession, the mark of a unique identity and one's masculinity or femininity. Those American Indian tribes that had the custom of never revealing true names undoubtedly avoided considerable psychological damage.

Questions for Study and Discussion

1. What is Farb's contention in this selection? Where is it revealed? For what reason does he divide and classify children's insults? (Glossary: *Thesis*)

2. Why does Farb feel that name-calling should not be dismissed lightly?

3. Farb states that children "regard names based on physical peculiarities as the most cutting." Why do suppose this might be true?

4. What principle of division does Farb use to establish his four categories of children's insults? What are the categories, and how does he order them? Be prepared to cite examples from the text.

5. List some insults that you remember from your own childhood or adolescence. Classify the insults according to Farb's system. Do any items on your list not fit into one of his categories? What new categories can you establish?

Vocabulary

Refer to your dictionary to define the following words as they are used in this selection. Then use each word in a sentence of your own.

subtle (1)	sibling (2)
peculiarities (2)	vulnerable (2)
deformities (2)	unique (2)

Suggested Writing Assignments

1. Using the following sentence as your thesis, write an essay that divides and classifies the students at your college or university:

   There are (number) types of students at (institution).

   Be sure to follow the guidelines for division and classification that appear on page 280.

2. Consider the following classes of items and determine at least two principles of division that can be used for each class. Then write a paragraph or two in which you classify one of the groups of items according to a single principle of division. For example, in discussing crime one could use the seriousness of the crime or the type of crime as principles of division. If the seriousness of the crime were used, this might yield two categories: felonies, or major crimes; and misdemeanors, or minor crimes. If the type of crime were used, this would yield categories such as burglary, murder, assault, larceny, and embezzlement.

   professional sports
   social sciences
   movies
   roommates
   cars
   slang used by college students

THE WAYS OF MEETING OPPRESSION

Martin Luther King, Jr.

*Martin Luther King, Jr. (1929–1968) was the lead-
ing spokesman for the rights of American blacks
during the 1950s and 1960s before he was assassi-
nated in 1968. He established the Southern
Christian Leadership Conference, organized
many civil rights demonstrations, and opposed
the Viet Nam War and the draft. In 1964 he was
awarded the Nobel Prize for Peace. In the following essay, taken from his book* Stride Toward
Freedom *(1958), King classifies the three ways
oppressed people throughout history have reacted to their oppressors.*

Oppressed people deal with their oppression in three char- 1
acteristic ways. One way is acquiescence: the oppressed
resign themselves to their doom. They tacitly adjust themselves
to oppression, and thereby become conditioned to it. In every
movement toward freedom some of the oppressed prefer to remain oppressed. Almost 2800 years ago Moses set out to lead
the children of Israel from the slavery of Egypt to the freedom
of the promised land. He soon discovered that slaves do not always welcome their deliverers. They become accustomed to being slaves. They would rather bear those ills they have, as
Shakespeare pointed out, than flee to others that they know not
of. They prefer the "fleshpots of Egypt" to the ordeals of eman-
cipation.

There is such a thing as the freedom of exhaustion. Some 2
people are so worn down by the yoke of oppression that they
give up. A few years ago in the slum areas of Atlanta, a Negro
guitarist used to sing almost daily: "Been down so long that
down don't bother me." This is the type of negative freedom
and resignation that often engulfs the life of the oppressed.

But this is not the way out. To accept passively an unjust sys- 3
tem is to cooperate with that system; thereby the oppressed be-

come as evil as the oppressor. Noncooperation with evil is as much a moral obligation as is cooperation with good. The oppressed must never allow the conscience of the oppressor to slumber. Religion reminds every man that he is his brother's keeper. To accept injustice or segregation passively is to say to the oppressor that his actions are morally right. It is a way of allowing his conscience to fall asleep. At this moment the oppressed fails to be his brother's keeper. So acquiescence— while often the easier way—is not the moral way. It is the way of the coward. The Negro cannot win the respect of his oppressor by acquiescing; he merely increases the oppressor's arrogance and contempt. Acquiescence is interpreted as proof of the Negro's inferiority. The Negro cannot win the respect of the white people of the South or the peoples of the world if he is willing to sell the future of his children for his personal and immediate comfort and safety.

A second way that oppressed people sometimes deal with oppression is to resort to physical violence and corroding hatred. Violence often brings about momentary results. Nations have frequently won their independence in battle. But in spite of temporary victories, violence never brings permanent peace. It solves no social problem; it merely creates new and more complicated ones.

Violence as a way of achieving racial justice is both impractical and immoral. It is impractical because it is a descending spiral ending in destruction for all. The old law of an eye for an eye leaves everybody blind. It is immoral because it seeks to humiliate the opponent rather than win his understanding; it seeks to annihilate rather than to convert. Violence is immoral because it thrives on hatred rather than love. It destroys community and makes brotherhood impossible. It leaves society in monologue rather than dialogue. Violence ends by defeating itself. It creates bitterness in the survivors and brutality in the destroyers. A voice echoes through time saying to every potential Peter, "Put up your sword."* History is cluttered with the wreckage of nations that failed to follow this command.

---

*The apostle Peter had drawn his sword to defend Christ from arrest. The voice was Christ's, who surrendered himself for trial and crucifixion (John 18:11).

If the American Negro and other victims of oppression suc-   6
cumb to the temptation of using violence in the struggle for
freedom, future generations will be the recipients of a desolate
night of bitterness, and our chief legacy to them will be an end-
less reign of meaningless chaos. Violence is not the way.

The third way open to oppressed people in their quest for   7
freedom is the way of nonviolent resistance. Like the synthesis
in Hegelian philosophy, the principle of nonviolent resistance
seeks to reconcile the truths of two opposites—the acquiescence and violence—while avoiding the extremes and immoral-
ities of both. The nonviolent resister agrees with the person
who acquiesces that one should not be physically aggressive
toward his opponent; but he balances the equation by agreeing
with the person of violence that evil must be resisted. He
avoids the nonresistance of the former and the violent resistance of the latter. With nonviolent resistance, no individual or
group need submit to any wrong, nor need anyone resort to violence in order to right a wrong.

It seems to me that this is the method that must guide the   8
actions of the Negro in the present crisis in race relations.
Through nonviolent resistance the Negro will be able to rise to
the noble height of opposing the unjust system while loving the
perpetrators of the system. The Negro must work passionately
and unrelentingly for full stature as a citizen, but he must not
use inferior methods to gain it. He must never come to terms
with falsehood, malice, hate, or destruction.

Nonviolent resistance makes it possible for the Negro to re-   9
main in the South and struggle for his rights. The Negro's problem will not be solved by running away. He cannot listen to the
glib suggestion of those who would urge him to migrate en
masse to other sections of the country. By grasping his great
opportunity in the South he can make a lasting contribution to
the moral strength of the nation and set a sublime example of
courage for generations yet unborn.

By nonviolent resistance, the Negro can also enlist all men of   10
good will in his struggle for equality. The problem is not a
purely racial one, with Negroes set against whites. In the end,
it is not a struggle between people at all, but a tension between
justice and injustice. Nonviolent resistance is not aimed
against oppressors but against oppression. Under its banner
consciences, not racial groups, are enlisted.

Questions for Study and Discussion

1. What are the disadvantages that King sees in meeting oppression with acquiescence or with violence? *I + gets worse*
2. What is King's purpose in writing this essay? How does classifying the three types of resistance to oppression serve this purpose? (Glossary: *Purpose*) *Just say people that violence don't solve anything. It makes it clear to understand and apply it to society.*
3. What principle of division does King use in this essay? *Racial*
4. Why do you suppose that King discusses acquiescence, violence, and nonviolent resistance in that order? (Glossary: *Organization*) *Because is you meet, become enemies, then return as friends*
5. King states that he favors nonviolent resistance over the other two ways of meeting oppression. Look closely at the words he uses to describe nonviolent resistance and those he uses to describe acquiescence and violence. How does his choice of words contribute to his argument? Show examples. (Glossary: *Connotation/Denotation*)

Vocabulary

Refer to your dictionary to define the following words as they are used in this selection. Then use each word in a sentence of your own.

acquiescence (1)   desolate (6)
tacitly (1)   synthesis (7)
corroding (4)   sublime (9)
annihilate (5)

Suggested Writing Assignments

1. Write an essay about a problem of some sort in which you use division and classification to discuss various possible solutions. You might discuss something personal such as the problems of giving up smoking or something that concerns everyone such as the difficulties of coping with limited supplies of oil and gasoline or other natural resources. Whatever your topic, use an appropriate principle of division to establish categories that suit the purpose of your discussion.

2. Consider any one of the following topics for an essay of classification:

movies
college courses
spectators
lifestyles
country music
newspapers
pets
grandparents

FRIENDS, GOOD FRIENDS
—AND SUCH GOOD FRIENDS

Judith Viorst

*Judith Viorst has written several volumes of
light verse as well as many articles that have appeared in popular magazines. The following essay appeared in her regular column in* Redbook.
*In it she analyzes and classifies the various types
of friends that a person can have. As you read the
essay, assess its validity by trying to place your
friends in Viorst's categories.*

Women are friends, I once would have said, when they totally love and support and trust each other, and bare to
each other the secrets of their souls, and run—no questions
asked—to help each other, and tell harsh truths to each other
(no, you can't wear that dress unless you lose ten pounds first)
when harsh truths must be told.

Women are friends, I once would have said, when they share
the same affection for Ingmar Bergman, plus train rides, cats,
warm rain, charades, Camus, and hate with equal ardor New-
ark and Brussels sprouts and Lawrence Welk and camping.

In other words, I once would have said that a friend is a
friend all the way, but now I believe that's a narrow point of
view. For the friendships I have and the friendships I see are
conducted at many levels of intensity, serve many different
functions, meet different needs and range from those as all-the-
way as the friendship of the soul sisters mentioned above to
that of the most nonchalant and casual playmates.

Consider these varieties of friendship:

1. Convenience friends. These are women with whom, if our
paths weren't crossing all the time, we'd have no particular
reason to be friends: a next-door neighbor, a woman in our car
pool, the mother of one of our children's closest friends or
maybe some mommy with whom we serve juice and cookies
each week at the Glenwood Co-op Nursery.

Convenience friends are convenient indeed. They'll lend us   6
their cups and silverware for a party. They'll drive our kids to
soccer when we're sick. They'll take us to pick up our car when
we need a lift to the garage. They'll even take our cats when we
go on vacation. As we will for them.

But we don't, with convenience friends, ever come too close   7
or tell too much; we maintain our public face and emotional
distance. "Which means," says Elaine, "that I'll talk about being overweight but not about being depressed. Which means
I'll admit being mad but not blind with rage. Which means that
I might say that we're pinched this month but never that I'm
worried sick over money."

But which doesn't mean that there isn't sufficient value to be   8
found in these friendships of mutual aid, in convenience
friends.

2. Special-interest friends. These friendships aren't inti-   9
mate, and they needn't involve kids or silverware or cats. Their
value lies in some interest jointly shared. And so we may have
an office friend or a yoga friend or a tennis friend or a friend
from the Women's Democratic Club.

"I've got one woman friend," says Joyce, "who likes, as I do,   10
to take psychology courses. Which makes it nice for me—and
nice for her. It's fun to go with someone you know and it's fun
to discuss what you've learned, driving back from the classes."
And for the most part, she says, that's all they discuss.

"I'd say that what we're doing is *doing* together, not being to-   11
gether," Suzanne says of her Tuesday-doubles friends. "It's
mainly a tennis relationship, but we play together well. And I
guess we all need to have a couple of playmates."

I agree.   12

My playmate is a shopping friend, a woman of marvelous   13
taste, a woman who knows exactly *where* to buy *what*, and furthermore is a woman who always knows beyond a doubt what
one ought to be buying. I don't have the time to keep up with
what's new in eyeshadow, hemlines and shoes and whether the
smock look is in or finished already. But since (oh, shame!) I
care a lot about eyeshadow, hemlines and shoes, and since I
don't *want* to wear smocks if the smock look is finished, I'm
very glad to have a shopping friend.

3. Historical friends. We all have a friend who knew us when   14

. . . maybe way back in Miss Meltzer's second grade, when our family lived in that three-room flat in Brooklyn, when our dad was out of work for seven months, when our brother Allie got in that fight where they had to call the police, when our sister married the endodontist from Yonkers and when, the morning after we lost our virginity, she was the first, the only, friend we told.

The years have gone by and we've gone separate ways and we've little in common now, but we're still an intimate part of each other's past. And so whenever we go to Detroit we always go to visit this friend of our girlhood. Who knows how we looked before our teeth were straightened. Who knows how we talked before our voice got un-Brooklyned. Who knows what we ate before we learned about artichokes. And who, by her presence, puts us in touch with an earlier part of ourself, a part of ourself it's important never to lose. 15

"What this friend means to me and what I mean to her," says Grace, "is having a sister without sibling rivalry. We know the texture of each other's lives. She remembers my grandmother's cabbage soup. I remember the way her uncle played the piano. There's simply no other friend who remembers those things." 16

4. Crossroads friends. Like historical friends, our crossroads friends are important for *what was*—for the friendship we shared at a crucial, now past, time of life. A time, perhaps, when we roomed in college together; or worked as eager young singles in the Big City together; or went together, as my friend Elizabeth and I did, through pregnancy, birth and that scary first year of new motherhood. 17

Crossroads friends forge powerful links, links strong enough to endure with not much more contact than once-a-year letters at Christmas. And out of respect for those crossroads years, for those dramas and dreams we once shared, we will always be friends. 18

5. Cross-generational friends. Historical friends and crossroads friends seem to maintain a special kind of intimacy—dormant but always ready to be revived—and though we may rarely meet, whenever we do connect, it's personal and intense. Another kind of intimacy exists in the friendships that form across generations in what one woman calls her daughter-mother and her mother-daughter relationships. 19

Evelyn's friend is her mother's age—"but I share so much more than I ever could with my mother"—a woman she talks to of music, of books and of life. "What I get from her is the benefit of her experience. What she gets—and enjoys—from me is a youthful perspective. It's a pleasure for both of us."   20

I have in my own life a precious friend, a woman of 65 who has lived very hard, who is wise, who listens well; who has been where I am and can help me understand it; and who represents not only an ultimate ideal mother to me but also the person I'd like to be when I grow up.   21

In our daughter role we tend to do more than our share of self-revelation; in our mother role we tend to receive what's revealed. It's another kind of pleasure—playing wise mother to a questing younger person. It's another very lovely kind of friendship.   22

6. Part-of-a-couple friends. Some of the women we call our friends we never see alone—we see them as part of a couple at couples' parties. And though we share interests in many things and respect each other's views, we aren't moved to deepen the relationship. Whatever the reason, a lack of time or—and this is more likely—a lack of chemistry, our friendship remains in the context of a group. But the fact that our feeling on seeing each other is always, "I'm *so* glad she's here" and the fact that we spend half the evening talking together says that this too, in its own way, counts as a friendship.   23

(Other part-of-a-couple friends are the friends that came with the marriage, and some of these are friends we could live without. But sometimes, alas, she married our husband's best friend; and sometimes, alas, she *is* our husband's best friend. And so we find ourself dealing with her, somewhat against our will, in a spirit of what I'll call *reluctant* friendship.)   24

7. Men who are friends. I wanted to write just of women friends, but the women I've talked to won't let me—they say I must mention man-woman friendships too. For these friendships can be just as close and as dear as those that we form with women. Listen to Lucy's description of one such friendship: 25

"We've found we have things to talk about that are different from what he talks about with my husband and different from what I talk about with his wife. So sometimes we call on the   26 phone or meet for lunch. There are similar intellectual interests—we always pass on to each other the books that we love—but there's also something tender and caring too."

In a couple of crises, Lucy says, "he offered himself for talking and for helping. And when someone died in his family he wanted me there. The sexual, flirty part of our friendship is very small, but *some*—just enough to make it fun and different." She thinks—and I agree—that the sexual part, though small, is always *some*, is always there when a man and a woman are friends.

It's only in the past few years that I've made friends with men, in the sense of a friendship that's *mine*, not just part of two couples. And achieving with them the ease and the trust I've found with women friends has value indeed. Under the dryer at home last week, putting on mascara and rouge, I comfortably sat and talked with a fellow named Peter. Peter, I finally decided, could handle the shock of me minus mascara under the dryer. Because we care for each other. Because we're friends.

8. There are medium friends, and pretty good friends, and very good friends indeed, and these friendships are defined by their level of intimacy. And what we'll reveal at each of these levels of intimacy is calibrated with care. We might tell a medium friend, for example, that yesterday we had a fight with our husband. And we might tell a pretty good friend that this fight with our husband made us so mad that we slept on the couch. And we might tell a very good friend that the reason we got so mad in that fight that we slept on the couch had something to do with that girl who works in his office. But it's only to our very best friends that we're willing to tell all, to tell what's going on with that girl in his office.

The best of friends, I still believe, totally love and support and trust each other, and bare to each other the secrets of their souls, and run—no questions asked—to help each other, and tell harsh truths to each other when they must be told.

But we needn't agree about everything (only 12-year-old girl friends agree about *everything*) to tolerate each other's point of view. To accept without judgment. To give and to take without ever keeping score. And to *be* there, as I am for them and as they are for me, to comfort our sorrows, to celebrate our joys.

Questions for Study and Discussion

1. What is Viorst's purpose in this essay? Why is division and classification an appropriate strategy for her to use? (Glossary: *Purpose*) ~To show diff types friendships~ ~It shows character~

2. Into what categories does Viorst divide her friends? ~Good friends + very good friends~

3. What principles of division does Viorst use to establish her categories of friends? Where does she state these principles?

4. Discuss the ways in which Viorst makes her categories distinct and memorable. ~The names she gave to the diff friendships~

5. Viorst wrote this essay for *Redbook*, and so her audience was women between the ages of twenty-five and thirty-five. If she had been writing on the same topic for an audience of men of the same age, how might her categories have been different? How might her examples have been different? (Glossary: *Audience*) ~She would have mentioned more about men + their friendships, but not all because men are sometimes self-centered.~

Vocabulary

Refer to your dictionary to define the following words as they are used in this selection. Then use each word in a sentence of your own.

ardor (2)   forge (18)
nonchalant (3)   dormant (19)
sibling (16)   perspective (20)

Suggested Writing Assignments

1. If for any reason you dislike or disagree with Viorst's classification of friends, write a classification essay of your own on the same topic. In preparation for writing, you may wish to interview your classmates and dorm members for their ideas on the various types of friends a person can have.

2. The following (p. 295) is a basic exercise in classification. By determining the features that the figures have in common, establish the general class to which they all belong. Next, establish subclasses by determining the distinctive features

that distinguish one subclass from another. Finally, place each figure in an appropriate subclass within your classification system. You may wish to compare your classification system with those developed by other members of your class and to discuss any differences that exist.

16

COMPARISON AND CONTRAST

A *comparison* points out the ways that two or more persons, places, or things are alike. A *contrast* points out how they differ. The subjects of a comparison or contrast should be in the same class or general category; if they have nothing in common, there is no good reason for setting them side by side.

The function of any comparison or contrast is to clarify and explain. The writer's purpose may be simply to inform, or to make readers aware of similarities or differences that are interesting and significant in themselves. Or, the writer may explain something unfamiliar by comparing it with something very familiar, perhaps explaining squash by comparing it with tennis. Finally, the writer can point out the superiority of one thing by contrasting it with another—for example, showing that one product is the best by contrasting it with all its competitors.

As a writer, you have two main options for organizing a comparison or contrast: the subject-by-subject pattern or the point-by-point pattern. For a short essay comparing and contrasting the Atlanta Braves and the Los Angeles Dodgers, you would probably follow the *subject-by-subject* pattern of organization. By this pattern you first discuss the points you wish to make about one team, and then go on to discuss the corresponding points for the other team. An outline of your essay might look like this:

    I. Atlanta Braves
       A. Pitching
       B. Fielding
       C. Hitting
   II. Los Angeles Dodgers
       A. Pitching
       B. Fielding
       C. Hitting

The subject-by-subject pattern presents a unified discussion of each team by placing the emphasis on the teams and not on the three points of comparison. Since these points are relatively few, readers should easily remember what was said about the Braves' pitching when you later discuss the Dodgers' pitching and should be able to make the appropriate connections between them.

For a somewhat longer essay comparing and contrasting solar energy and wind energy, however, you should consider the *point-by-point* pattern of organization. With this pattern, your essay is organized according to the various points of comparison. Discussion alternates between solar and wind energy for each point of comparison. An outline of your essay might look like this:

I. Installation Expenses
    A. Solar
    B. Wind
	IV. Convenience
	    A. Solar
	    B. Wind

II. Efficiency
    A. Solar
    B. Wind
	V. Maintenance
	    A. Solar
	    B. Wind

III. Operating Costs
    A. Solar
    B. Wind
	VI. Safety
	    A. Solar
	    B. Wind

The point-by-point pattern allows the writer to make immediate comparisons between solar and wind energy, thus enabling readers to consider each of the similarities and differences separately.

Each organizational pattern has its advantages. In general, the subject-by-subject pattern is useful in short essays where there are few points to be considered, whereas the point-by-point pattern is preferable in long essays where there are numerous points under consideration.

A good essay of comparison and contrast tells readers something significant that they do not already know. That is, it must do more than merely point out the obvious. As a rule, therefore, writers tend to draw contrasts between things that are usually perceived as being similar or comparisons between things usually perceived as different. In fact, comparison and contrast often go together. For example, an essay about Minneapolis and St. Paul might begin by showing how much they are alike, but end with a series of contrasts revealing how much they differ. Or, a consumer magazine might report the contrasting claims made by six car manufacturers, and then go on to demonstrate that the cars all actually do much the same thing in the same way.

THAT LEAN AND HUNGRY LOOK

Suzanne Britt

Suzanne Britt makes her home in Raleigh, North Carolina, where she is a freelance writer. In 1983 she published Show & Tell, *a collection of her characteristically informal essays. The following essay first appeared in* Newsweek *and became the basis for her book,* Skinny People Are Dull and Crunchy Like Carrots *(1982), titled after a line in the essay. As you read her essay, notice the way that Britt has organized the points of her contrast of fat and thin people.*

Caesar was right. Thin people need watching. I've been watching them for most of my adult life, and I don't like what I see. When these narrow fellows spring at me, I quiver to my toes. Thin people come in all personalities, most of them menacing. You've got your "together" thin person, your mechanical thin person, your condescending thin person, your tsk-tsk thin person, your efficiency-expert thin person. All of them are dangerous.

In the first place, thin people aren't fun. They don't know how to goof off, at least in the best, fat sense of the word. They've always got to be adoing. Give them a coffee break, and they'll jog around the block. Supply them with a quiet evening at home, and they'll fix the screen door and lick S&H green stamps. They say things like "there aren't enough hours in the day." Fat people never say that. Fat people think the day is too damn long already.

Thin people make me tired. They've got speedy little metabolisms that cause them to bustle briskly. They're forever rubbing their bony hands together and eyeing new problems to "tackle." I like to surround myself with sluggish, inert, easygoing fat people, the kind who believe that if you clean it up today, it'll just get dirty again tomorrow.

Some people say the business about the jolly fat person is a myth, that all of us chubbies are neurotic, sick, sad people. I disagree. Fat people may not be chortling all day long, but they're a hell of a lot *nicer* than the wizened and shriveled. Thin people turn surly, mean, and hard at a young age because they never learn the value of a hot-fudge sundae for easing tension. Thin people don't like gooey soft things because they themselves are neither gooey nor soft. They are crunchy and dull, like carrots. They go straight to the heart of the matter while fat people let things stay all blurry and hazy and vague, the way things actually are. Thin people want to face the truth. Fat people know there is no truth. One of my thin friends is always staring at complex, unsolvable problems and saying, "The key thing is. . . ." Fat people never say that. They know there isn't any such thing as the key thing about anything.

Thin people believe in logic. Fat people see all sides. The 5 sides fat people see are rounded blobs, usually gray, always nebulous and truly not worth worrying about. But the thin person persists. "If you consume more calories than you burn," says one of my thin friends, "you will gain weight. It's that simple." Fat people always grin when they hear statements like that. They know better.

Fat people realize that life is illogical and unfair. They know 6 very well that God is not in his heaven and all is not right with the world. If God was up there, fat people could have two doughnuts and a big orange drink anytime they wanted it.

Thin people have a long list of logical things they are always 7 spouting off to me. They hold up one finger at a time as they reel off these things, so I won't lose track. They speak slowly as if to a young child. The list is long and full of holes. It contains tidbits like "get a grip on yourself," "cigarettes kill," "cholesterol clogs," "fit as a fiddle," "ducks in a row," "organize," and "sound fiscal management." Phrases like that.

They think these 2,000-point plans lead to happiness. Fat people 8 know happiness is elusive at best and even if they could get the kind thin people talk about, they wouldn't want it. Wisely, fat people see that such programs are too dull, too hard, too off the mark. They are never better than a whole cheesecake.

Fat people know all about the mystery of life. They are the 9 ones acquainted with the night, with luck, with fate, with playing it by ear. One thin person I know once suggested that we arrange all the parts of a jigsaw puzzle into groups according to size, shape, and color. He figured this would cut the time needed to complete the puzzle by at least 50 percent. I said I wouldn't do it. One, I like to muddle through. Two, what good would it do to finish early? Three, the jigsaw puzzle isn't the important thing. The important thing is the fun of four people (one thin person included) sitting around a card table, working a jigsaw puzzle. My thin friend had no use for my list. Instead of joining us, he went outside and mulched the boxwoods. The three remaining fat people finished the puzzle and made chocolate, double-fudged brownies to celebrate.

The main problem with thin people is they oppress. Their   10
good intentions, bony torsos, tight ships, neat corners, cerebral machinations, and pat solutions loom like dark clouds over the loose, comfortable, spread-out, soft world of the fat. Long after fat people have removed their coats and shoes and put their feet up on the coffee table, thin people are still sitting on the edge of the sofa, looking neat as a pin, discussing rutabagas. Fat people are heavily into fits of laughter, slapping their thighs and whooping it up, while thin people are still politely waiting for the punch line.

Thin people are downers. They like math and morality and   11
reasoned evaluation of the limitations of human beings. They have their skinny little acts together. They expound, prognose, probe, and prick.

Fat people are convivial. They will like you even if you're ir-   12
regular and have acne. They will come up with a good reason why you never wrote the great American novel. They will cry in your beer with you. They will put your name in the pot. They will let you off the hook. Fat people will gab, giggle, guffaw, gallumph, gyrate, and gossip. They are generous, giving, and gallant. They are gluttonous and goodly and great. What you want when you're down is soft and jiggly, not muscled and stable. Fat people know this. Fat people have plenty of room. Fat people will take you in.

Questions for Study and Discussion

1. Does Britt use a subject-by-subject or a point-by-point pattern of organization to contrast fat and thin people? Explain. What points of contrast does Britt discuss?

2. What is Britt's purpose in this essay? (Glossary: *Purpose*) Is she serious, partially serious, mostly humorous? Are fat and thin people really her subject?

3. Britt makes effective use of the short sentence. Identify examples of sentences with three or fewer words and explain what function they serve. (Glossary: *Effective Sentences*)

4. Britt uses many clichés in her essay. Identify at least a dozen examples. What do you suppose is her purpose in using them? (Glossary: *Cliché*)

5. It is somewhat unusual for an essayist to use alliteration (the repetition of initial consonant sounds), a technique more commonly found in poetry. Where has Britt used alliteration and why do you suppose she has used this particular technique?

Vocabulary

Refer to your dictionary to define the following words as they are used in this selection. Then use each word in a sentence of your own.

menacing (1)	nebulous (5)
adoing (2)	rutabagas (10)
metabolism (3)	prognose (11)
inert (3)	convivial (12)
chortling (4)	gallant (12)

Suggested Writing Assignments

1. Write a counter-argument in favor of thin people, using comparison and contrast and modeled on Britt's "That Lean and Hungry Look."

2. Reread paragraphs 3–6, and notice how these paragraphs are developed by contrasting the features of thin and fat people. Select two items from the following categories—people, products, events, institutions, places—and make a list of their contrasting features. Then write an essay modeled on Britt's, using the entries on your list.

BING AND ELVIS

Russell Baker

Russell Baker writes a syndicated column for
The New York Times *for which he was awarded
a Pulitzer Prize in 1979. In the following selection, which first appeared in the* Times *shortly
after Bing Crosby's death in 1977, Baker com-
pares and contrasts two of our most popular entertainers and in the process tells us something
about the generations that produced them.*

The grieving for Elvis Presley and the commercial exploita- 1
tion of his death were still not ended when we heard of
Bing Crosby's death the other day. Here is a generational puzzle. Those of an age to mourn Elvis must marvel that their el-
ders could really have cared about Bing, just as the Crosby generation a few weeks ago wondered what all the to-do was about
when Elvis died.

Each man was a mass culture hero to his generation, but it 2
tells us something of the difference between generations that
each man's admirers would be hard-pressed to understand why
the other could mean very much to his devotees.

There were similarities that ought to tell us something. Both 3
came from obscurity to national recognition while quite young
and became very rich. Both lacked formal music education and
went on to movie careers despite lack of acting skills. Both developed distinctive musical styles which were originally
scorned by critics and subsequently studied as pioneer devel-
opments in the art of popular song.

In short, each man's career followed the mythic rags-to- 4
triumph pattern in which adversity is conquered, detractors
are given their comeuppance and estates, fancy cars and world
tours become the reward of perseverance. Traditionally this
was supposed to be the history of the American business
striver, but in our era of committee capitalism it occurs most
often in the mass entertainment field, and so we look less and

less to the board room for our heroes and more and more to the microphone.

Both Crosby and Presley were creations of the microphone. It made it possible for people with frail voices not only to be heard beyond the third row but also to caress millions. Crosby was among the first to understand that the microphone made it possible to sing to multitudes by singing to a single person in a small room.

Presley cuddled his microphone like a lover. With Crosby the microphone was usually concealed, but Presley brought it out on stage, detached it from its fitting, stroked it, pressed it to his mouth. It was a surrogate for his listener, and he made love to it unashamedly.

The difference between Presley and Crosby, however, reflected generational differences which spoke of changing values in American life. Crosby's music was soothing; Presley's was disturbing. It is too easy to be glib about this, to say that Crosby was singing to, first, Depression America and, then, to wartime America, and that his audience had all the disturbance they could handle in their daily lives without buying more at the record shop and movie theater.

Crosby's fans talk about how "relaxed" he was, how "natural," how "casual and easy going." By the time Presley began causing sensations, the entire country had become relaxed, casual and easy going, and its younger people seemed to be tired of it, for Elvis's act was anything but soothing and scarcely what a parent of that placid age would have called "natural" for a young man.

Elvis was unseemly, loud, gaudy, sexual—that gyrating pelvis!—in short, disturbing. He not only disturbed parents who thought music by Crosby was soothing but also reminded their young that they were full of the turmoil of youth and an appetite for excitement. At a time when the country had a population coming of age with no memory of troubled times, Presley spoke to a yearning for disturbance.

It probably helped that Elvis's music made Mom and Dad climb the wall. In any case, people who admired Elvis never talk about how relaxed and easy going he made them feel. They are more likely to tell you he introduced them to something new and exciting.

To explain each man in terms of changes in economic and po- 11
litical life probably oversimplifies the matter. Something in the
culture was also changing. Crosby's music, for example, paid
great attention to the importance of lyrics. The "message" of
the song was as essential to the audience as the tune. The
words were usually inane and witless, but Crosby—like Sinatra
a little later—made them vital. People remembered them, sang
them. Words still had meaning.

Although many of Presley's songs were highly lyrical, in most 12
it wasn't the words that moved audiences; it was the "sound."
Rock 'n' roll, of which he was the great popularizer, was a
"sound" event. Song stopped being song and turned into
"sound," at least until the Beatles came along and solved the
problem of making words sing to the new beat.

Thus a group like the Rolling Stones, whose lyrics are often 13
elaborate, seems to the Crosby-tuned ear to be shouting only
gibberish, a sort of accompanying background noise in a
"sound" experience. The Crosby generation has trouble hearing rock because it makes the mistake of trying to understand
the words. The Presley generation has trouble with Crosby because it finds the sound unstimulating and cannot be touched
by the inanity of the words. The mutual deafness may be a measure of how far we have come from really troubled times and of
how deeply we have come to mistrust the value of words.

Questions for Study and Discussion

1. What similarities between Crosby and Presley does Russell
   Baker see? What differences does he see? Why does he consider the similarities between these two singers before considering their differences?
2. What conclusion does Baker draw from his comparison and
   contrast of the two entertainers?
3. Does Baker use a point-by-point or a subject-by-subject pattern of organization in his essay? Why is the pattern that he
   uses particularly effective for the subject matter?
4. Though the tone in Baker's essay is serious and reflective, it

remains basically informal. Identify specific words that help to establish this tone. (Glossary: *Tone*)

Vocabulary

Refer to your dictionary to define the following words as they are used in this selection. Then use each word in a sentence of your own.

mythic (4)   glib (7)
adversity (4)   placid (8)
surrogate (6)   inane (11)

Suggested Writing Assignments

1. Compare and contrast any two popular singers or singing groups. In selecting a topic you should consider (1) what your purpose will be, (2) whether you will emphasize similarities or differences, (3) what specific points you will discuss, and (4) what organizational pattern will best suit your purpose.

2. Select one of the following topics for an essay of comparison and contrast.

   two cities
   two friends
   two ways to heat a home
   two restaurants
   two actors or actresses
   two books by the same author
   two mountains

THE BRIGHT CHILD
AND THE DULL CHILD

John Holt

*A former elementary and secondary school teacher, John Holt also taught at Harvard and the University of California at Berkeley. Through his books—*How Children Fail *(1964),* What I Do on Monday *(1970),* How Children Learn *(1970), and* Escape from Childhood *(1976)—Holt has been recognized as a thoughtful critic of the philosophy and methods of American education. In the following selection Holt draws upon his many years of experience in the classroom, to sharply contrast the behavior patterns of the bright child with those of the dull child.*

Years of watching and comparing bright children and the not-bright, or less bright, have shown that they are very different kinds of people. The bright child is curious about life and reality, eager to get in touch with it, embrace it, unite himself with it. There is no wall, no barrier between him and life. The dull child is far less curious, far less interested in what goes on and what is real, more inclined to live in worlds of fantasy. The bright child likes to experiment, to try things out. He lives by the maxim that there is more than one way to skin a cat. If he can't do something one way, he'll try another. The dull child is usually afraid to try at all. It takes a good deal of urging to get him to try even once; if that try fails, he is through.

The bright child is patient. He can tolerate uncertainty and failure, and will keep trying until he gets an answer. When all his experiments fail, he can even admit to himself and others that for the time being he is not going to get an answer. This may annoy him, but he can wait. Very often, he does not want to be told how to do the problem or solve the puzzle he has struggled with, because he does not want to be cheated out of the chance to figure it out for himself in the future. Not so the dull child. He cannot stand uncertainty or failure. To him, an unanswered question is not a challenge or an opportunity, but a threat. If he can't find the answer quickly, it must be given to him, and quickly; and he must have answers for everything. Such are the children of whom a second-grade teacher once said, "But my children *like* to have questions for which there is only one answer." They did; and by a mysterious coincidence, so did she.

The bright child is willing to go ahead on the basis of incomplete understanding and information. He will take risks, sail uncharted seas, explore when the landscape is dim, the landmarks few, the light poor. To give only one example, he will often read books he does not understand in the hope that after a while enough understanding will emerge to make it worth while to go on. In this spirit some of my fifth graders tried to read *Moby Dick*. But the dull child will go ahead only when he thinks he knows exactly where he stands and exactly what is ahead of him. If he does not feel he knows exactly what an experience will be like, and if it will not be exactly like other experiences he already knows, he wants no part of it. For while the bright child feels that the universe is, on the whole, a sensible, reasonable, and trustworthy place, the dull child feels that it is senseless, unpredictable, and treacherous. He feels that he can never tell what may happen, particularly in a new situation, except that it will probably be bad.

Questions for Study and Discussion

1. List the main differences that Holt sees between the "bright child" and the "dull child."

2. Holt uses a point-by-point pattern of organization to discuss differences between the "bright child" and the "dull child." What would have been gained or lost with a subject-by-subject pattern of organization?

3. When using a point-by-point pattern of organization, the writer must take care to use transitions to guide the reader and ensure paragraph coherence. Cite examples of the vari-

ous transitional devices Holt uses in paragraph 3. (Glossary: *Transitions*)

Vocabulary

Refer to your dictionary to define the following words as they are used in this selection. Then use each word in a sentence of your own.

inclined (1)   treacherous (3)
maxim (1)

Suggested Writing Assignments

1. Using Holt's essay as a model, write an essay in which you compare and contrast any one of the following pairs:

   the athletic/nonathletic child
   the well-adjusted/maladjusted child
   the overachieving/underachieving child
   the artistic/unartistic child
   the handicapped/normal child
   the alienated/socially-active child
   the shy/aggressive child

2. Write a short essay in which you use a point-by-point pattern of organization to compare or contrast any one of the following pairs for purposes of showing that one is superior to the other:

   Back to the Future and *Gone With the Wind*
   a sociology course and a psychology course
   hot dogs and hamburgers
   poker and bridge
   Florida and California
   the Yankees and the Red Sox

FABLE FOR TOMORROW

Rachel Carson

Naturalist Rachel Carson (1907–1964) wrote The Sea Around Us *(1951),* Under the Sea Wind *(1952), and* The Edge of the Sea *(1955), sensitive investigations of marine life. But it was* Silent Spring *(1962), her study of herbicides and insecticides, that made Carson a controversial figure. Once denounced as an alarmist, she is now regarded as an early prophet of the ecology movement. In the following fable taken from* Silent Spring, *Carson uses contrast to show her readers the devastating effects of indiscriminate use of pesticides.*

There was once a town in the heart of America where all life 1 seemed to live in harmony with its surroundings. The town lay in the midst of a checkerboard of prosperous farms, with fields of grain and hillsides of orchards where, in spring, white clouds of bloom drifted above the green fields. In autumn, oak and maple and birch set up a blaze of color that flamed and flickered across a backdrop of pines. Then foxes barked in the hills and deer silently crossed the fields, half hidden in the mists of the fall mornings.

Along the roads, laurel, viburnum and alder, great ferns and 2 wildflowers delighted the traveler's eye through much of the year. Even in winter the roadsides were places of beauty, where countless birds came to feed on the berries and on the seed heads of the dried weeds rising above the snow. The countryside was, in fact, famous for the abundance and variety of its bird life, and when the flood of migrants was pouring through in spring and fall people traveled from great distances to observe them. Others came to fish the streams, which flowed clear and cold out of the hills and contained shady pools where trout lay. So it had been from the days many years ago when the first settlers raised their houses, sank their wells, and built their barns.

Then a strange blight crept over the area and everything be- 3 gan to change. Some evil spell had settled on the community: mysterious maladies swept the flocks of chickens; the cattle and sheep sickened and died. Everywhere was a shadow of death. The farmers spoke of much illness among their families. In the town the doctors had become more and more puzzled by new kinds of sickness appearing among their patients. There had been several sudden and unexplained deaths, not only among adults but even among children, who would be stricken suddenly while at play and die within a few hours.

There was a strange stillness. The birds, for example— 4 where had they gone? Many people spoke of them, puzzled and disturbed. The feeding stations in the backyards were deserted. The few birds seen anywhere were moribund; they trembled violently and could not fly. It was a spring without voices. On the mornings that had once throbbed with the dawn chorus of robins, catbirds, doves, jays, wrens, and scores of other bird voices there was now no sound; only silence lay over the fields and woods and marsh.

On the farms the hens brooded, but no chicks hatched. The 5 farmers complained that they were unable to raise any pigs— the litters were small and the young survived only a few days. The apple trees were coming into bloom but no bees droned among the blossoms, so there was no pollination and there would be no fruit.

The roadsides, once so attractive, were now lined with 6 browned and withered vegetation as though swept by fire. These, too, were silent, deserted by all living things. Even the streams were now lifeless. Anglers no longer visited them, for all the fish had died.

In the gutters under the eaves and between the shingles of 7 the roofs, a white granular powder still showed a few patches; some weeks before it had fallen like snow upon the roofs and the lawns, the fields and streams.

No witchcraft, no enemy action had silenced the rebirth of 8 new life in this stricken world. The people had done it themselves.

This town does not actually exist, but it might easily have a 9 thousand counterparts in America or elsewhere in the world. I know of no community that has experienced all the misfortunes I describe. Yet every one of these disasters has actually happened somewhere, and many real communities have already suffered a substantial number of them. A grim specter has crept upon us almost unnoticed, and this imagined tragedy may easily become a stark reality we all shall know.

Questions for Study and Discussion

1. A fable is a short narrative that makes an edifying or cautionary point. What is the point of Carson's fable?
2. How do comparison and contrast help Carson make her point?
3. Does Carson use a point-by-point or a subject-by-subject method of organization in this selection? How is the pattern of organization Carson uses appropriate for her purpose? Be prepared to cite examples from the text.

Vocabulary

Refer to your dictionary to define the following words as they are used in this selection. Then use each word in a sentence of your own.

migrants (2)   moribund (4)
blight (3)   specter (9)
maladies (3)

Suggested Writing Assignments

1. Write an essay modeled after Carson's in which you show how a particular place or area changed character for some reason (for example, as a result of herbicides, gentrification, urbanization, commercialization, strip mining, highway development, hurricane, etc.). Describe the area before and after the change, and be sure to give your reaction to the change either implicitly or explicitly.

2. Using one of the following "before and after" situations, write a short essay of comparison and/or contrast.

before and after a diet
before and after urban renewal
before and after Christmas
before and after beginning college
before and after a final exam

17

CAUSE AND EFFECT

Every time you try to answer a question that asks *why*, you engage in the process of *causal analysis*—you attempt to determine a *cause* or series of causes for a particular *effect*. When you try to answer a question that asks *what if*, you attempt to determine what effect will result from a particular cause. You will have frequent opportunity to use cause and effect analysis in the writing that you will do in college. For example, in history you might be asked to determine the causes of the Seven-Day War between Egypt and Israel; in political science you might be asked to determine the reasons why Ronald Reagan won the 1984 Presidential election; and, in sociology you might be asked to predict the effect that changes in Social Security legislation would have on senior citizens.

Determining causes and effects is usually thought-provoking and quite complex. One reason for this is that there are two types of causes: *immediate causes*, which are readily apparent because they are closest to the effect, and *ultimate causes*, which, being somewhat removed, are not so apparent and perhaps even hidden. Furthermore, ultimate causes may bring about effects which themselves become immediate causes, thus creating a *causal chain*. For example, consider the following causal chain: Sally, a computer salesperson, prepared extensively for a meeting with an important client (ultimate cause), impressed the client (immediate cause), and made a very large sale (effect). The chain did not stop there: The large sale caused her to be promoted by her employer (effect).

A second reason why causal analysis can be so complex is that an effect may have any number of possible or actual causes, and a cause may have any number of possible or actual effects. An upset stomach may be caused by eating spoiled food, but it may also be caused by overeating, flu, allergy, nervousness, pregnancy, or any combination of factors. Similarly, the high cost of electricity may have multiple effects: higher profits for utility companies, fewer sales of electrical appliances, higher prices for other products, and the development of alternative sources of energy.

Sound reasoning and logic, while present in all good writing, are central to any causal analysis. Writers of believable causal analysis examine their material objectively and develop their essays carefully. They are convinced by their own examination of the material, but are not afraid to admit other possible causes and effects. Above all, they do not let their own prejudices interfere with the logic of their analyses and presentations.

Because people are accustomed to thinking of causes with their effects, they sometimes commit an error in logic known as the "after this, therefore because of this" fallacy (in Latin, *post hoc, ergo propter hoc*). This fallacy leads people to believe that because one event occurred after another event the first event somehow caused the second; that is, they sometimes make causal connections that are not proven. For example, if students began to perform better after a free breakfast program was instituted at their school, one could not assume that the improvement was caused by the breakfast program. There could of course be any number of other causes for this effect, and a responsible writer on the subject would analyze and consider them all before suggesting the cause.

NEVER GET SICK IN JULY

Marilyn Machlowitz

Marilyn Machlowitz earned her doctorate in psychology at Yale and is now a management psychologist. She contributes a regular column to Working Woman *magazine, has written* Workaholics *(1980), and is at work on a new book dealing with the consequences of succeeding at an early age. Notice in the following selection first published in* Esquire *magazine in July, 1978, how Machlowitz analyzes the various reasons why it is a bad idea to get sick in July.*

One Harvard medical school professor warns his students   1
to stay home—as he does—on the Fourth of July. He fears
he will become one of the holiday's highway casualties and
wind up in an emergency room with an inexperienced intern
"practicing" medicine on *him.*

Just the mention of July makes medical students, nurses, in-   2
terns, residents, and "real doctors" roll their eyes. While hospital administrators maintain that nothing is amiss that month,
members of the medical profession know what happens when
the house staff turns over and the interns take over each July 1.

This July 1, more than 13,000 new doctors will invade over   3
600 hospitals across the country. Within minutes they will be
overwhelmed: last July 1, less than a month after finishing
medical school, Dr. John Baumann, then twenty-five, walked
into Washington, D.C.'s, Walter Reed Army Medical Center,
where he was immediately faced with caring for "eighteen of
the sickest people I had ever seen."

Pity the patient who serves as guinea pig at ten A.M.—or three   4
A.M.—that first day. Indeed, according to Dr. Russell K. Laros,
Jr., professor and vice-chairman of obstetrics, gynecology, and
reproductive sciences at the University of California, San Francisco, "There is no question that patients throughout the country are mismanaged during July. Without the most meticulous
supervision," he adds, "serious errors can be made."

And they are. Internship provides the first chance to practice   5
one's illegible scrawl on prescription blanks, a golden opportunity to make lots of mistakes. Interns—who are still known to
most people by that name, even though they are now officially
called first-year residents—have ordered the wrong drug in the
wrong dosage to be administered the wrong way at the wrong
times to the wrong patient. While minor mistakes are most
common, serious errors are the sources of hospital horror stories. One intern prescribed an anti-depressant without knowing that it would inactivate the patient's previously prescribed
antihypertensive medication.* The patient then experienced a
rapid increase in blood pressure and suffered a stroke.

When interns do not know what to do, when they cannot cov-   6
ertly consult *The Washington Manual* (a handbook of medical
therapeutics), they can always order tests. The first time one intern attempted to perform a pleural biopsy—a fairly difficult
procedure—he punctured the patient's lung. When an acquaintance of mine entered an emergency room one Friday
night in July with what was only an advanced case of the flu,
she wound up having a spinal tap. While negative findings are
often necessary to rule out alternative diagnoses, some of the
tests are really unwarranted. Interns admit that the results are
required only so they can cover themselves in case a resident or
attending physician decides to give them the third degree.

Interns' hours only increase their inadequacy. Dr. Jay   7
Dobkin, president of the Physicians National Housestaff Association, a Washington-based organization representing 12,000
interns and residents, says that "working conditions . . . directly impact and influence the quality of patient care. After
thirty-six hours 'on,' most interns find their abilities compro-
mised." Indeed, their schedules (they average 110 hours a
week) and their salaries (last year, they averaged $13,145) make
interns the chief source of cheap labor. No other hospital personnel will do as much "scut" work—drawing blood, for
instance—or dirty work, such as manually disimpacting severely constipated patients.

Even private patients fall prey to interns, because many phy-   8
sicians prefer being affiliated with hospitals that have interns

---

*A depressant medicine used to lower high blood pressure.

to perform these routine duties around the clock. One way to reduce the likelihood of falling into the hands of an intern is to rely upon a physician in group practice whose partners can provide substitute coverage. Then, too, it probably pays to select a physician who has hospital privileges at the best teaching institution in town. There, at least, you are unlikely to encounter any interns who slept through school, as some medical students admit they do: only the most able students survive the computer-matching process to win the prestigious positions at university hospitals.

It may be reassuring to remember that while veteran nurses   9
joke about scheduling their vacations to start July 1, they monitor interns most carefully and manage to catch many mistakes. Residents bear much more responsibility for supervision and surveillance, and Dr. Lawrence Boxt, president of the 5,000-member, Manhattan-based Committee of Interns and Residents and a resident himself, emphasizes that residents are especially vigilant during July. One of the interns he represents agreed: "You're watched like a hawk. You have so much support and backup. They're not going to let you kill anybody." So no one who requires emergency medical attention should hesitate to be hospitalized in July.

I asked Dr. Boxt whether he also had any advice for someone   10
about to enter a hospital for elective surgery.

"Yes," he said. "Stay away."   11

Questions for Study and Discussion

1. What, according to Machlowitz, are the immediate causes of the problems many hospitals experience during the month of July?

2. What does she say are the causes of intern inadequacy? How does she substantiate the cause and effect relationship?

3. What suggestions does Machlowitz give for minimizing patient risk during the month of July?

4. How would you interpret Dr. Boxt's answer to the final question Machlowitz asks him?

Vocabulary

Refer to your dictionary to define the following words as they are used in this selection. Then use each word in a sentence of your own.

meticulous (4)	affiliated (8)
diagnoses (6)	prestigious (8)
unwarranted (6)	vigilant (9)
compromised (7)	

Suggested Writing Assignments

1. Write an essay in which you argue for changes in the ways hospitals handle the "July" problem. Make sure your proposals are realistic, clearly stated, and have some chance of producing the desired effects. You may wish to consider some possible objections to your proposals and how they might be overcome.

2. There is often more than one cause for an event. Make a list of at least six possible causes for one of the following:

   a quarrel with a friend

   an upset victory in a football game

   a well-done exam

   a broken leg

   a change of major

Examine your list, and identify the causes which seem most probable. Which of these are immediate causes and which are ultimate causes? Using this material, write a short cause and effect essay.

THE COLLAPSE OF PUBLIC SCHOOLS

John C. Sawhill

Beginning his career in a New York brokerage firm, John C. Sawhill worked as a management consultant and later became deputy director of the Federal Energy Administration. From 1975 to 1979 he served as the president of New York University. In 1979 Sawhill returned to government service, joining the Carter Administration in the Department of Energy. In the following selection Sawhill looks at a number of causes for the failure of public schools to provide good education. He concludes with some suggestions for change.

For more than two decades, America's public schools have 1
been expected to cure society's discontents. In the mid-Fifties, we demanded that our schools create a harmony among races that existed nowhere else in American life. In the mid-Sixties, when our young were engaged in a rebellion that seemed to threaten virtually every ideal we embraced as a nation, we insisted that the schools restore social order and preserve the status quo. In the mid-Seventies, we instructed our schools to go one step further—to look first to the wants of the individual, to nurture a child's discovery of self, while at the same time distracting him from his attempts to reduce his school to rubble.

Clearly, this prolonged and ill-advised effort to make the edu- 2
cational system the principal tool for social change has contributed to such problems as the sharply increased incidence of functional illiteracy.

To rehabilitate our schools, we must look to the hard reali- 3
ties of *why* our system of public education is not working and learn from them.

As we examine the performance of our schools, six basic 4
truths—most of them a result of our mixing altruism and education—emerge time and again.

1.   *Schools are asked to do too much*. Racial, economic, and sexual inequalities; poor parenting; malnutrition; crime; and a lengthy list of other social disorders unquestionably affect an individual's capacity to participate in society. But while education can enhance the student's ability to cope with, and to change, the conditions of life around him, it cannot, in and of itself, make them better. In thrusting the schools to the forefront of social change, we have diverted their energies from their basic purpose—education.

The issue of acculturation of ethnic minorities provides a case in point. Greater emphasis has been placed on bilingual education in the public schools as the number and variety of ethnic minorities have grown in the nation. We are insisting both that the schools improve the way they teach English, so that language is removed as a barrier to learning, and that they increase the number of courses taught in students' native tongues, so that the pace of learning begun in their homelands continues uninterrupted. The conflict that such demands create can be seen in Chicago, where, as a condition of $90 million in aid, the federal government exacted a pledge that the public schools offer bilingual courses in 20 languages, from Arabic to Vietnamese.

While we do not yet know what effect the study of major courses in a native tongue has on a child's ability to learn English, we may be allowed the suspicion that it will prove as counter-productive as it sounds. In addition, the burden these extra courses place on the schools is obvious.

Once we stop asking the schools to do too much, they can get on with solving the more acute problem of performing their basic task—that of education—more effectively.

2.   *Students cannot learn what they are not taught*. Current dismay over public education centers on the fact that substantial numbers of our children cannot perform even the most basic functions of reading, writing, and mathematics. Such poor performance is understandable, however, when we recognize that proficiency in basic skills no longer is required of public school students.

"Minimum competency" is the result of the schools' misguided efforts to serve two masters at the same time. On one hand, they are trying to respond to the public demand for sound, basic education by requiring a specific level of achievement in certain subjects. On the other hand, in their attempt to correct social inequities, schools are often setting standards so low as to be meaningless and even detrimental.

Although the concept of minimum competency is not inherently bad, it does require careful implementation. The depth to which public education can sink under the weight of problematic minimum-competency levels was demonstrated in New York this past spring when educators and others engaged in a spirited debate over the question of whether freshman reading standards are too *high* for graduating seniors. What began as a tool for ensuring performance has become an excuse for failure. This situation must be corrected.

Electives are sometimes used by schools as another means of preventing students from failing when they cannot educate them. Nationally, we can see a trend that moves even further away from requiring certain basics and toward instituting yet more electives—courses that range from studies amplifying basic skills to programs that can only be described as the marginalia of pop culture.

In Massachusetts, state educators compared a survey of elective courses developed between 1971 and 1976 with an analysis of Scholastic Achievement Test scores for students in 43 high schools. In this five-year period there was a 50 percent increase in English electives alone. The educators found that students with more electives showed greater than average declines in SAT scores.

Similarly, in New York, where the documented trend has been away from academic basics in recent years, two-thirds of the graduates of city high schools required additional pre-college study upon entering the City University.

In contrast, a survey of 34 high schools in which students have maintained or improved their SAT scores revealed that these schools encourage enrollment in advanced academic courses and allow electives to be taken only in addition to required classes rather than as a substitute for them.

Thus we must temper our dismay at our children's inability to read, write, and solve simple mathematical problems with the recognition that little goes on in the classroom to provide them with the skills to do better.

3. *We do not know what makes for an effective learning experi-* [17]
ence. With the possible exception of one-to-one teaching, virtually all of our theories about factors that contribute to productive instruction have not held up. Even our most cherished socio-educational assumption—that racial and social integration contributes to learning (provided half of the class is white)—runs counter to the reality of public schools, where students are put in classes according to their abilities; ethnic minorities are thus effectively resegregated and educational inadequacies perpetuated.

As long as schools are diverted by social concerns from the [18] experimentation essential to improving their performance, our students and teachers will continue to stumble through a succession of educational theories, reinventing the wheel daily out of necessity and, worse, becoming more entrenched in classroom practices that produce no positive results.

4. *What is good for the teacher is not always good for the pu-* [19]
pil. Increasingly in recent years, teachers have argued that higher salaries attract better teachers. Smaller classes, they have said, more time to prepare for class, and publicly financed teacher training improve the performance of those already in the profession. The result, our teachers tell us, is better education for our children. None of these assertions is supported by fact.

Teachers' salaries have risen steadily during the past 20 [20] years. In the classroom, the ratio of one teacher for every 30 students in 1955 had dropped to one for every 20 by 1976. There has also been a substantial increase in the amount of time teachers spend outside the classroom in course preparation and professional training. Yet students are performing dismally on almost every test we have thus far devised to measure their academic competence.

As is the case with the learning experience itself, we must [21] recognize finally that we do not know what makes a teacher effective.

5. *The way we finance public education is discriminatory and* [22]
contributes to chaos in the schools. Getting and spending the money to finance our public schools are among the most serious problems we face as a nation today.

Taxation of private property in itself has become an explosive issue. Reliance on property taxes discriminates against our cities and poorer suburban and rural areas. Property-poor localities must tax themselves at a higher rate to generate the same amount of tax dollars as their property-rich neighbors. Those who can afford to, move to areas where taxes are lower, and the money available for public education is thus further eroded in those localities where it is most needed.   23

Efforts have been made in the state courts and legislatures to equalize funding. While these efforts generally have resulted in increased aid to poorer districts, they have not addressed the major issue of linking public education to property taxes.   24

Meanwhile, increases in property taxes meet with growing resistance. The "taxpayers' revolt" is surprising only in that it did not surface sooner. Neither the very poor nor the very rich pay as much of the cost of education as the middle-class property owner.   25

The inequities of the property tax are also felt acutely by older property owners who enjoy only indirectly the benefits of public education. Many of those who must survive on fixed incomes have found that the value of their once-modest homes has tripled and even quadrupled in recent years. The result: steep increases in taxes that their incomes cannot grow to match.   26

While we have yet to see what long-term effects the taxpayers' revolt will have on public education, Cleveland provided us with a clue when voter rejection of a bond issue closed the schools twice in one year, left the city $130 million in debt, and pushed teachers' salaries months in arrears.   27

Getting the money to finance public education, however, is only half of the problem we face. Spending it wisely is equally important and sometimes even more perplexing.   28

Why is it, with increased teachers' salaries and per-pupil expenditures, that our students perform so poorly? Again, the answer can be found in our zeal to correct social disorders. Schools in localities with large low-income and minority populations must provide costly social services to their students, leaving even less money for actual education.   29

6. *Someone must be in charge.* Local, state, and federal gov-   30

ernment; community groups; unions; educational theorists; parents; and even students have all taken a crack at running our schools, and the results are about the same. None has run them well. Schools and their employees' unions have developed intricate bureaucracies of their own, which spend more time explaining their failures than seeking solutions to the problems they face.

The responsibility for making decisions, controlling re- 31 sources, and planning and implementing programs has been taken away from principals and teachers and dispersed throughout the educational bureaucracy, from the local school system all the way to the federal government.

We cannot expect our schools to function well when those 32 most directly involved lack the authority to manage them effectively.

Acceptance of these six realities will not provide all the an- 33 swers to the problems our schools face today. But they do suggest directions we might pursue:

We must recognize that schools exist to educate, and that the 34 task is monumental enough without the attempt to right the social wrongs that have originated elsewhere.

We must recognize that—if the function of education is to en- 35 able us to become the most that we can be—there is no such thing as a minimum acceptable standard.

We must insist that time and money be used to strengthen ba- 36 sic academic curricula.

We must scrutinize our beliefs about what makes for an ef- 37 fective learning experience and discard those that have proved ineffective and wasteful; further, we cannot rely on teachers and educational theorists alone in making such decisions.

We must revolutionize the way in which schools are financed 38 and establish firm priorities for spending.

And finally, we must return the management of our schools 39 to those most directly involved in the delivery of educational services to the public.

Our schools provide a key to the future of society. We must 40 take control of them, watch over them, and nurture them if they are to be set right again. To do less is to invite disaster upon ourselves, our children, and our nation.

Questions for Study and Discussion

1. What is the author's purpose? Why does cause and effect analysis suit his purpose? (Glossary: *Purpose*)
2. What, according to Sawhill, is the cause for the failure of our public schools?
3. What are the six basic truths that Sawhill says "emerge time and again" when we examine why our schools do not work?
4. What is the relationship between the six truths that Sawhill discusses and the suggestions he makes at the end of the essay for improving the performance of our schools?
5. What effect has increased teachers' salaries and per-pupil expenditures had on academic performance? Has Sawhill presented sufficient evidence to substantiate his claims?

Vocabulary

Refer to your dictionary to define the following words as they are used in this selection. Then use each word in a sentence of your own.

virtually (1)	proficiency (9)
status quo (1)	detrimental (10)
enhance (5)	inherently (11)
acculturation (6)	scrutinize (37)

Suggested Writing Assignments

1. Write an essay in which you state what you think were the major problems of the high school you attended, what caused them, and how they can be resolved.
2. Write an essay in which you analyze the most significant reasons why you went to college. You may wish to discuss such matters as your high school experience, people and events that influenced your decision, and your goals in college as well as in later life.

WHEN TELEVISION IS A SCHOOL FOR CRIMINALS

Grant Hendricks

Grant Hendricks is serving a life sentence in Michigan's Marquette maximum-security prison. When he submitted the following article to TV Guide for publication, the editors found the results of his research so surprising that they verified the facts for themselves before publishing the article. Hendricks contends that penitentiary inmates watch television not only to pass the time but also to learn new techniques for committing yet more crimes—that television may, in fact, be a school for criminals.

For years, psychologists and sociologists have tried to find some connection between crime and violence on television and crime and violence in American society. To date, no one has been able to prove—or disprove—that link. But perhaps the scientists, with their academic approaches, have been unable to mine the mother lode of information on violence, crime and television available in our prison systems.

I'm not about to dismiss the scientists' findings, but as a prisoner serving a life sentence in Michigan's Marquette maximum-security prison, I believe I can add a new dimension to the subject. Cons speak much more openly to one of their own than to outsiders. And because of this, I spent three weeks last summer conducting an informal survey of 208 of the 688 inmates here at Marquette, asking them what they felt about the correlation between the crime and violence they see on television and the crime and violence they have practiced as a way of life.

Making this survey, I talked to my fellow prisoners in the mess hall, in the prison yard, in the factory and in my cell block. I asked them, on a confidential basis, whether or not their criminal activities have ever been influenced by what they see on TV. A surprising 9 out of 10 told me that they have actually learned new tricks and improved their criminal expertise by watching crime programs. Four out of 10 said that they have attempted specific crimes they saw on television crime dramas, although they also admit that only about one-third of these attempts were successful.

Perhaps even more surprising is the fact that here at Marquette, where 459 of us have television sets in our individual cells, hooked up to a cable system, many cons sit and take notes while watching *Baretta, Kojak, Police Woman, Switch* and other TV crime shows. As one of my buddies said recently: "It's like you have a lot of intelligent, creative minds—all those Hollywood writers—working for *you.* They keep coming up with new ideas. They'll lay it all out for you, too: show you the type of evidence the cops look for—how they track you, and so on." 4

What kinds of lessons have been learned by TV-watching criminals? Here are some examples. 5

One of my prison-yard mates told me he "successfully" pulled off several burglaries, all patterned on a caper from *Police Woman.* 6

Another robbed a sporting-goods store by following the *modus operandi** he saw on an *Adam-12* episode. 7

By copying a *Paper Moon* scheme, one con man boasts he pulled off a successful bunco fraud—for which he has never been caught (he's currently serving time for another crime). 8

Of course, television doesn't guarantee that the crime you pull off will be successful. One inmate told me he attempted to rip off a dope house, modeling his plan on a *Baretta* script. But the heroin dealers he tried to rob called the cops and he was caught. Another prison-yard acquaintance mentioned that, using a *Starsky & Hutch* plot, he tried to rob a nightclub. But to his horror, the place was owned by underworld people. "I'm lucky to still be alive," he said. 9

On the question of violence, however, a much smaller number of Marquette inmates feel they were influenced by watching anything on television. Of the 59 men I interviewed who 10

---

*(Latin) *modus operandi,* or method of operation.

have committed rape, only 1 out of 20 said that he felt inspired or motivated to commit rape as a result of something he saw on television. Forty-seven of the 208 men I spoke to said that at one time or another they had killed another person. Of those, 31 are now serving life sentences for either first- or second-degree murder. Of these 31, only 2 said their crimes had been television-influenced. But of the 148 men who admitted to committing assault, about 1 out of 6 indicated that his crime had been inspired or motivated by something he saw on TV.

Still, one prisoner after another will tell you how he has been   11
inspired, motivated and helped by television. And crime shows and TV-movies are not the only sources of information. CBS's *60 Minutes* provides choice viewing for Marquette's criminal population. One con told me: "They recently did a segment on *60 Minutes* on how easy it was to get phony IDs. Just like the hit man in 'Day of the Jackal,' but on *60 Minutes* it wasn't fiction—it was for real. After watching that show, you knew how to go out and score a whole new personality on paper—credit cards, driver's license, everything. It was fantastic."

Sometimes, watching television helps you learn to think on   12
your feet. Like an old friend of mine named Shakey, who once escaped from the North Dakota State Penitentiary. While he hid in the basement of a private residence, they were putting up roadblocks all around the city of Bismarck. But Shakey was smart. He knew that there had to be some way for him to extricate himself from this mess. Then, all of a sudden it occurred to him: Shakey remembered a caper film he'd seen on television once, in which a fugitive had managed to breach several roadblocks by using an emergency vehicle.

With this basic plan in mind, he proceeded to the Bismarck   13
City Hospital and, pretending to be hysterical, he stammered to the first white-coated attendant he met that his brother was lying trapped beneath an overturned farm tractor about 12 miles or so from town. He then climbed into the back of the ambulance, and with red lights blazing and siren screaming, the vehicle drove right through two roadblocks—and safely out of Bismarck.

Two days or so later, Shakey arrived back on the same ranch   14
in Montana where he'd worked before his jail sentence. The foreman even gave him his job again. But Shakey was so proud

of what he'd done that he made one big mistake: he boasted about his escape from the North Dakota state prison, and in the end he was turned over to the authorities, who sent him back to North Dakota—and prison. . . .

An 18-year-old inmate told me that while watching an old *Adam-12* show, he had learned exactly how to break open pay-phone coin boxes. He thought it seemed like a pretty good idea for picking up a couple of hundred dollars a day, so he gave it a try. To his surprise and consternation, the writers of *Adam-12* had failed to explain that Ma Bell has a silent alarm system built into her pay phones. If you start tampering with one, the operator can notify the police within seconds—even giving them the location of the phone being ripped off. He was arrested on his first attempt and received a one-year sentence. 15

Another prisoner told me that he had learned to hot-wire cars at the age of 14 by watching one of his favorite TV shows. A week later he stole his first car—his mother's. Five years later he was in Federal prison for transporting stolen vehicles across state lines. 16

This man, at the age of 34, has spent 15 years behind bars. According to him, "TV has taught me how to steal cars, how to break into establishments, how to go about robbing people, even how to roll a drunk. Once, after watching a *Hawaii Five-O*, I robbed a gas station. The show showed me how to do it. Nowadays [he's serving a term for attempted rape] I watch TV in my house [cell] from 4 P.M. until midnight. I just sit back and take notes. I see 'em doing it this way or that way, you know, and I tell myself that I'll do it the same way when I get out. You could probably pick any 10 guys in here and ask 'em and they'd tell you the same thing. Everybody's picking up on what's on the TV." . . . 17

One of my friends here in Marquette says that TV is just a reflection of what's happening "out there." According to him, "The only difference is that the people out there haven't been caught—and we have. But our reaction to things is basically the same. Like when they showed the movie 'Death Wish' here, the people reacted the same way they did on the outside—they applauded Charles Bronson when he wasted all the criminals. The crooks applauded Bronson!" 18

Still, my research—informal though it is—shows that criminals look at television differently than straight people. Outside, TV is entertainment. Here, it helps the time go by. But it is also educational. As one con told me, television has been beneficial to his career in crime by teaching him all the things *not* to do. Another mentioned that he's learned a lot about how cops think and work by watching crime-drama shows. In the prison factory, one guy said that he's seen how various alarm systems operate by watching TV; and here in my cell block somebody said that because of television shows, he's been kept up-to-date on modern police procedures and equipment.

Another con told me: "In the last five to seven years we've learned that the criminal's worst enemy is the snitch. TV has built that up. On *Starsky & Hutch* they've even made a sympathetic character out of a snitch. So we react to that in here. Now the general feeling is that if you use a partner to commit a crime, you kill him afterwards so there's nobody to snitch on you."

For most of us cons in Marquette, it would be hard to do time without TV. It's a window on the world for us. We see the news shows, we watch sports and some of us take great pains to keep tuned into the crime shows. When I asked one con if he felt that watching TV crime shows in prison would be beneficial to his career, he just smiled and said, "Hey, I sit and take notes—do my homework, you know? No way would I sit in my cell and waste my time watching comedies for five hours—no way!"

Questions for Study and Discussion

1. What is Hendricks's purpose in this essay? Where does he state his purpose? (Glossary: *Purpose*)
2. What particular cause and effect relationship does the author set out to establish in the essay? Does the essay seem sound and logical? Why or why not?
3. For what purpose does Hendricks use examples in this essay? (Glossary: *Example*)
4. What does Hendricks gain by quoting his fellow inmates rather than paraphrasing them? (Glossary: *Dialogue*)

5. How objective is Hendricks in this essay? Is he a disinterested observer?

Vocabulary

Refer to your dictionary to define the following words as they are used in this selection. Then use each word in a sentence of your own.

correlation (2)   hysterical (13)
extricate (12)   consternation (15)

Suggested Writing Assignments

1. Much attention has been focused on the issue of violence on television. Write a cause and effect essay using the following statement as your thesis:

   Television teaches us that violence is an acceptable way to deal with those who disagree with us or who keep us from having our own way.

2. Write an essay in which you discuss the effects of television on you or on American society. You may wish to focus on the specific influences of one of the following aspects of television:

   advertising
   sports broadcasts
   cultural programming
   talk shows
   national or international news
   children's programming
   educational television
   situation comedies

WHO'S AFRAID OF MATH, AND WHY?

Sheila Tobias

Sheila Tobias served as Associate Provost of Wesleyan University, where she became interested in the reasons why certain students, notably women, choose not to pursue careers in math or math-related fields. On the basis of her research, Tobias, a "mathematics avoider" herself, founded the Math Clinic at Wesleyan. She is the author of Overcoming Math Anxiety *(1978), from which this essay is taken. As you read the essay, notice how Tobias systematically analyzes the possible causes of "math anxiety."*

The first thing people remember about failing at math is that it felt like sudden death. Whether the incident occurred while learning "word problems" in sixth grade, coping with equations in high school, or first confronting calculus and statistics in college, failure came suddenly and in a very frightening way. An idea or a new operation was not just difficult, it was impossible! And, instead of asking questions or taking the lesson slowly, most people remember having had the feeling that they would never go any further in mathematics. If we assume that the curriculum was reasonable, and that the new idea was but the next in a series of learnable concepts, the feeling of utter defeat was simply not rational; yet "math anxious" college students and adults have revealed that no matter how much the teacher reassured them, they could not overcome that feeling.

A common myth about the nature of mathematical ability holds that one either has or does not have a mathematical mind. Mathematical imagination and an intuitive grasp of mathematical principles may well be needed to do advanced research, but why should people who can do college-level work in other subjects not be able to do college-level math as well? Rates of learning may vary. Competency under time pressure may differ. Certainly low self-esteem will get in the way. But where is the evidence that a student needs a "mathematical mind" in order to succeed at learning math?

Consider the effects of this mythology. Since only a few people are supposed to have this mathematical mind, part of what makes us so passive in the face of our difficulties in learning mathematics is that we suspect all the while we may not be one of "them," and we spend our time waiting to find out when our nonmathematical minds will be exposed. Since our limit will eventually be reached, we see no point in being methodical or in attending to detail. We are grateful when we survive fractions, word problems, or geometry. If that certain moment of failure hasn't struck yet, it is only temporarily postponed.

Parents, especially parents of girls, often expect their children to be nonmathematical. Parents are either poor at math and had their own sudden-death experiences, or, if math came easily for them, they do not know how it feels to be slow. In either case, they unwittingly foster the idea that a mathematical mind is something one either has or does not have.

Mathematics and Sex

Although fear of math is not a purely female phenomenon, girls tend to drop out of math sooner than boys, and adult women experience an aversion to math and math-related activities that is akin to anxiety. A 1972 survey of the amount of high school mathematics taken by incoming freshmen at Berkeley revealed that while 57 percent of the boys had taken four years of high school math, only 8 percent of the girls had had the same amount of preparation. Without four years of high school math, students at Berkeley, and at most other colleges and universities, are ineligible for the calculus sequence, unlikely to attempt chemistry or physics, and inadequately prepared for statistics and economics.

Unable to elect these entry-level courses, the remaining 92 percent of the girls will be limited, presumably, to the career choices that are considered feminine: the humanities, guidance and counseling, elementary school teaching, foreign languages, and the fine arts.

Boys and girls may be born alike with respect to math, but certain sex differences in performance emerge early according to several respected studies, and these differences remain through adulthood. They are:

1. Girls compute better than boys (elementary school and on).
2. Boys solve word problems better than girls (from age thirteen on).
3. Boys take more math than girls (from age sixteen on).
4. Girls learn to hate math sooner and possibly for different reasons.

Why the differences in performance? One reason is the amount of math learned and used at play. Another may be the difference in male-female maturation. If girls do better than boys at all elementary school tasks, then they may compute better for no other reason than that arithmetic is part of the elementary school curriculum. As boys and girls grow older, girls become, under pressure, academically less competitive. Thus, the falling off of girls' math performance between ages ten and fifteen may be because:

1. Math gets harder in each successive year and requires more work and commitment.
2. Both boys and girls are pressured, beginning at age ten, not to excel in areas designated by society to be outside their sex-role domains.
3. Thus girls have a good excuse to avoid the painful struggle with math; boys don't.

Such a model may explain girls' lower achievement in math overall, but why should girls even younger than ten have difficulty in problem-solving? In her review of the research on sex differences, psychologist Eleanor Maccoby noted that girls are generally more conforming, more suggestible, and more dependent upon the opinion of others than boys (all learned, not innate, behaviors). Being so, they may not be as willing to take risks or to think for themselves, two behaviors that are necessary in solving problems. Indeed, in one test of third-graders, girls were found to be not nearly as willing to estimate, to make judgments about "possible right answers," or to work with systems they had never seen before. Their very success at doing what is expected of them up to that time seems to get in the way of their doing something new.

If readiness to do word problems, to take one example, is as   10
much a function of readiness to take risks as it is of "reasoning
ability," then mathematics performance certainly requires
more than memory, computation, and reasoning. The differences in math performance between boys and girls—no matter
how consistently those differences show up— cannot be attrib-
uted simply to differences in innate ability.

Still, if one were to ask the victims themselves, they would   11
probably disagree: they would say their problems with math
have to do with the way they are "wired." They feel they are
somehow missing something—one ability or several—that
other people have. Although women want to believe they are
not mentally inferior to men, many fear that, where math is
concerned, they really are. Thus, we have to consider seriously
whether mathematical ability has a biological basis, not only
because a number of researchers believe this to be so, but because a number of victims agree with them.

The Arguments from Biology

The search for some biological basis for math ability or dis-   12
ability is fraught with logical and experimental difficulties.
Since not all math under-achievers are women, and not all
women are mathematics-avoidant, poor performance in math
is unlikely to be due to some genetic or hormonal difference between the sexes. Moreover, no amount of research so far has
unearthed a "mathematical competency" in some tangible,
measurable substance in the body. Since "masculinity" cannot
be injected into women to test whether or not it improves their
mathematics, the theories that attribute such ability to genes
or hormones must depend for their proof on circumstantial evidence. So long as about 7 percent of the Ph.D.'s in mathematics
are earned by women, we have to conclude either that these
women have genes, hormones, and brain organization different
from those of the rest of us, or that certain positive experiences
in their lives have largely undone the negative fact that they are
female, or both.

Genetically, the only difference between males and females   13
(albeit a significant and pervasive one) is the presence of two
chromosomes designated X in every female cell. Normal males
exhibit an X-Y combination. Because some kinds of mental re-

tardation are associated with sex-chromosomal anomalies, a number of researchers have sought a converse linkage between specific abilities and the presence or absence of the second X. But the linkage between genetics and mathematics is not supported by conclusive evidence.

Since intensified hormonal activity commences at adolescence, a time during which girls seem to lose interest in mathematics, much more has been made of the unequal amounts in females and males of the sex-linked hormones androgen and estrogen. Biological researchers have linked estrogen—the female hormone—with "simple repetitive tasks," and androgen—the male hormone—with "complex restructuring tasks." The assumption here is not only that such specific talents are biologically based (probably undemonstrable) but also that one cannot be good at *both* repetitive and restructuring kinds of assignments.   14

Sex Roles and Mathematics Competence

The fact that many girls tend to lose interest in math at the age they reach puberty (junior high school) suggests that puberty might in some sense cause girls to fall behind in math. Several explanations come to mind: the influence of hormones, more intensified sex-role socialization, or some extracurricular learning experience exclusive to boys of that age.   15

One group of seventh-graders in a private school in New England gave a clue as to what children themselves think about all of this. When asked why girls do as well as boys in math until the sixth grade, while sixth-grade boys do better from that point on, the girls responded: "Oh, that's easy. After sixth grade, we have to do real math." The answer to why "real math" should be considered to be "for boys" and not "for girls" can be found not in the realm of biology but only in the realm of ideology of sex differences.   16

Parents, peers, and teachers forgive a girl when she does badly in math at school, encouraging her to do well in other subjects instead. " 'There, there.' my mother used to say when I failed at math," one woman says. "But I got a talking-to when I did badly in French." Lynn Fox, who directs a program for mathematically gifted junior high boys and girls on the campus of Johns Hopkins University, has trouble recruiting girls and   17 keeping them in her program. Some parents prevent their daughters from participating altogether for fear that excellence in math will make them too different. The girls themselves are often reluctant to continue with mathematics, Fox reports, because they fear social ostracism.

Where do these associations come from? 18

The association of masculinity with mathematics sometimes 19 extends from the discipline to those who practice it. Students, asked on a questionnaire what characteristics they associate with a mathematician (as contrasted with a "writer"), selected terms such as rational, cautious, wise, and responsible. The writer, on the other hand, in addition to being seen as individualistic and independent, was also described as warm, interested in people, and altogether more compatible with a feminine ideal.

As a result of this psychological conditioning, a young 20 woman may consider math and math-related fields to be inimical to femininity. In an interesting study of West German teenagers, Erika Schildkamp-Kuendiger found that girls who identified themselves with the feminine ideal underachieved in mathematics, that is, did less well than would have been expected of them based on general intelligence and performance in other subjects.

Street Mathematics: Things, Motion, Scores

Not all the skills that are necessary for learning mathematics 21 are learned in school. Measuring, computing, and manipulating objects that have dimensions and dynamic properties of their own are part of the everyday life of children. Children who miss out on these experiences may not be well primed for math in school.

Feminists have complained for a long time that playing with 22 dolls is one way of convincing impressionable little girls that they may only be mothers or housewives—or, as in the case of the Barbie doll, "pinup girls"—when they grow up. But dollplaying may have even more serious consequences for little girls than that. Do girls find out about gravity and distance and shapes and sizes playing with dolls? Probably not.

A curious boy, if his parents are tolerant, will have taken 23 apart a number of household and play objects by the time he is ten, and, if his parents are lucky, he may even have put them back together again. In all of this he is learning things that will be useful in physics and math. Taking parts out that have to go back in requires some examination of form. Building something that stays up or at least stays put for some time involves working with structure.

Sports is another source of math-related concepts for chil- 24
dren which tends to favor boys. Getting to first base on a not very well hit grounder is a lesson in time, speed, and distance. Intercepting a football thrown through the air requires some rapid intuitive eye calculations based on the ball's direction, speed, and trajectory. Since physics is partly concerned with velocities, trajectories, and collisions of objects, much of the math taught to prepare a student for physics deals with relationships and formulas that can be used to express motion and acceleration.

What, then, can we conclude about mathematics and sex? If 25
math anxiety is in part the result of math avoidance, why not require girls to take as much math as they can possibly master? If being the only girl in "trig" is the reason so many women drop math at the end of high school, why not provide psychological counseling and support for those young women who wish to go on? Since ability in mathematics is considered by many to be unfeminine, perhaps fear of success, more than any bodily or mental dysfunction, may interfere with girls' ability to learn math.

Questions for Study and Discussion

1. Tobias states that girls suffer more than boys from math anxiety. What does she say causes girls to be more fearful than boys?

2. What evidence does Tobias use to establish the main cause and effect relationship in this essay? Is her evidence sufficient? If not, what else might she have added? (Glossary: *Evidence*)

3. Why does Tobias downplay sex differences as a cause for differences in mathematical performance?

4. Tobias states, "A common myth about the nature of mathematical ability holds that one either has or does not have a mathematical mind." What does she think are the effects of this myth?

5. What is the cause and effect relationship discussed in paragraphs 15–20? What function does paragraph 18 serve in the development of that relationship?

Vocabulary

Refer to your dictionary to define the following words as they are used in this selection. Then use each word in a sentence of your own.

curriculum (1)   innate (9)
myth (2)   commences (14)
intuitive (2)   compatible (19)
unwittingly (4)   inimical (20)
aversion (5)

Suggested Writing Assignments

1. How do you feel about mathematics? Write a short essay discussing the reasons for your attitude. What *caused* you to feel the way that you do?

2. If you were able to find the ideal job after college, what would that job be? Write an essay explaining why you think a particular job would be best for you and, more importantly, explain what forces (causes) in your life have led you to that career choice (effect). For example, you may want to be an automobile salesman because your uncle is an automobile salesman, or you have spent time in his office and you know what he does, or you enjoy being around cars and working with people.

18

ARGUMENT

Argumentation is the attempt to persuade a reader to accept your point of view, to make a decision, or to pursue a particular course of action. Because the writer of an argument is often interested in explaining a subject, as well as in advocating a particular view, argumentation frequently adopts other rhetorical strategies. Nevertheless, it is the attempt to convince, not to explain, that is most important in an argumentative essay.

There are two basic types of argumentation: logical and persuasive. In *logical argumentation* the writer appeals to the reader's rational or intellectual faculties to convince him of the truth of a particular statement or belief. In *persuasive argumentation*, on the other hand, the writer appeals to the reader's emotions and opinions to move the reader to action. These two types of argumentation are seldom found in their pure forms, and the degree to which one or the other is emphasized in written work depends on the writer's subject, specific purpose, and intended audience. Although you may occasionally need or want to appeal to your readers' emotions, most often in your college work you will need to rely only on the fundamental techniques of logical argumentation.

There are two types of reasoning common to essays of argumentation: induction and deduction. *Inductive reasoning*, the more common type, moves from a set of specific examples to a general statement. In doing so, the writer makes what is known as an *inductive leap* from the evidence to the generalization. For example, after examining enrollment statistics, we can conclude that students do not like to take courses offered early in the morning or late in the afternoon. *Deductive reasoning*, on the other hand, moves from a general statement to a specific conclusion. It works on the model of the *syllogism*, a simple three-part argument that consists of a major premise, a minor premise, and a conclusion, as in the following example:

a. All women are mortal. (major premise)

b. Judy is a woman. (minor premise)
c. Judy is mortal. (conclusion)

A well-constructed argument avoids *logical fallacies*, flaws in the reasoning that will render the argument invalid. Following are some of the most common logical fallacies:

1. *Oversimplification.* The tendency to provide simple solutions to complex problems. "The reason we have inflation today is that OPEC has unreasonably raised the price of oil."

2. *Hasty Generalization.* A generalization that is based on too little evidence or on evidence that is not representative. "It was the best movie I saw this year, and so it should get an Academy Award."

3. *Post hoc, ergo propter hoc* ("After this, therefore because of this"). Confusing chance or coincidence with causation. Because one event comes after another one, it does not necessarily mean that the first event caused the second. "Ever since I went to the hockey game I've had a cold." The assumption here is that going to the hockey game had something to do with the speaker's cold when, in fact, there might be a different, or many different, causes for the cold.

4. *Begging the question.* Assuming in a premise that which needs to be proven. "Conservation is the only means of meeting the energy crisis; therefore, we should seek out methods to conserve energy."

5. *False analogy.* Making a misleading analogy between logically unconnected ideas. "Of course he'll make a fine coach. He was an all-star basketball player."

6. *Either/or thinking.* The tendency to see an issue as having only two sides. "Used car salesmen are either honest or crooked."

7. *Non sequitur* ("It does not follow"). An inference or conclusion that does not follow from established premises or evidence. "She is a sincere speaker; she must know what she is talking about."

As you write your argumentative essays, you should keep the following advice in mind. Somewhere near the beginning of your essay, you should identify the issue to be discussed, explain why you think it is important, and point out what interest you and your readers share in the issue. Then, in the body of your essay, you should organize the various points of your argument. You may move from your least important point to your most important point, from the most familiar to the least familiar, from the easiest to accept or comprehend to the most difficult. For each point in your argument, you should provide sufficient appropriate supporting evidence—facts and statistics, illustrative examples and narratives, quotations from authorities. In addition, you should acknowledge the strongest opposing arguments and explain why you believe your position is more valid.

Be sure that you neither overstate nor understate your position. It is always wise to let the evidence convince your reader. Overstatement not only annoys readers but, more important, raises serious doubts about your own confidence in the power of your facts and reasoning. At the same time, no writer persuades by excessively understating or qualifying information with words and phrases such as *perhaps, maybe, I think, sometimes, most often, nearly always,* or *in my opinion.* The result sounds not rational and sensible but indecisive and fuzzy.

WHY I WANT TO HAVE A FAMILY

Lisa Brown

When she wrote the following essay, Lisa Brown was a junior majoring in American Studies at the University of Texas. In her essay, which was published as a "My Turn" column in the October, 1984, issue of Newsweek on Campus, *she argues that many women in their drive to success have overlooked the potential for fulfillment inherent in good relationships and family life.*

For years the theory of higher education operated something like this: men went to college to get rich, and women went to college to marry rich men. It was a wonderful little setup, almost mathematical in its precision. To disturb it would have been to rock an American institution.

During the '60s, though, this theory lost much of its luster. As the nation began to recognize the idiocy of relegating women to a secondary role, women soon joined men in what once were male-only pursuits. This rebellious decade pushed women toward independence, showed them their potential and compelled them to take charge of their lives. Many women took the opportunity and ran with it. Since then feminine autonomy has been the rule, not the exception, at least among college women.

That's the good news. The bad news is that the invisible push has turned into a shove. Some women are downright obsessive about success, to the point of becoming insular monuments to selfishness and fierce bravado, the condescending sort that hawks: "I don't need *anybody*. So there." These women dismiss children and marriage as unbearably outdated and potentially harmful to their up-and-coming careers. This notion of independence smacks of egocentrism. What do these women fear? Why can't they slow down long enough to remember that relationships and a family life are not inherently awful things?

Granted that for centuries women were on the receiving end of some shabby treatment. Now, in an attempt to liberate college women from the constraints that forced them almost exclusively into teaching or nursing as a career outside the home—always subject to the primary career of motherhood—some women have gone too far. Any notion of motherhood seems to be regarded as an unpleasant reminder of the past, when homemakers were imprisoned by husbands, tots and household chores. In short, many women consider motherhood a time-consuming obstacle to the great joy of working outside the home.

The rise of feminism isn't the only answer. Growing up has   5
something to do with it, too. Most people find themselves in a bind as they hit their late 20s: they consider the ideals they grew up with and find that these don't necessarily mix with the ones they've acquired. The easiest thing to do, it sometimes seems, is to throw out the precepts their parents taught. Growing up, my friends and I were enchanted by the idea of starting new traditions. We didn't want self-worth to be contingent upon whether there was a man or child around the house to make us feel wanted.

I began to reconsider my values after my sister and a friend   6
had babies. I was entertained by their pregnancies and fascinated by the births; I was also thankful that I wasn't the one who had to change the diapers every day. I was a doting aunt only when I wanted to be. As my sister's and friend's lives changed, though, my attitude changed. I saw their days flip-flop between frustration and joy. Though these two women lost the freedom to run off to the beach or to a bar, they gained something else—an abstract happiness that reveals itself when they talk about Jessica's or Amanda's latest escapade or vocabulary addition. Still in their 20s, they shuffle work and motherhood with the skill of poker players. I admire them, and I marvel at their kids. Spending time with the Jessicas and Amandas of the world teaches us patience and sensitivity and gives us a clue into our own pasts. Children are also reminders that there is a future and that we must work to ensure its quality.

Now I feel challenged by the idea of becoming a parent. I   7
want to decorate a nursery and design Halloween costumes; I want to answer my children's questions and help them learn to read. I want to be unselfish. But I've spent most of my life

working in the opposite direction: toward independence, no emotional or financial strings attached. When I told a friend—one who likes kids but never, ever wants them—that I'd decided to accommodate motherhood, she accused me of undermining my career, my future, my life. "If that's all you want, then why are you even in college?" she asked.

The answer's simple: I want to be a smart mommy. I have   8
solid career plans and look forward to working. I make a distinction between wanting kids and wanting nothing but kids. And I've accepted that I'll have to give up a few years of full-time work to allow time for being pregnant and buying Pampers. As for undermining my life, I'm proud of my decision because I think it's evidence that the women's movement is working. While liberating women from the traditional child-bearing role, the movement has given respectability to motherhood by recognizing that it's not a brainless task like dishwashing. At the same time, women who choose not to have children are not treated as oddities. That certainly wasn't the case even 15 years ago. While the graying, middle-aged bachelor was respected, the female equivalent—tagged a spinster—was automatically suspect.

Today, women have choices: about careers, their bodies, chil-   9
dren. I am grateful that women are no longer forced into motherhood as a function of their biology; it's senseless to assume that having a uterus qualifies anyone to be a good parent. By the same token, it is ridiculous for women to abandon all maternal desire because it might jeopardize personal success. Some women make the decision to go childless without ever analyzing their true needs or desires. They forget that motherhood can add to personal fulfillment.

I wish those fiercely independent women wouldn't look down   10
upon those of us who, for whatever reason, choose to forgo much of the excitement that runs in tandem with being single, liberated and educated. Excitement also fills a family life; it just comes in different ways.

I'm not in college because I'll learn how to make tastier pot   11
roast. I'm a student because I want to make sense of the world and of myself. By doing so, I think I'll be better prepared to be a mother to the new lives that I might bring into the world. I'll

also be a better me. It's a package deal I don't want to turn down.

Questions for Study and Discussion

1. What is Brown arguing for in this essay? What does she say prompted a change in her attitude? (Glossary: *Attitude*)
2. Against what group is Brown arguing? What does she find wrong with the beliefs of that group?
3. What reasons does she provide for wanting to have a family?
4. Explain how the first sentences in paragraphs 3 and 5 function. (Glossary: *Transitions*)
5. How would you describe Brown's tone in this essay? (Glossary: *Tone*)
6. For what audience do you think this essay is intended? Do you think men would be as interested as women in the author's viewpoint? Explain. (Glossary: *Audience*)

Vocabulary

Refer to your dictionary to define the following words as they are used in this selection. Then use each word in a sentence of your own.

relegating (2)	precepts (5)
autonomy (2)	contingent (5)
insular (3)	doting (6)
bravado (3)	tandem (10)

Suggested Writing Assignments

1. Write an essay in which you argue any one of the following positions with regard to the women's movement: it has gone too far; it is out of control; it is misdirected; it hasn't gone far enough or done enough; it needs to reach more women and men; it should lower its sights; a position of your own

different from the above. Whichever position you argue, be sure that you provide sufficient evidence to support your point of view.

2. Fill in the following statement and write an argument in support of it.

The purpose of a college education is to _____

_____.

PAIN IS NOT THE ULTIMATE ENEMY

Norman Cousins

*After attending Columbia University, Norman
Cousins began a long, industrious career as an
educator, journalist, and writer. He is perhaps
best known as the former editor of* Saturday Review, *a position he held for thirty-eight years. He
has written many books, among them his very
successful* Anatomy of An Illness as Perceived
by the Patient: Reflections on Healing and Re-
generation *(1979), a widely read account of how
he coped with a nearly fatal illness. In the following essay, Cousins tells about the nature of
pain and explains how painkillers work; he attempts to persuade us that we should not seek to
deaden pain but to relieve its causes.*

Americans are probably the most pain-conscious people on   1
the face of the earth. For years we have had it drummed
into us—in print, on radio, over television, in everyday
conversation—that any hint of pain is to be banished as though
it were the ultimate evil. As a result, we are becoming a nation
of pill-grabbers and hypochondriacs, escalating the slightest
ache into a searing ordeal.

We know very little about pain and what we don't know   2
makes it hurt all the more. Indeed, no form of illiteracy in the
United States is so widespread or costly as ignorance about
pain—what it is, what causes it, how to deal with it without
panic. Almost everyone can rattle off the names of at least a
dozen drugs that can deaden pain from every conceivable
cause—all the way from headaches to hemorrhoids. There is
far less knowledge about the fact that about 90 percent of pain
is self-limiting, that it is not always an indication of poor
health, and that, most frequently, it is the result of tension,
stress, worry, idleness, boredom, frustration, suppressed rage,
insufficient sleep, overeating, poorly balanced diet, smoking,

excessive drinking, inadequate exercise, stale air, or any of the other abuses encountered by the human body in modern society.

The most ignored fact of all about pain is that the best way to eliminate it is to eliminate the abuse. Instead, many people reach almost instinctively for the painkillers—aspirins, barbiturates, codeines, tranquilizers, sleeping pills, and dozens of other analgesics or desensitizing drugs. 3

Most doctors are profoundly troubled over the extent to which the medical profession today is taking on the trappings of a pain-killing industry. Their offices are overloaded with people who are morbidly but mistakenly convinced that something dreadful is about to happen to them. It is all too evident that the campaign to get people to run to a doctor at the first sign of pain has boomeranged. Physicians find it difficult to give adequate attention to patients genuinely in need of expert diagnosis and treatment because their time is soaked up by people who have nothing wrong with them except a temporary indisposition or a psychogenic ache. 4

Patients tend to feel indignant and insulted if the physician tells them he can find no organic cause for the pain. They tend to interpret the term "psychogenic" to mean that they are complaining of nonexistent symptoms. They need to be educated about the fact that many forms of pain have no underlying physical cause but are the result, as mentioned earlier, of tension, stress, or hostile factors in the general environment. Sometimes a pain may be a manifestation of "conversion hysteria," . . . the name given by Jean Charcot to physical symptoms that have their origins in emotional disturbances. 5

Obviously, it is folly for an individual to ignore symptoms that could be a warning of a potentially serious illness. Some people are so terrified of getting bad news from a doctor that they allow their malaise to worsen, sometimes past the point of no return. Total neglect is not the answer to hypochondria. The only answer has to be increased education about the way the human body works, so that more people will be able to steer an intelligent course between promiscuous pill-popping and irresponsible disregard of genuine symptoms. 6

Of all forms of pain, none is more important for the individual to understand than the "threshold" variety. Almost every- 7 one has a telltale ache that is triggered whenever tension or fatigue reaches a certain point. It can take the form of a migraine-type headache or a squeezing pain deep in the abdomen or cramps or a pain in the lower back or even pain in the joints. The individual who has learned how to make the correlation between such threshold pains and their cause doesn't panic when they occur; he or she does something about relieving the stress and tension. Then, if the pain persists despite the absence of apparent cause, the individual will telephone the doctor.

If ignorance about the nature of pain is widespread, igno-   8
rance about the way pain-killing drugs work is even more so. What is not generally understood is that many of the vaunted pain-killing drugs conceal the pain without correcting the underlying condition. They deaden the mechanism in the body that alerts the brain to the fact that something may be wrong. The body can pay a high price for suppression of pain without regard to its basic cause.

Professional athletes are sometimes severely disadvantaged   9
by trainers whose job it is to keep them in action. The more famous the athlete, the greater the risk that he or she may be subjected to extreme medical measures when injury strikes. The star baseball pitcher whose arm is sore because of a torn muscle or tissue damage may need sustained rest more than anything else. But his team is battling for a place in the World Series; so the trainer or team doctor, called upon to work his magic, reaches for a strong dose of butazolidine or other powerful pain suppressants. Presto, the pain disappears! The pitcher takes his place on the mound and does superbly. That could be the last game, however, in which he is able to throw a ball with full strength. The drugs didn't repair the torn muscle or cause the damaged tissue to heal. What they did was to mask the pain, enabling the pitcher to throw hard, further damaging the torn muscle. Little wonder that so many star athletes are cut down in their prime, more the victims of overzealous treatment of their injuries than of the injuries themselves.

The king of all painkillers, of course, is aspirin. The U.S.   10
Food and Drug Administration permits aspirin to be sold without prescription, but the drug, contrary to popular belief, can be dangerous and, in sustained doses, potentially lethal. Aspi-

rin is self-administered by more people than any other drug in the world. Some people are aspirin-poppers, taking ten or more a day. What they don't know is that the smallest dose can cause internal bleeding. Even more serious perhaps is the fact that aspirin is <u>antagonistic to collagen,</u> which has a key role in the formation of connective tissue. Since many forms of arthritis involve disintegration of the connective tissue, the steady use of aspirin can actually intensify the underlying arthritic condition. . . .

Aspirin is not the only pain-killing drug, of course, that is known to have dangerous side effects. Dr. Daphne A. Roe, of Cornell University, at a medical meeting in New York City in 1974, presented startling evidence of a wide range of hazards associated with sedatives and other pain suppressants. Some of these drugs seriously interfere with the ability of the body to metabolize food properly, producing malnutrition. In some instances, there is also the danger of bone-marrow depression, interfering with the ability of the body to replenish its blood supply.   11

Pain-killing drugs are among the greatest advances in the history of medicine. Properly used, they can be a boon in alleviating suffering and in treating disease. But their indiscriminate and promiscuous use is making psychological cripples and chronic ailers out of millions of people. The unremitting barrage of advertising for pain-killing drugs, especially over television, has set the stage for a mass anxiety neurosis. Almost from the moment children are old enough to sit up-right in front of a television screen, they are being indoctrinated into the hypochondriac's clamorous and morbid world. Little wonder so many people fear pain more than death itself.   12

It might be a good idea if concerned physicians and educators could get together to make knowledge about pain an important part of the regular school curriculum. As for the populace at large, perhaps some of the same techniques used by public-service agencies to make people cancer-conscious can be used to counteract the growing terror of pain and illness in general. People ought to know that nothing is more remarkable about the human body than its recuperative drive, given a modicum of respect. If our broadcasting stations cannot provide equal time for responses to the pain-killing advertisements,   13 they might at least set aside a few minutes each day for common-sense remarks on the subject of pain. As for the Food and Drug Administration, it might be interesting to know why an agency that has so energetically warned the American people against taking vitamins without prescriptions is doing so little to control over-the-counter sales each year of billions of pain-killing pills, some of which can do more harm than the pain they are supposed to suppress.

Questions for Study and Discussion

1. What is Cousins's purpose in this essay? What does he want us to believe? What does he want us to do? (Glossary: *Purpose*)
2. If "pain is not the ultimate enemy," what, according to Cousins, is?
3. What does the example of the star baseball pitcher contribute to the persuasiveness of the essay?
4. What in Cousins's tone—his attitude toward his subject and audience—particularly contributes to the persuasiveness of the essay? Cite examples from the selection. (Glossary: *Tone*)
5. One strategy Cousins uses to develop his argument is causal analysis. Identify the passages in which he uses causal analysis. How exactly does it serve his argument? (Glossary: *Cause and Effect*)
6. For what audience do you suppose Cousins wrote this essay? In your opinion, would most readers be convinced by what Cousins says about pain? Are you convinced? Why, or why not? (Glossary: *Audience*)

Vocabulary

Refer to your dictionary to define the following words as they are used in this selection. Then use each word in a sentence of your own.

hypochondriacs (1)   lethal (10)
searing (1)   antagonistic (10)
promiscuous (6)   neurosis (12)
overzealous (9)

Suggested Writing Assignments

1. Write a persuasive essay in which you support or refute the following proposition: Television advertising is in large part responsible for Americans' belief that pain is the ultimate enemy.

2. What is the most effective way to bring about social change and to influence societal attitudes? Concentrating on the sorts of changes you have witnessed over the last ten years, write an essay in which you describe how best to influence public opinion.

WHAT'S WRONG WITH BLACK ENGLISH

Rachel L. Jones

*Rachel L. Jones was a sophomore at Southern Il-
linois University when she published the following essay in* Newsweek *in December 1982. Jones
argues against the popularly held belief of both
her fellow black students and black authorities
that speaking "white English" is a betrayal of
her blackness.*

William Labov, a noted linguist, once said about the use   1
of black English, "It is the goal of most black Americans to acquire full control of the standard language without
giving up their own culture." He also suggested that there are
certain advantages to having two ways to express one's feelings. I wonder if the good doctor might also consider the goals
of those black Americans who have full control of standard English but who are every now and then troubled by that colorful,
grammar-to-the-winds patois that is black English. Case in
point—me.

I'm a 21-year-old black born to a family that would probably   2
be considered lower-middle class—which in my mind is a polite
way of describing a condition only slightly better than poverty.
Let's just say we rarely if ever did the winter-vacation thing in
the Caribbean. I've often had to defend my humble beginnings
to a most unlikely group of people for an even less likely reason. Because of the way I talk, some of my black peers look at
me sideways and ask, "Why do you talk like you're white?"

The first time it happened to me I was nine years old. Cor-   3
nered in the school bathroom by the class bully and her side-
kick, I was offered the opportunity to swallow a few of my
teeth unless I satisfactorily explained why I always got good
grades, why I talked "proper" or "white." I had no ready answer for her, save the fact that my mother had from the time I
was old enough to talk stressed the importance of reading and

learning, or that L. Frank Baum and Ray Bradbury were my closest companions. I read all my older brothers' and sisters' literature textbooks more faithfully than they did, and even lightweights like the Bobbsey Twins and Trixie Belden were allowed into my bookish inner circle. I don't remember exactly what I told those girls, but I somehow talked my way out of a beating.

I was reminded once again of my "white pipes" problem while apartment hunting in Evanston, Ill., last winter. I doggedly made out lists of available places and called all around. I would immediately be invited over—and immediately turned down. The thinly concealed looks of shock when the front door opened clued me in, along with the flustered instances of "just getting off the phone with the girl who was ahead of you and she wants the rooms." When I finally found a place to live, my roommate stirred up old memories when she remarked a few months later, "You know, I was surprised when I first saw you. You sounded white over the phone." Tell me another one, sister.

I should've asked her a question I've wanted an answer to for years: how does one "talk white"? The silly side of me pictures a rabid white foam spewing forth when I speak. I don't use Valley Girl jargon, so that's not what's meant in my case. Actually, I've pretty much deduced what people mean when they say that to me, and the implications are really frightening.

It means that I'm articulate and well-versed. It means that I can talk as freely about John Steinbeck as I can about Rick James. It means that "ain't" and "he be" are not staples of my vocabulary and are only used around family and friends. (It is almost Jekyll and Hyde-ish the way I can slip out of academic abstractions into a long, lean, double-negative-filled dialogue, but I've come to terms with that aspect of my personality.) As a child, I found it hard to believe that's what people meant by "talking proper"; that would've meant that good grades and standard English were equated with white skin, and that went against everything I'd ever been taught. Running into the same type of mentality as an adult has confirmed the depressing reality that for many blacks, standard English is not only unfamiliar, it is socially unacceptable.

James Baldwin once defended black English by saying it had ₇
added "vitality to the language," and even went so far as to label it a language in its own right, saying, "Language [i.e., black
English] is a political instrument" and a "vivid and crucial key
to identity." But did Malcolm X urge blacks to take power in
this country "any way y'all can"? Did Martin Luther King Jr.
say to blacks, "I has been to the mountaintop, and I done seed
the Promised Land"? Toni Morrison, Alice Walker and James
Baldwin did not achieve their eloquence, grace and stature by
using only black English in their writing. Andrew Young, Tom
Bradley and Barbara Jordan did not acquire political power by
saying, "Y'all crazy if you ain't gon vote for me." They all have
full command of standard English, and I don't think that
knowledge takes away from their blackness or commitment to
black people.

I know from experience that it's important for black people, ₈
stripped of culture and heritage, to have something they can
point to and say, "This is ours, *we* can comprehend it, *we* alone
can speak it with a soulful flourish." I'd be lying if I said that
the rhythms of my people caught up in "some serious rap"
don't sound natural and right to me sometimes. But how heart-
warming is it for those same brothers when they hit the pavement searching for employment? Studies have proven that the
use of ethnic dialects decreases power in the marketplace. "I
be" is acceptable on the corner, but not with the boss.

Am I letting capitalistic, European-oriented thinking fog the ₉
issue? Am I selling out blacks to an ideal of assimilating, being
as much like white as possible? I have not formed a personal
political ideology, but I do know this: it hurts me to hear black
children use black English, knowing that they will be at yet another disadvantage in an educational system already full of
stumbling blocks. It hurts me to sit in lecture halls and hear fellow black students complain that the professor "be tripping
dem out using big words dey can't understand." And what
hurts most is to be stripped of my own blackness simply because I know my way around the English language.

I would have to disagree with Labov in one respect. My goal ₁₀
is not so much to acquire full control of both standard and
black English, but to one day see more black people less depen-

dent on a dialect that excludes them from full participation in the world we live in. I don't think I talk white, I think I talk right.

Questions for Study and Discussion

1. What is Jones's purpose in this essay? (Glossary: *Purpose*) For what is she arguing?
2. What purpose is served by Jones's title? Does the title indicate that she will be arguing for or against black English?
3. What citations to authorities has Jones used and for what specific reasons has she used each? (Glossary: *Evidence*)
4. What is black English? Where does Jones provide a definition of the term? (Glossary: *Definition*)
5. How has Jones used narration to help her case? (Glossary: *Narration*)

Vocabulary

Refer to your dictionary to define the following words as they are used in this selection. Then use each word in a sentence of your own.

linguist (1)	deduced (5)
patois (1)	staples (6)
doggedly (4)	dialect (10)
rabid (5)	

Suggested Writing Assignments

1. Much has been written since the late 60s on how black English should be regarded linguistically, socially, educationally, and personally. The subject is sometimes called bidialectalism or bilingualism. Review some aspect of this controversy as presented in newspapers and popular magazines, and come to some conclusions of your own regarding the issues. You may find it helpful to consult the *Reader's*

Guide to Periodical Literature in the reference section of your school library. Finally, write an argument based on your own views. Be sure to provide as much evidence as possible to support your conclusions.

2. The title of Rachel Jones's essay suggests a formula for other possible arguments. Using the "What's Wrong with _____" as a title, write an argumentative essay on any one of the following topics:

    the sale of over-the-counter tranquilizers
    United States military involvement in Central America
    gentrification
    the 55-mile-per-hour speed limit
    diets
    gun control
    cheating
    salt/sugar

LOTTERIES CHEAT, CORRUPT THE PEOPLE

George F. Will

*Born in 1941 in Champaign, Illinois, George F.
Will attended Trinity College in Hartford, Connecticut, and Princeton University before going
on to teach political science at Michigan State
University and the University of Toronto. Will is
best known for his syndicated newspaper
column and his biweekly column in* Newsweek.
*He has collected his columns in two books and
has written another book on politics,* Statecraft
as Soulcraft: What Government Does *(1983). In
the following selection, Will takes issue with
government-run lotteries and the delusions they
encourage.*

On the outskirts of this city of insurance companies, there   1
is another, less useful, business based on an understanding of probabilities. It is a jai alai fronton, a cavernous court
where athletes play a fast game for the entertainment of gamblers and the benefit of, among others, the state treasury.

Half the states have legal betting in casinos, at horse or dog   2
tracks, off-track betting parlors, jai alai frontons, or in state-
run lotteries. Only Connecticut has four (the last four) kinds of
gambling, and there is talk of promoting the other two.

Not coincidentally, Connecticut is one of just seven states   3
still fiercely determined not to have an income tax. Gambling
taxes yielded $76.4 million last year, which is not a large slice
of Connecticut's $2.1 billion budget, but it would be missed,
and is growing.

Last year Americans legally wagered $15 billion, up 8 per-   4
cent over 1976. Lotteries took in 24 percent more. Stiffening resistance to taxes is encouraging states to seek revenues from

gambling, and thus to encourage gambling. There are three rationalizations for this:

State-run gambling controls illegal gambling. 5

Gambling is a painless way to raise revenues. 6

Gambling is a "victimless" recreation, and thus is a matter of 7 moral indifference.

Actually, there is evidence that legal gambling increases the 8 respectability of gambling, and increases public interest in gambling. This creates new gamblers, some of whom move on to illegal gambling, which generally offers better odds. And as a revenue-raising device, gambling is severely regressive.

Gamblers are drawn disproportionately from minority and 9 poor populations that can ill-afford to gamble, that are especially susceptible to the lure of gambling, and that especially need a government that will not collaborate with gambling entrepreneurs, as in jai alai, and that will not become a gambling entrepreneur through a state lottery.

A depressing number of gamblers have no margin for eco- 10 nomic losses and little understanding of the probability of losses. Between 1975 and 1977 there was a 140 percent increase in spending to advertise lotteries—lotteries in which more than 99.9 percent of all players are losers. Such advertising is apt to be especially effective, and cruel, among people whose tribulations make them susceptible to dreams of sudden relief.

Grocery money is risked for such relief. Some grocers in 11 Hartford's poorer neighborhoods report that receipts decline during jai-alai season. Aside from the injury gamblers do to their dependents, there is a more subtle but more comprehensive injury done by gambling. It is the injury done to society's sense of elemental equities. Gambling blurs the distinction between well-earned and "ill-gotten" gains.

Gambling is debased speculation, a lust for sudden wealth 12 that is not connected with the process of making society more productive of goods and services. Government support of gambling gives a legitimating imprimatur to the pursuit of wealth without work.

"It is," said Jefferson, "the manners and spirit of a people 13 which preserves a republic in vigor." Jefferson believed in the virtue-instilling effects of agricultural labor. Andrew Jackson denounced the Bank of the United States as a "monster" because increased credit creation meant increased speculation. Martin Van Buren warned against "a craving desire . . . for sudden wealth." The early nineteenth century belief was that citizens could be distinguished by the moral worth of the way they acquired wealth; and physical labor was considered the most ennobling labor.

It is perhaps a bit late to worry about all this: the United States is a developed capitalist society of a sort Jefferson would have feared if he had been able to imagine it. But those who cherish capitalism should note that the moral weakness of capitalism derives, in part, from the belief that too much wealth is allocated in "speculative" ways, capriciously, to people who earn their bread neither by the sweat of their brows nor by wrinkling their brows for socially useful purposes. 14

Of course, any economy produces windfalls. As a town grows, some land values soar. And some investors (like many non-investors) regard stock trading as a form of roulette. 15

But state-sanctioned gambling institutionalizes windfalls, whets the public appetite for them, and encourages the delusion that they are more frequent than they really are. Thus do states simultaneously cheat and corrupt their citizens. 16

Questions for Study and Discussion

1. The city that Will refers to in paragraph 1 is later revealed to be Hartford, Connecticut, long regarded as the nation's insurance capital. Why does Will make this reference to insurance companies? Is buying insurance a form of gambling? Explain.

2. Why does Will think that state-run lotteries "cheat and corrupt" society?

3. Where, specifically, has Will answered each of the three "rationalizations" he presents in paragraphs 5–7? On which point does he spend the most time? Why?

4. Do you feel Will's evidence in paragraph 11 is convincing? Why, or why not? (Glossary: *Evidence*)

5. What purpose is served by paragraph 14? Is Will against capitalism because it relies on speculation? Explain.
6. Why do you suppose Will's paragraphs are so short?

Vocabulary

Refer to your dictionary to define the following words as they are used in this selection. Then use each word in a sentence of your own.

probabilities (1)	debased (12)
rationalizations (4)	imprimatur (12)
entrepreneurs (9)	windfalls (15)
tribulations (10)	whets (16)

Suggested Writing Assignments

1. Argue for or against government-run lotteries, bingo, or other form of gambling in your state.
2. Anyone who is against a lottery might feel differently if he or she had bought a $1 ticket and won a million dollars. But should our attitude and actions regarding issues be based on whether or not we stand to gain personally? Make the case for deciding important issues on the basis of principles, however arguable they might be, and not on an individual, case-by-case basis. Think about the possible objections to such a belief and how you might answer these objections in your essay.

THE PENALTY OF DEATH

H. L. Mencken

H. L. Mencken (1880–1956) was born in Baltimore, Maryland. As a newspaper and magazine journalist, he is best remembered today for his sardonic wit and irreverence for what he called the American "booboisie." He attracted a national audience as a literary critic for the American Mercury, *which he founded and for which he wrote on everything from politics to music. The following selection, an argument in favor of the death penalty, is taken from* Prejudices, Sixth Series *(1926), the last in a series of essay collections that expose literary, political, and sociological pretensions.*

Of the arguments against capital punishment that issue   1
from uplifters, two are commonly heard most often, to
wit:

1. That hanging a man (or frying him or gassing him) is a
   dreadful business, degrading to those who have to do it and
   revolting to those who have to witness it.
2. That it is useless, for it does not deter others from the same
   crime.

The first of these arguments, it seems to me, is plainly too   2
weak to need serious refutation. All it says, in brief, is that the
work of the hangman is unpleasant. Granted. But suppose it is?
It may be quite necessary to society for all that. There are, indeed, many other jobs that are unpleasant, and yet no one
thinks of abolishing them—that of the plumber, that of the sol-
dier, that of the garbage-man, that of the priest hearing confessions, that of the sand-hog, and so on. Moreover, what evidence
is there that any actual hangman complains of his work? I have
heard none. On the contrary, I have known many who delighted
in their ancient art, and practised it proudly.

In the second argument of the abolitionists there is rather   3
more force, but even here, I believe, the ground under them is
shaky. Their fundamental error consists in assuming that the
whole aim of punishing criminals is to deter other (potential)
criminals—that we hang or electrocute A simply in order to so
alarm B that he will not kill C. This, I believe, is an assumption
which confuses a part with the whole. Deterrence, obviously, is
one of the aims of punishment, but it is surely not the only one.
On the contrary, there are at least half a dozen, and some are
probably quite as important. At least one of them, practically
considered, is *more* important. Commonly, it is described as revenge, but revenge is really not the word for it. I borrow a better term from the late Aristotle: *katharsis. Katharsis*, so used,
means a salubrious discharge of emotions, a healthy letting off
of steam. A school-boy, disliking his teacher, deposits a tack
upon the pedagogical chair; the teacher jumps and the boy
laughs. This is *katharsis*. What I contend is that one of the
prime objects of all judicial punishments is to afford the same
grateful relief *(a)* to the immediate victims of the criminal pun-
ished, and *(b)* to the general body of moral and timorous men.

These persons, and particularly the first group, are con-   4
cerned only indirectly with deterring other criminals. The
thing they crave primarily is the satisfaction of seeing the criminal actually before them suffer as he made them suffer. What
they want is the peace of mind that goes with the feeling that
accounts are squared. Until they get that satisfaction they are
in a state of emotional tension, and hence unhappy. The instant
they get it they are comfortable. I do not argue that this yearning is noble; I simply argue that it is almost universal among
human beings. In the face of injuries that are unimportant and
can be borne without damage it may yield to higher impulses;
that is to say, it may yield to what is called Christian charity.
But when the injury is serious Christianity is adjourned, and
even saints reach for their sidearms. It is plainly asking too
much of human nature to expect it to conquer so natural an impulse. A keeps a store and has a bookkeeper, B. B steals $700,
employs it in playing at dice or bingo, and is cleaned out. What
is A to do? Let B go? If he does he will be unable to sleep at
night. The sense of injury, of injustice, of frustration will haunt
him like pruritus. So he turns B over to the police, and they

hustle B to prison. Thereafter A can sleep. More, he has pleasant dreams. He pictures B chained to the wall of a dungeon a hundred feet underground, devoured by rats and scorpions. It is so agreeable that it makes him forget his $700. He has got his *katharsis.*

The same thing precisely takes place on a larger scale when there is a crime which destroys a whole community's sense of security. Every law-abiding citizen feels menaced and frustrated until the criminals have been struck down—until the communal capacity to get even with them, and more than even, has been dramatically demonstrated. Here, manifestly, the business of deterring others is no more than an afterthought. The main thing is to destroy the concrete scoundrels whose act has alarmed everyone, and thus made everyone unhappy. Until they are brought to book that unhappiness continues; when the law has been executed upon them there is a sigh of relief. In other words, there is *katharsis.*

I know of no public demand for the death penalty for ordinary crimes, even for ordinary homicides. Its infliction would shock all men of normal decency of feeling. But for crimes involving the deliberate and inexcusable taking of human life, by men openly defiant of all civilized order—for such crimes it seems, to nine men out of ten, a just and proper punishment. Any lesser penalty leaves them feeling that the criminal has got the better of society—that he is free to add insult to injury by laughing. That feeling can be dissipated only by a recourse to *katharsis,* the invention of the aforesaid Aristotle. It is more effectively and economically achieved, as human nature now is, by wafting the criminal to realms of bliss.

The real objection to capital punishment doesn't lie against the actual extermination of the condemned, but against our brutal American habit of putting it off so long. After all, every one of us must die soon or late, and a murderer, it must be assumed, is one who makes that sad fact the cornerstone of his metaphysic. But it is one thing to die, and quite another thing to lie for long months and even years under the shadow of death. No sane man would choose such a finish. All of us, despite the Prayer Book, long for a swift and unexpected end. Unhappily, a murderer, under the irrational American system, is tortured for what, to him, must seem a whole series of eternities. For

months on end he sits in prison while his lawyers carry on their
idiotic buffoonery with writs, injunctions, mandamuses, and
appeals. In order to get his money (or that of his friends) they
have to feed him with hope. Now and then, by the imbecility of
a judge or some trick of juridic science, they actually justify it.
But let us say that, his money all gone, they finally throw up
their hands. Their client is now ready for the rope or the chair.
But he must still wait for months before it fetches him.

That wait, I believe, is horribly cruel. I have seen more than   8
one man sitting in the death-house, and I don't want to see any
more. Worse, it is wholly useless. Why should he wait at all?
Why not hang him the day after the last court dissipates his
last hope? Why torture him as not even cannibals would torture their victims? The common answer is that he must have
time to make his peace with God. But how long does that take?
It may be accomplished, I believe, in two hours quite as comfortably as in two years. There are, indeed, no temporal limitations upon God. He could forgive a whole herd of murderers in
a millionth of a second. More, it has been done.

Questions for Study and Discussion

1. What is Mencken's purpose in this essay? Does he have
   more than one purpose? Explain. (Glossary: *Purpose*)
2. Where does Mencken refute objections to his argument?
3. If his first point does not need any refutation as he says,
   what is the function of Mencken's second paragraph?
4. Where in his essay does Mencken use definition, and for
   what purpose? (Glossary: *Definition*)
5. At what points in the essay does Mencken use humor? Is his
   use of humor appropriate in the context of this essay? Explain.
6. In paragraph 7 Mencken says that the "real objection to
   capital punishment" is in "our brutal American habit of
   putting it off so long." What evidence does he offer to support this claim? Do you believe Mencken is correct in his
   contention? Explain. (Glossary: *Evidence*)

Vocabulary

Refer to your dictionary to define the following words as they are used in this selection. Then use each word in a sentence of your own.

abolitionists (3)   pruritis (4)
deterrence (3)   wafting (6)
salubrious (3)   metaphysic (7)
timorous (3)   buffoonery (7)
crave (4)   imbecility (7)
adjourned (4)   juridic (7)

Suggested Writing Assignments

1. Mencken's essay was published in 1926, but the debate concerning capital punishment continues. Research some of the current opinions and arguments as reported in recent articles and books, and write an argument for or against capital punishment. You should, of course, properly document the sources of any ideas and evidence that are not original to you.

2. Mencken contends that the problem with capital punishment is "our brutal American habit of putting it off so long." While it may be true that men and women on death row do suffer immeasurably because of the uncertainty of their fate, few people who are concerned with the capital punishment issue refer to this problem in their arguments. Nevertheless, the American judicial and penal systems are themselves far from free of controversy. Arguments concern the fairness, legality, ethics, efficiency, effectiveness, and cost, among other factors, of each system. Research any one of these problem areas, or a concern of your own, and write an argument about it. For example, you may wish to argue that the judicial appeals process is too long and too complex, that plea bargaining is wrong, that prisons do not do the job for which they were intended, that prisons are a place for criminals to learn how to be better criminals, or that the judicial process ignores the victim.

THE DECLARATION OF INDEPENDENCE

Thomas Jefferson

President, governor, statesman, lawyer, architect, philosopher, and writer, Thomas Jefferson (1743–1826) was a seminal figure in the early history of our country. In 1776 Jefferson drafted the Declaration of Independence. Although it was revised by Benjamin Franklin and other colleagues at the Continental Congress, the document retains in its sound logic and forceful, direct style the unmistakable qualities of Jefferson's prose. In 1809, after two terms as president, Jefferson retired to Monticello, a home he had designed and helped build. Ten years later he founded the University of Virginia. Jefferson died at Monticello on July 4, 1826, the fiftieth anniversary of the signing of the Declaration of Independence.

When in the course of human events, it becomes necessary for one people to dissolve the political bands which have connected them with another, and to assume among the Powers of the earth, the separate and equal station to which the Laws of Nature and of Nature's God entitle them, a decent respect to the opinions of mankind requires that they should declare the causes which impel them to the separation.

We hold these truths to be self-evident, that all men are created equal, that they are endowed by their Creator with certain unalienable Rights, that among these are Life, Liberty and the pursuit of Happiness. That to secure these rights, Governments are instituted among Men deriving their just powers from the consent of the governed. That whenever any Form of Government becomes destructive of these ends, it is the Right of the People to alter or to abolish it, and to institute new Government, laying its foundation on such principles and organizing its powers in such form, as to them shall seem most likely to effect their Safety and Happiness. Prudence, indeed, will dictate that Governments long established should not be changed for light and transient causes; and accordingly all experience hath shown, that mankind are more disposed to suffer, while evils are sufferable, than to right themselves by abolishing the forms to which they are accustomed. But when a long train of abuses and usurpations pursuing invariably the same Object evinces a design to reduce them under absolute Despotism, it is their right, it is their duty, to throw off such government, and to provide new Guards for their future security. Such has been the patient sufferance of these Colonies; and such is now the necessity which constrains them to alter their former Systems of Government. The history of the present King of Great Britain is a history of repeated injuries and usurpations, all having in direct object the establishment of an absolute Tyranny over these States. To prove this, let Facts be submitted to a candid world.

He has refused his Assent to Laws, the most wholesome and necessary for the public good. 3

He has forbidden his Governors to pass Laws of immediate and pressing importance, unless suspended in their operation till his Assent should be obtained; and when so suspended, he has utterly neglected to attend to them. 4

He has refused to pass other Laws for the accommodation of large districts of people, unless those people would relinquish the right of Representation in the Legislature, a right inestimable to them and formidable to tyrants only. 5

He has called together legislative bodies at places unusual, uncomfortable, and distant from the depository of their Public Records, for the sole purpose of fatiguing them into compliance with his measures. 6

He has dissolved Representative Houses repeatedly, for opposing with manly firmness his invasions on the rights of the people. 7

He has refused for a long time, after such dissolutions, to cause others to be elected; whereby the Legislative Powers, incapable of Annihilation, have returned to the People at large for their exercise; the State remaining in the mean time exposed to all the dangers of invasion from without, and convulsions within. 8

He has endeavoured to prevent the population of these States; for that purpose obstructing the Laws of Naturalization 9 of Foreigners; refusing to pass others to encourage their migration hither, and raising the conditions of new Appropriations of Lands.

He has obstructed the Administration of Justice, by refusing his Assent to Laws for establishing Judiciary Powers. 10

He has made Judges dependent on his Will alone, for the tenure of their offices, and the amount and payment of their salaries. 11

He has erected a multitude of New Offices, and sent hither swarms of Officers to harass our People, and eat out their substance. 12

He has kept among us, in time of peace, Standing Armies without the Consent of our Legislature. 13

He has affected to render the Military independent of and superior to the Civil Power. 14

He has combined with others to subject us to jurisdictions foreign to our constitution, and unacknowledged by our laws; giving his Assent to their acts of pretended Legislation: 15

For quartering large bodies of armed troops among us: 16

For protecting them, by a mock Trial, from Punishment for any Murders which they should commit on the Inhabitants of these States: 17

For cutting off our Trade with all parts of the world: 18

For imposing Taxes on us without our Consent: 19

For depriving us in many cases, of the benefits of Trial by Jury: 20

For transporting us beyond Seas to be tried for pretended offenses: 21

For abolishing the free System of English Laws in a Neighbouring Province, establishing therein an Arbitrary government, and enlarging its boundaries so as to render it at once an example and fit instrument for introducing the same absolute rule into these Colonies: 22

For taking away our Charters, abolishing our most valuable Laws, and altering fundamentally the Forms of our Governments: 23

For suspending our own Legislatures, and declaring themselves invested with Power to legislate for us in all cases whatsoever. 24

He has abdicated Government here, by declaring us out of his Protection and waging War against us. 25

He has plundered our seas, ravaged our Coasts, burnt our 26 towns and destroyed the Lives of our people.

He is at this time transporting large Armies of foreign Merce- 27 naries to compleat works of death, desolation and tyranny, already begun with circumstances of Cruelty & perfidy scarcely paralleled in the most barbarous ages, and totally unworthy the Head of a civilized nation.

He has constrained our fellow Citizens taken Captive on the 28 high Seas to bear Arms against their Country, to become the executioners of their friends and Brethren, or to fall themselves by their Hands.

He has excited domestic insurrections amongst us, and has 29 endeavoured to bring on the inhabitants of our frontiers, the merciless Indian Savages, whose known rule of warfare, is an undistinguished destruction of all ages, sexes and conditions.

In every stage of these Oppressions We Have Petitioned for 30 Redress in the most humble terms: Our repeated petitions have been answered only by repeated injury. A Prince, whose character is thus marked by every act which may define a Tyrant, is unfit to be the ruler of a free People.

Nor have We been wanting in attention to our British breth- 31 ren. We have warned them from time to time of attempts by their legislature to extend an unwarrantable jurisdiction over us. We have reminded them of the circumstances of our emigration and settlement here. We have appealed to their native justice and magnanimity and we have conjured them by the ties of our common kindred to disavow these usurpations, which would inevitably interrupt our connections and correspondence. They too have been deaf to the voice of justice and of consanguinity. We must, therefore acquiesce in the necessity, which denounces our Separation, and hold them, as we hold the rest of mankind, Enemies in War, in Peace Friends.

We, therefore, the Representatives of the United States of 32 America, in General Congress, Assembled, appealing to the Supreme Judge of the world for the rectitude of our intentions, do, in the Name, and by Authority of the good People of these Colonies, solemnly publish and declare, That these United Colonies are, and of Right ought to be Free and Independent States; that they are Absolved from all Allegiance to the British Crown, and that all political connection between them and the State of Great Britain, is and ought to be totally dissolved; and that as Free and Independent States, they have full power to levy War, conclude Peace, contract Alliances, establish Commerce, and to do all other Acts and Things which Independent States may of right do. And for the support of this Declaration, with a firm reliance on the protection of Divine Providence, we mutually pledge to each other our lives, our Fortunes and our sacred Honor.

Questions for Study and Discussion

1. In paragraph 2, Jefferson presents certain "self-evident" truths. What are these truths, and how are they related to his argument? Do you consider them self-evident?

2. The Declaration of Independence is a deductive argument; it can, therefore, be presented in the form of a syllogism. What are the major premise, the minor premise, and the conclusion of Jefferson's argument? (Glossary: *Syllogism*)

3. The list of charges against the king is given as evidence in support of Jefferson's minor premise. Does he offer any evidence in support of his major premise? (Glossary: *Evidence*)

4. How, specifically, does Jefferson refute the possible charge that the colonists had not tried to solve their problems by less drastic means?

5. Where in the Declaration does Jefferson use parallel structure? What does he achieve by using it? (Glossary: *Parallelism*)

6. While the basic structure of the Declaration reflects sound deductive reasoning, Jefferson's language, particularly when he lists the charges against the king, tends to be emotional. Identify as many examples of this emotional language as you can, and discuss possible reasons why Jefferson uses this kind of language. (Glossary: *Diction*)

Vocabulary

Refer to your dictionary to define the following words as they are used in this selection. Then use each word in a sentence of your own.

prudence (2)   conjured (31)
transient (2)   acquiesce (31)
convulsions (8)   rectitude (32)
abdicated (25)

Suggested Writing Assignments

1. In recent years, and particularly during the administration of President Jimmy Carter, the issue of human rights was much discussed. Review the arguments for and against our country's active and outspoken promotion of the human rights issue as reported in the press. Then write an argument of your own in favor of the renewal of a strong human rights policy on the part of our nation's leaders.

2. Using one of the subjects listed below, develop a thesis, and then write an essay in which you argue in support of that thesis.

   the minimum wage
   social security
   capital punishment
   the erosion of individual rights
   welfare
   separation of church and state
   First Amendment rights

GLOSSARY OF USEFUL TERMS

Abstract   See *Concrete/Abstract.*

Allusion   An allusion is a passing reference to a familiar person, place, or thing often drawn from history, the Bible, mythology, or literature. An allusion is an economical way for a writer to capture the essence of an idea, atmosphere, emotion, or historical era, as in "The scandal was his Watergate," or "He saw himself as a modern Job," or "The campaign ended not with a bang but a whimper." An allusion should be familiar to the reader; if it is not, it will add nothing to the meaning.

Analogy   Analogy is a special form of comparison in which the writer explains something unfamiliar by comparing it to something familiar: "A transmission line is simply a pipeline for electricity. In the case of a water pipeline, more water will flow through the pipe as water pressure increases. The same is true of electricity in a transmission line."

Anecdote   An anecdote is a short narrative about an amusing or interesting event. Writers often use anecdotes to begin essays as well as to illustrate certain points.

Appropriateness   See *Diction.*

Argumentation   Argumentation is one of the four basic types of prose. (Narration, description, and exposition are the other three.) To argue is to attempt to persuade a reader to agree with a point of view, to make a given decision, or to pursue a particular course of action. There are two basic types of argumentation: logical and persuasive. See the introduction to Chapter 18 (pp. 342–344) for a detailed discussion of argumentation.

Attitude   A writer's attitude reflects his or her opinion of a subject. The writer can think very positively or very negatively about a subject, or somewhere in between. See also *Tone.*

Audience   An audience is the intended readership for a piece of writing. For example, the readers of a national weekly newsmagazine come from all walks of life and have diverse interests, opinions, and educational backgrounds. In contrast, the readership for an organic chemistry journal is made up of people whose interests and education are quite similar. The essays in *Models for Writers* are intended for general readers, intelligent people who may lack specific information about the subject being discussed.

Beginnings   See *Beginnings and Endings.*

Beginnings and Endings   A *beginning* is that sentence, group of sentences, or section that introduces an essay. Good beginnings usually identify the thesis or controlling idea, attempt to interest readers, and establish a tone.

An *ending* is that sentence or group of sentences which brings an essay to a close. Good endings are purposeful and well planned. They can be a summary, a concluding example, an anecdote, a quotation. Endings satisfy readers when they are the natural outgrowths of the essays themselves and give the readers a sense of finality or completion. Good essays do not simply stop; they conclude. See the introduction to Chapter 4 for a detailed discussion of *Beginnings and Endings.*

Cause and Effect   Cause-and-effect analysis is a type of exposition that explains the reasons for an occurrence or the consequences of an action. See the introduction to Chapter 17 (pp. 315–316) for a detailed discussion of cause and effect. See also *Exposition.*

Classification   See *Division and Classification.*

Cliché   A cliché is an expression that has become ineffective through overuse. Expressions such as *quick as a flash, jump for joy*, and *slow as molasses* are clichés. Writers normally avoid such trite expressions and seek instead to express themselves in fresh and forceful language. See also *Diction.*

Coherence   Coherence is a quality of good writing that results when all sentences, paragraphs, and longer divisions of an essay are naturally connected. Coherent writing is achieved through (1) a logical sequence of ideas (arranged in chronological order, spatial order, order of importance, or some other appropriate order), (2) the purposeful repetition of key words and ideas, (3) a pace suitable for your topic and your reader, and (4) the use of transitional words and expressions. Coherence should not be confused with unity. (See *Unity.*) See also *Transitions.*

Colloquial Expressions   A colloquial expression is characteristic of or appropriate to spoken language or to writing that seeks its effect. Colloquial expressions are informal, as *chem, gym, come up with, be at loose ends, won't,* and *photo* illustrate.

See also *Diction.* Thus, colloquial expressions are acceptable in formal writing only if they are used purposefully.

Comparison and Contrast   Comparison and contrast is a type of exposition in which the writer points out the similarities and differences between two or more subjects in the same class or category. The function of any comparison and contrast is to clarify—to reach some conclusion about the items being compared and contrasted. See the introduction to Chapter 16 (pp. 297–299) for a detailed discussion of comparison and contrast. See also *Exposition.*

Conclusions   See *Beginnings and Endings.*

Concrete   See *Concrete/Abstract.*

Concrete/Abstract   A concrete word names a specific object, person, place, or action that can be directly perceived by the senses: *car, bread, building, book, John F. Kennedy, Chicago,* or *hiking.* An abstract word, in contrast, refers to general qualities, conditions, ideas, actions, or relationships which cannot be directly perceived by the senses: *bravery, dedication, excellence, anxiety, stress, thinking,* or *hatred.* See also the introduction to Chapter 8 (pp. 137–142).

Connotation   See *Connotation/Denotation.*

Connotation/Denotation   Both connotation and denotation refer to the meanings of words. Denotation is the dictionary meaning of a word, the literal meaning. Connotation, on the other hand, is the implied or suggested meaning of a word. For example, the denotation of *lamb* is "a young sheep." The connotations of lamb are numerous: *gentle, docile, weak, peaceful, blessed, sacrificial, blood, spring, frisky, pure, innocent,* and so on. See also the introduction to Chapter 8 (pp. 137–142).

Controlling Idea   See *Thesis.*

Coordination   Coordination is the joining of grammatical constructions of the same rank (e.g., words, phrases, clauses) to indicate that they are of equal importance. For example, *They ate hotdogs,* and *we ate hamburgers.* See the introduction to Chapter 7 (pp. 117–121). See also *Subordination.*

Deduction   Deduction is the process of reasoning from stated premises to a conclusion which follows necessarily. This form of reasoning moves from the general to the specific. See the introduction to Chapter 18 (pp. 342–344) for a discussion of deductive reasoning and its relation to argumentation. See also *Syllogism.*

Definition   Definition is one of the types of exposition. Definition is a statement of the meaning of a word. A definition may be either brief or extended, part of an essay or an entire essay itself. See the introduction to Chapter 14 (pp. 266–267) for a detailed discussion of definition. See also *Exposition.*

Denotation   See *Connotation/Denotation.*

Description   Description is one of the four basic types of prose. (Narration, exposition, and argumentation are the other three.) Description tells how a person, place, or thing is perceived by the five senses. See the introduction to Chapter 12 (pp. 229–230) for a detailed discussion of description.

Dialogue   Conversation of two or more people as represented in writing. Dialogue is what people say directly to one another.

Diction   Diction refers to a writer's choice and use of words. Good diction is precise and appropriate—the words mean exactly what the writer intends, and the words are well suited to the writer's subject, intended audience, and purpose in writing. The word-conscious writer knows that there are differences among *aged, old,* and *elderly; blue, navy,* and *azure;* and *disturbed, angry,* and *irritated.* Furthermore, this writer knows in which situation to use each word. See the introduction to Chapter 8 (pp. 137–142) for a detailed discussion of diction. See also *Cliché, Colloquial Expressions, Connotation/Denotation, Jargon, Slang.*

Division and Classification   Division and classification is one of the types of exposition. When dividing and classifying, the writer first establishes categories and then arranges or sorts people, places, or things into these categories according to their different characteristics, thus making them more manageable for the writer and more understandable and meaningful for the reader. See the introduction to Chapter 15 (pp. 279–280) for a detailed discussion of division and classification. See also *Exposition.*

Dominant Impression   A dominant impression is the single mood, atmosphere, or quality a writer emphasizes in a piece of descriptive writing. The dominant impression is created through the careful selection of details and is, of course, influenced by the writer's subject, audience, and purpose. See also the introduction to Chapter 12 (pp. 229–230).

Endings   See *Beginnings and Endings.*

Evaluation   An evaluation of a piece of writing is an assessment of its effectiveness or merit. In evaluating a piece of writing, one should ask the following questions: What is the writer's purpose? Is it a worthwhile purpose? Does the writer achieve the purpose? Is the writer's information sufficient and accurate? What are the strengths of the essay? What are its weaknesses? Depending on the type of writing and the purpose, more specific questions can also be asked. For example, with an argument one could ask: Does the writer follow the principles of logical thinking? Is the writer's evidence sufficient and convincing?

Evidence   Evidence is the information on which a judgment or argument is based or by which proof or probability is established. Evidence usually takes the form of statistics, facts, names, examples or illustrations, and opinions of authorities.

Example   An example illustrates a larger idea or represents something of which it is a part. An example is a basic means of developing or clarifying an idea. Furthermore, examples enable writers to show and not simply to tell readers what they mean. See also the introduction to Chapter 10 (pp. 177–179).

Exposition   Exposition is one of the four basic types of prose. (Narration, description, and argumentation are the other three.) The purpose of exposition is to clarify, explain, and inform. The methods of exposition presented in *Models for Writers* are process analysis, definition, illustration, classification, comparison and contrast, and cause and effect. For a detailed discussion of these methods of exposition, see the appropriate section introduction.

Fallacy   See *Logical Fallacies.*

Figures of Speech   Figures of speech are brief, imaginative comparisons which highlight the similarities between things that are basically dissimilar. They make writing vivid, interesting, and memorable. The most common figures of speech are:

> *Simile:* An explicit comparison introduced by *like* or *as.* "The fighter's hands were like stone."
> *Metaphor:* An implied comparison which makes one thing the equivalent of another. "All the world's a stage."
> *Personification:* A special kind of simile or metaphor in which human traits are assigned to an inanimate object. "The engine coughed and then stopped."

See the introduction to Chapter 9 (pp. 161–162) for a detailed discussion of figurative language.

Focus   Focus is the limitation that a writer gives his or her subject. The writer's task is to select a manageable topic given the constraints of time, space, and purpose. For example, within the general subject of sports, a writer could focus on government support of amateur athletes or narrow the focus further to government support of Olympic athletes.

General   See *Specific/General.*

Idiom   An idiom is a word or phrase that is used habitually with special meaning. The meaning of an idiom is not always readily apparent to nonnative speakers of that language. For example, *catch cold, hold a job, make up your mind,* and *give them a hand* are all idioms in English.

Illustration   Illustration is the use of examples to explain, elucidate, or corroborate. Writers rely heavily on illustration to make their ideas both clear and concrete. See the introduction to Chapter 10 (pp. 177–179) for a detailed discussion of illustration.

Induction   Induction is the process of reasoning to a conclusion about all members of a class through an examination of only a few members of the class. This form of reasoning moves from the particular to the general. See the introduction to Chapter 18 (pp. 342–344) for a discussion of inductive reasoning and its relation to argumentation.

Inductive Leap   An inductive leap is the point at which a writer of an argument, having presented sufficient evidence, moves to a generalization or conclusion. See also *Induction.*

Introductions   See *Beginnings and Endings.*

Irony   The use of words to suggest something different from their literal meaning. For example, when Jonathan Swift proposes in *A Modest Proposal* that Ireland's problems could be solved if the people of Ireland fattened their babies and sold them to the English landlords for food, he meant that almost any other solution would be preferable. A writer can use irony to establish a special relationship with the reader and to add an extra dimension or twist to the meaning. See also the introduction to Chapter 8 (pp. 137–142).

Jargon   Jargon, or technical language, is the special vocabulary of a trade, profession, or group. Doctors, construction workers, lawyers, and teachers, for example, all have a specialized vocabulary that they use "on the job." See also *Diction*.

Logical Argumentation See *Argumentation*.

Logical Fallacies A logical fallacy is an error in reasoning that renders an argument invalid. See the introduction to Chapter 18 (pp. 342–344) for a discussion of the more common logical fallacies.

Logical Reasoning See *Deduction* and *Induction*.

Metaphor See *Figures of Speech*.

Narration One of the four basic types of prose. (Description, exposition, and argumentation are the other three.) To narrate is to tell a story, to tell what happened. While narration is most often used in fiction, it is also important in expository writing, either by itself or in conjunction with other types of prose. See the introduction to Chapter 11 (pp. 200–201) for a detailed discussion of narration.

Opinion An opinion is a belief or conclusion, which may or may not be substantiated by positive knowledge or proof. (If not substantiated, an opinion is a prejudice.) Even when based on evidence and sound reasoning, an opinion is personal and can be changed, and is therefore less persuasive than facts and arguments.

Organization Organization is the pattern of order that the writer imposes on his or her material. Some often used patterns of organization include: time order, space order, and order of importance. See the introduction to Chapter 3 (pp. 42–43) for a more detailed discussion of organization.

Paradox A paradox is a seemingly contradictory statement that is nonetheless true. For example, *"we little know what we have until we lose it"* is a paradoxical statement.

Paragraph The paragraph, the single most important unit of thought in an essay, is a series of closely related sentences. These sentences adequately develop the central or controlling idea of the paragraph. This central or controlling idea, usually stated in a topic sentence, is necessarily related to the purpose of the whole composition. A well-written paragraph has several distinguishing characteristics: a clearly stated or implied topic sentence, adequate development, unity, coherence, and an appropriate organizational strategy. See the introduction to Chapter 5 (pp. 83–85) for a detailed discussion of paragraphs.

Parallelism Parallel structure is the repetition of word order or grammatical form either within a single sentence or in several sentences that develop the same central idea. As a rhetorical device, parallelism can aid coherence and add emphasis. Roosevelt's statement, "I see one third of the nation ill-housed, ill-clad, and ill-nourished," illustrates effective parallelism.

Personification See *Figures of Speech*.

Persuasive Argumentation See *Argumentation*.

Point of View Point of view refers to the grammatical person in an essay. For example, first-person point of view uses the pronoun *I* and is commonly found in autobiography and the personal essay; third-person point of view uses the pronouns *he, she,* or *it* and is commonly found in objective writing. See the introduction to Chapter 11 (pp. 200–201) for a discussion of point of view in narration.

Process Analysis Process analysis is a type of exposition. Process analysis answers the question *how* and explains how something works or gives step-by-step directions for doing something. See the introduction to Chapter 13 (pp. 251–252) for a detailed discussion of process analysis. See also *Exposition*.

Purpose Purpose is what the writer wants to accomplish in a particular piece of writing. Purposeful writing seeks to *relate* (narration), to *describe* (description), to *explain* (process analysis, definition, classification, comparison and contrast, and cause and effect), or to *convince* (argumentation).

Rhetorical Question A rhetorical question is asked but requires no answer from the reader. "When will nuclear proliferation end?" is such a question. Writers use rhetorical questions to introduce topics they plan to discuss or to emphasize important points.

Satire A literary form that uses wit, irony, or sarcasm to expose vice or folly. Satire is frequently used to inform or bring about change and not simply to entertain the reader.

Sentence A sentence is a grammatical unit that expresses a complete thought. It consists of at least a subject (a noun) and a predicate (a verb). See the introduction to Chapter 7 (pp. 117–121) for a discussion of effective sentences.

Simile See *Figures of Speech*.

Slang Slang is the unconventional, very informal language of particular subgroups in our culture. Slang, such as *zonk, coke,* *split, rap, dude,* and *stoned,* is acceptable in formal writing only if it is used selectively for specific purposes.

Specific/General   General words name groups or classes of objects, qualities, or actions. Specific words, on the other hand, name individual objects, qualities, or actions within a class or group. To some extent the terms *general* and *specific* are relative. For example, *clothing* is a class of things. *Shirt,* however, is more specific than *clothing* but more general than *T-shirt.* See also *Diction.*

Strategy   A strategy is a means by which a writer achieves his or her purpose. Strategy includes the many rhetorical decisions that the writer makes about organization, paragraph structure, sentence structure, and diction. In terms of the whole essay, strategy refers to the principal rhetorical mode that a writer uses. If, for example, a writer wishes to show how to make chocolate chip cookies, the most effective strategy would be process analysis. If it is the writer's purpose to show why sales of American cars have declined in recent years, the most effective strategy would be cause-and-effect analysis.

Style   Style is the individual manner in which a writer expresses his or her ideas. Style is created by the author's particular choice of words, construction of sentences, and arrangement of ideas.

Subordination   Subordination is the use of grammatical constructions to make one part in a sentence dependent upon rather than equal to another. For example, the italicized clause in the following sentence is subordinate: They all cheered *when I finished the race.* See the introduction to Chapter 7 (pp. 117–121). See also *Coordination.*

Supporting Evidence   See *Evidence.*

Syllogism   A syllogism is an argument that utilizes deductive reasoning and consists of a major premise, a minor premise, and a conclusion. For example,

   All trees that lose leaves are deciduous. (major premise)
   Maple trees lose their leaves. (minor premise)
   Therefore, maple trees are deciduous. (conclusion)

See also *Deduction.*

Symbol   A symbol is a person, place, or thing that represents something beyond itself. For example, the eagle is a symbol of the United States, and the maple leaf, a symbol of Canada.

Syntax   Syntax refers to the way in which words are arranged to form phrases, clauses, and sentences, as well as to the grammatical relationship among the words themselves.

Technical Language   See *Jargon.*

Thesis   A thesis is the main idea of an essay, also known as the controlling idea. A thesis may sometimes be implied rather than stated directly in a thesis statement. See the introduction to Chapter 1 (pp. 11–12) for a detailed discussion of thesis.

Title   A title is a word or phrase set off at the beginning of an essay to identify the subject, to state the main idea of the essay, or to attract the reader's attention. A title may be explicit or suggestive. A subtitle, when used, explains or restricts the meaning of the main title.

Tone   Tone is the manner in which a writer relates to an audience, the "tone of voice" used to address readers. Tone may be friendly, serious, distant, angry, cheerful, bitter, cynical, enthusiastic, morbid, resentful, warm, playful, and so forth. A particular tone results from a writer's diction, sentence structure, purpose, and attitude toward the subject. See the introduction to Chapter 8 (pp. 137–142) for several examples that display different tones.

Topic Sentence   The topic sentence states the central idea of a paragraph and thus limits the content of the paragraph. Although the topic sentence normally appears at the beginning of the paragraph, it may appear at any other point, particularly if the writer is trying to create a special effect. Not all paragraphs contain topic sentences. See also *Paragraph.*

Transitions   Transitions are words or phrases that link sentences, paragraphs, and larger units of a composition in order to achieve coherence. These devices include parallelism, pronoun references, conjunctions, and the repetition of key ideas, as well as the many conventional transitional expressions such as *moreover, on the other hand, in addition, in contrast,* and *therefore.* See the introduction to Chapter 6 (pp. 100–102) for a detailed discussion of transitions. Also see *Coherence.*

Unity   Unity is that quality of oneness in an essay that results when all the words, sentences, and paragraphs contribute to the thesis. The elements of a unified essay do not distract the reader. Instead, they all harmoniously support a single idea or purpose. See the introduction to Chapter 2 (pp. 26–27) for a detailed discussion of unity.

Verb   Verbs can be classified as either strong verbs (*scream, pierce, gush, ravage,* and *amble*) or weak verbs (*be, has, get,* and *do*). Writers often prefer to use strong verbs in order to make writing more specific or more descriptive.

Voice   Verbs can be classified as being in either the active or the passive voice. In the active voice the doer of the action is the subject. In the passive voice the receiver of the action is the grammatical subject:

Active: Glenda questioned all of the children.

Passive: All of the children were questioned by Glenda.

Acknowledgments (Continued from p. iv)

"How to Take a Job Interview" by Kirby W. Stanat. © 1977, Raintree Publishers Inc. 330 East Kilbourn Avenue, Milwaukee, Wisconsin 53202.

"Rush Week" by Bob Greene from *American Beat.* Copyright © 1983 John Deadline Enterprises. Reprinted with the permission of Atheneum Publishers, Inc.

"Hugh Troy: World's Greatest Practical Joker" from *The People's Almanac #2* by David Wallechinsky, Irving Wallace, Alfred Rosa and Paul Eschholz. Copyright © 1978 by David Wallechinsky and Irving Wallace. By permission of William Morrow & Company.

5. Paragraphs

"Claude Fetridge's Infuriating Law" by H. Allen Smith. Reprinted with permission from June 1963 *Reader's Digest.* Copyright © 1963 by The Reader's Digest Assn., Inc.

"Americans and Physical Fitness" from *The Complete Book of Running,* by James F. Fixx. Copyright © 1977 by James F. Fixx. Reprinted by permission of Random House, Inc.

"Simplicity" by William Zinsser. Copyright © 1980 by William K. Zinsser. Reprinted by permission of the author.

6. Transitions

"Fresh Start" by Evelyn Herald. Reprinted by permission. © 1982 Evelyn J. Herald. All rights reserved.

"Baby Birds" by Gale Lawrence. From *The Beginning Naturalist.* Copyright © 1979 by Gale Lawrence. Reprinted with the permission of The New England Press, Inc.

"Auto-Suggestion" by Russell Baker. Copyright © 1979 by The New York Times Company. Reprinted by permission.

7. Effective Sentences

"Terror at Tinker Creek" by Annie Dillard. Pages 5–6 from *Pilgrim at Tinker Creek* by Annie Dillard. Copyright © 1974 by Annie Dillard. Reprinted by permission of Harper & Row, Publishers, Inc.

"Salvation" from *The Big Sea* by Langston Hughes. Copyright © 1940 by Langston Hughes. Reprinted by permission of Farrar, Straus and Giroux, Inc.

II. The Language of the Essay

8. Diction and Tone

"When Not to Call the Doctor" by Art Buchwald. Reprinted with permission of the author.

"On Being Seventeen, Bright and Unable to Read" by David Raymond. Copyright © 1976 by The New York Times Company. Reprinted by permission.

"The Flight of the Eagles" by N. Scott Momaday. Specified selection on pages 17–18 from *House Made of Dawn* by N. Scott Momaday. Copyright © 1966, 1967, 1968 by N. Scott Momaday. Reprinted by permission of Harper & Row, Publishers, Inc.

9. Figurative Language

"Nobel Prize Acceptance Speech" by William Faulkner from *Essays, Speeches and Public Letters* by William Faulkner, edited by James B. Meriwether. Courtesy of Random House, Inc.

"The Mississippi River" from *Life on the Mississippi* by Mark Twain. By permission of Harper & Row Publishers, Inc.

"Notes on Punctuation" from *The Medusa and the Snail* by Lewis Thomas. Copyright © 1979 by Lewis Thomas. Reprinted by permission of Viking Penguin Inc.

"The Death of Benny Paret" by Norman Mailer. Reprinted by permission of the author and the author's agents, Scott Meredith Literary Agency, Inc., 845 Third Avenue, New York, New York 10022.

III. Types of Essay

10. Illustration

"Referee: Roughest Role in Sports" by Bill Surface. Reprinted with permission from December 1976 *Reader's Digest*. Copyright © 1976 by The Reader's Digest Assn., Inc.

"One Environment, Many Worlds" from Judith and Herbert Kohl, *The View From the Oak*. Copyright © 1977 by Judith and Herbert Kohl. (San Francisco: Sierra Club Books, 1977) Reprinted with the permission of Sierra Club Books.

"At War With the System" (Original title "Businesses Wrong Him") by Enid Nemy. © 1974 by The New York Times Company. Reprinted with permission.

"This is Progress?" by Alan L. Otten. Reprinted by permission of *The Wall Street Journal*, © Dow Jones & Company, Inc. 1978. All Rights Reserved.

11. Narration

"Shame" from *Nigger: An Autobiography* by Dick Gregory with Robert Lipsyte. Copyright © 1964 by Dick Gregory Enterprises, Inc. Reprinted by permission of the publisher, E.P. Dutton, a division of New American Library.

"Thirty-Eight Who Saw Murder Didn't Call the Police" by Martin Gansberg. Copyright © 1964 by The New York Times Company. Reprinted by permission.

"How I Designed an A-Bomb in My Junior Year at Princeton" by John Aristotle Phillips and David Michaelis. Condensed from *Mushroom: The Story of the A-Bomb Kid* by John Aristotle Phillips and David Michaelis, as it appeared in *Reader's Digest*, under the title "How I Designed an A-Bomb in My Junior Year at Princeton." Copyright © 1978 by John Aristotle Phillips. By permission of William Morrow & Company.

"Momma, the Dentist, and Me" from *I Know Why the Caged Bird Sings*, by Maya Angelou. Copyright © 1969 by Maya Angelou. Reprinted by permission of Random House, Inc.

12. Description

"Subway Station" by Gilbert Highet. Reprinted by permission of Curtis Brown, Ltd. Copyright © 1957 by Gilbert Highet.

"The Sounds of the City" by James Tuite. Copyright © 1966 by The New York Times Company. Reprinted by permission.

"Unforgettable Miss Bessie" by Carl T. Rowan. Reprinted with permission from March 1985 *Reader's Digest*. Copyright © 1985 by The Reader's Digest Assn., Inc.

"My Friend, Albert Einstein" by Banesh Hoffmann. Reprinted with permission from January 1968 *Reader's Digest*. Copyright © 1968 by The Reader's Digest Assn., Inc.

13. Process Analysis

"How to Build a Fire in a Fireplace" by Bernard Gladstone. Copyright © 1972 by The New York Times Company. Reprinted by permission.

Inc. and renewed 1954 by H.L. Mencken. Reprinted from *A Mencken Chrestomathy*, by H.L. Mencken, by permission of the publisher.

"Lotteries Cheat, Corrupt the People" by George F. Will. © 1984, Washington Post Writers Group, reprinted with permission.

"What's Wrong With Black English" by Rachel L. Jones. Copyright 1982, by Newsweek, Inc. All Rights Reserved. Reprinted by Permission.

"Astro Tube" from *Wings and Things: Origami That Flies* by Stephen Weiss. Copyright © 1984 by Stephen Weiss, St. Martin's Press, Inc., New York.

INDEX OF AUTHORS, TITLES, AND RHETORICAL TERMS